P9-DHG-835

JLA: ULTRAMARINE CORPS

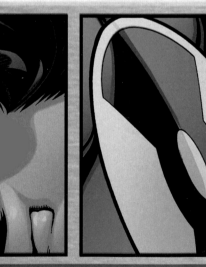

12/3/07 Ingram $14.99

Dan DiDio
SENIOR VP-EXECUTIVE EDITOR

Mike Carlin / Dan Raspler
EDITORS-ORIGINAL SERIES

Peter Tomasi
ASSOCIATE EDITOR-ORIGINAL SERIES

Michael Siglain
ASSISTANT EDITOR-ORIGINAL SERIES

Bob Joy
EDITOR-COLLECTED EDITION

Robbin Brosterman
SENIOR ART DIRECTOR

Paul Levitz
PRESIDENT & PUBLISHER

Georg Brewer
VP-DESIGN & DC DIRECT CREATIVE

Richard Bruning
SENIOR VP-CREATIVE DIRECTOR

Patrick Caldon
EXECUTIVE VP-FINANCE & OPERATIONS

Chris Caramalis
VP-FINANCE

John Cunningham
VP-MARKETING

Terri Cunningham
VP-MANAGING EDITOR

Alison Gill
VP-MANUFACTURING

Hank Kanalz
VP-GENERAL MANAGER, WILDSTORM

Jim Lee
EDITORIAL DIRECTOR-WILDSTORM

Paula Lowitt
SENIOR VP-BUSINESS & LEGAL AFFAIRS

MaryEllen McLaughlin
VP-ADVERTISING & CUSTOM PUBLISHING

John Nee
VP-BUSINESS DEVELOPMENT

Gregory Noveck
SENIOR VP-CREATIVE AFFAIRS

Sue Pohja
VP-BOOK TRADE SALES

Cheryl Rubin
SENIOR VP-BRAND MANAGEMENT

Jeff Trojan
VP-BUSINESS DEVELOPMENT, DC DIRECT

Bob Wayne
VP-SALES

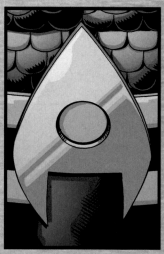

Ed McGuinness / Dexter Vines COVER ART
Amie Brockway-Metcalf PUBLICATION DESIGN

JLA: ULTRAMARINE CORPS

Published by DC Comics. Cover and compilation copyright © 2007 DC Comics. All Rights Reserved.

Originally published in single magazine form in JLA/WILDC.A.T.S 1, JLA SECRET FILES 2004 1,
JLA CLASSIFIED 1-3. Copyright © 1997 DC Comics and Regis Entertainment, 2004, 2005 DC Comics.
All Rights Reserved. All characters, their distinctive likenesses and related elements featured in this publication
are trademarks of DC Comics. The stories, characters and incidents featured in this publication are entirely
fictional. DC Comics does not read or accept unsolicited submissions of ideas, stories or artwork.

DC Comics, 1700 Broadway, New York, NY 10019.

A Warner Bros. Entertainment Company

Printed in Canada. First Printing.

ISBN: 1-4012-1564-5

ISBN 13: 978-1-4012-1564-4

JLA: ULTRAMARINE CORPS

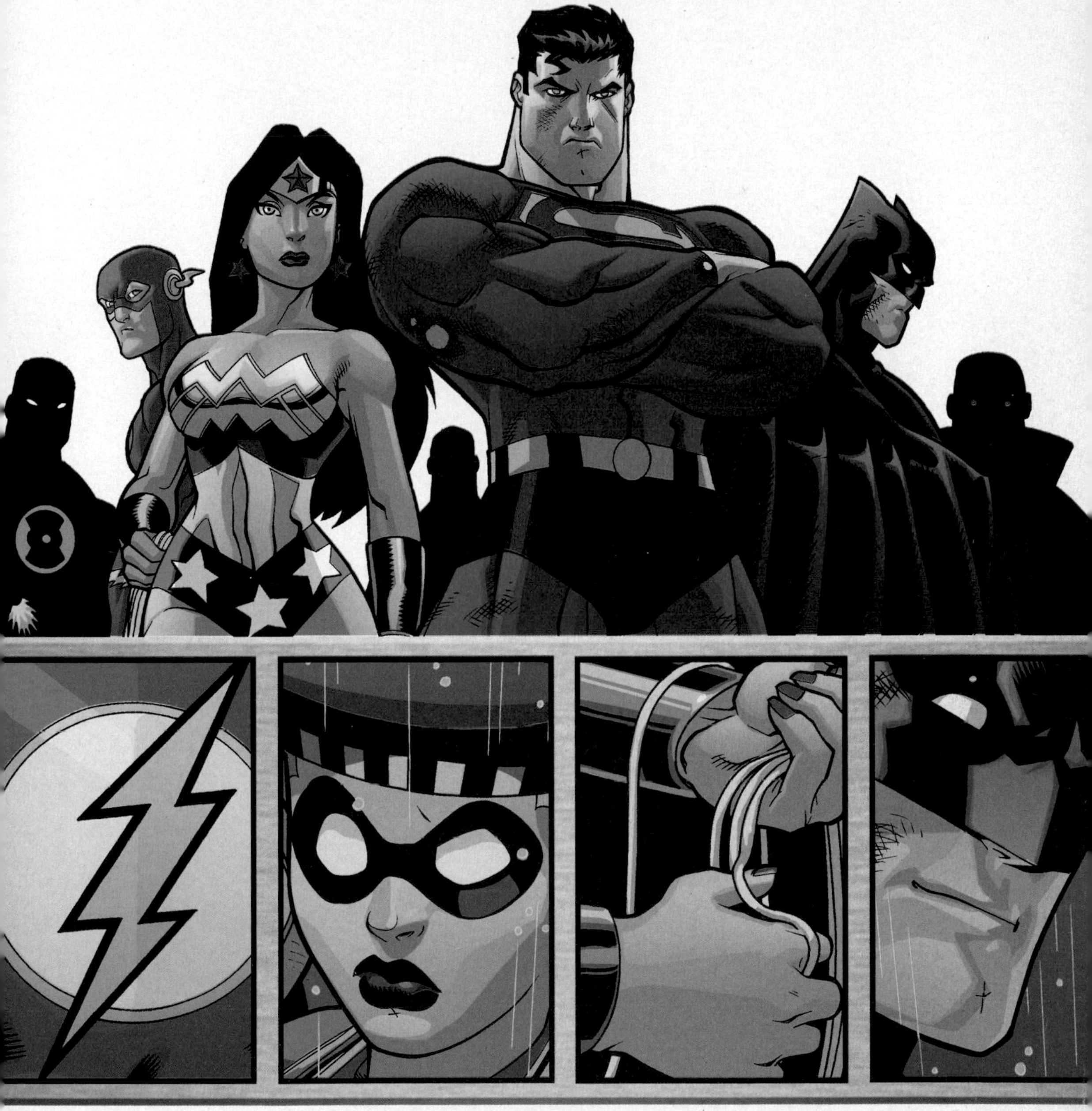

GRANT MORRISON WRITER
ED McGUINNESS PENCILS
DEXTER VINES INKER

DAVE McCAIG COLORIST
PHIL BALSMAN LETTERER
ULTRAMARINES PROFILE WRITTEN BY MIKE McAVENNIE

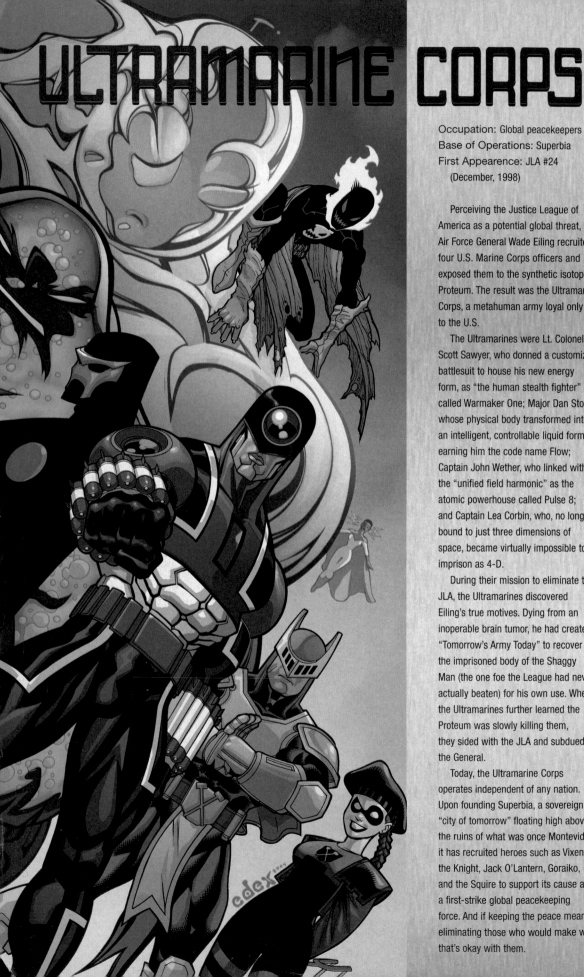

ULTRAMARINE CORPS

Occupation: Global peacekeepers
Base of Operations: Superbia
First Appearence: JLA #24
    (December, 1998)

Perceiving the Justice League of America as a potential global threat, Air Force General Wade Eiling recruited four U.S. Marine Corps officers and exposed them to the synthetic isotope Proteum. The result was the Ultramarine Corps, a metahuman army loyal only to the U.S.

The Ultramarines were Lt. Colonel Scott Sawyer, who donned a customized battlesuit to house his new energy form, as "the human stealth fighter" called Warmaker One; Major Dan Stone, whose physical body transformed into an intelligent, controllable liquid form, earning him the code name Flow; Captain John Wether, who linked with the "unified field harmonic" as the atomic powerhouse called Pulse 8; and Captain Lea Corbin, who, no longer bound to just three dimensions of space, became virtually impossible to imprison as 4-D.

During their mission to eliminate the JLA, the Ultramarines discovered Eiling's true motives. Dying from an inoperable brain tumor, he had created "Tomorrow's Army Today" to recover the imprisoned body of the Shaggy Man (the one foe the League had never actually beaten) for his own use. When the Ultramarines further learned the Proteum was slowly killing them, they sided with the JLA and subdued the General.

Today, the Ultramarine Corps operates independent of any nation. Upon founding Superbia, a sovereign "city of tomorrow" floating high above the ruins of what was once Montevideo, it has recruited heroes such as Vixen, the Knight, Jack O'Lantern, Goraiko, and the Squire to support its cause as a first-strike global peacekeeping force. And if keeping the peace means eliminating those who would make war, that's okay with them.

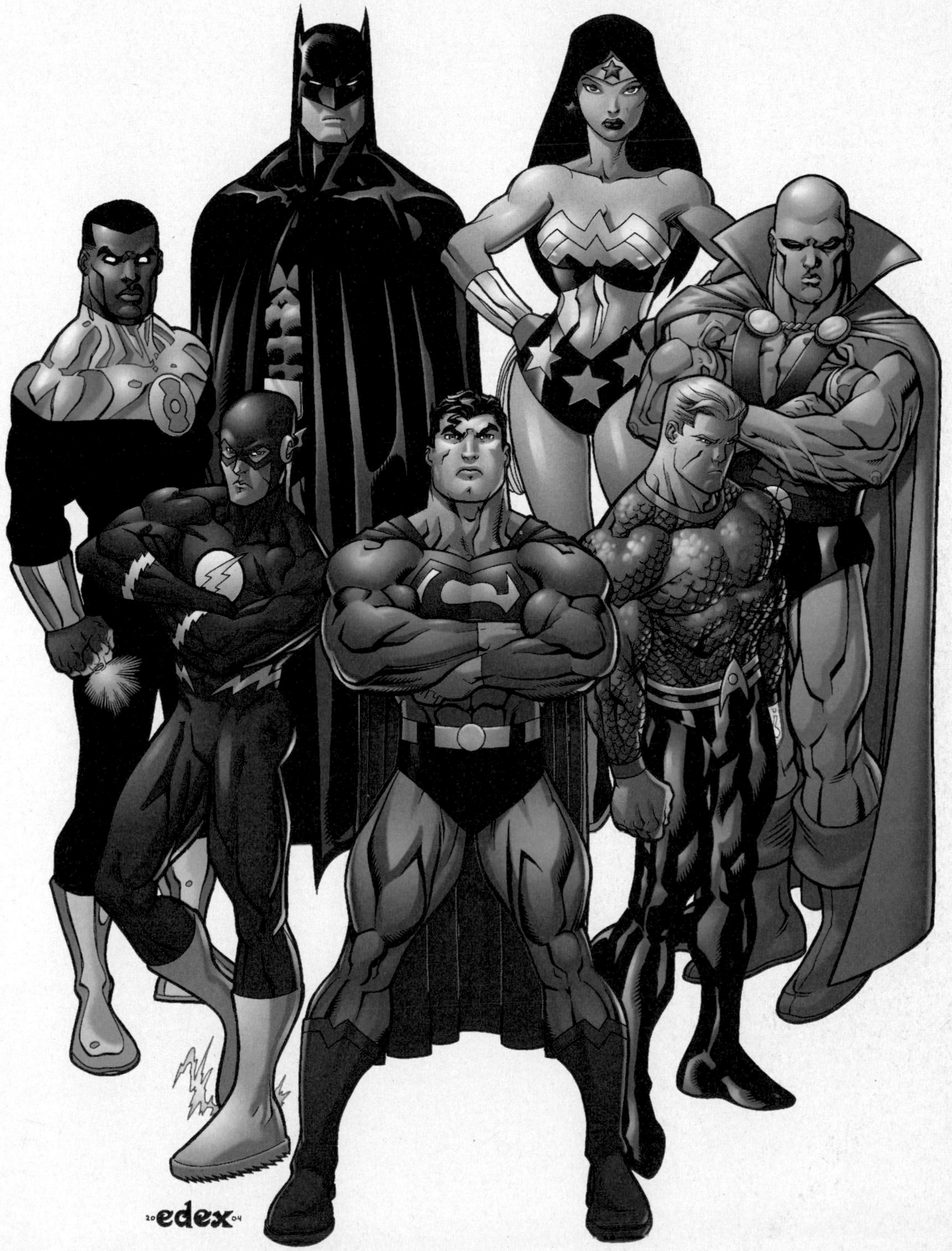
20 edex 04

JLA CLASSIFIED #1

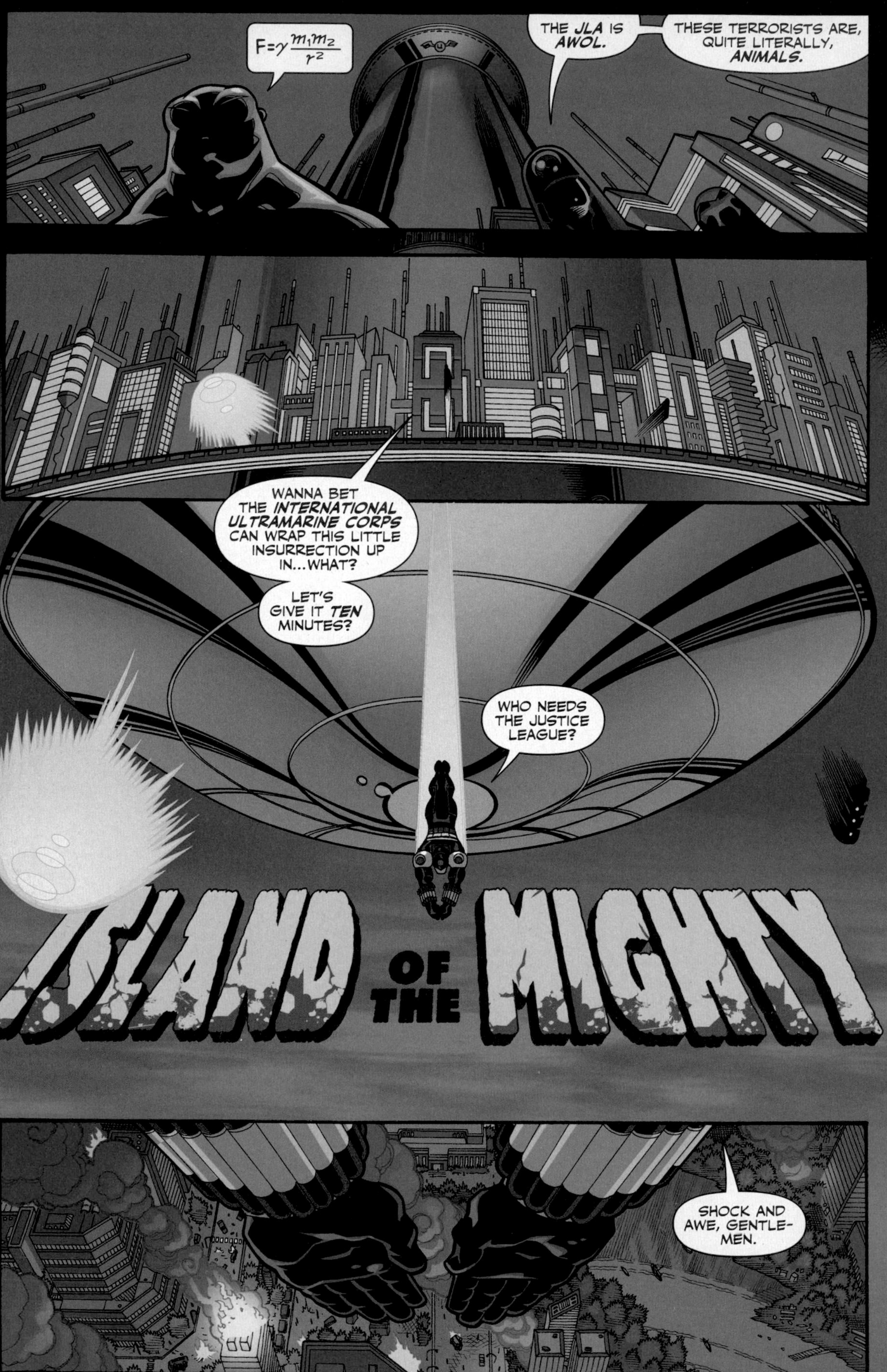

$F=\gamma \frac{m_1 m_2}{r^2}$
THE JLA IS AWOL.
THESE TERRORISTS ARE, QUITE LITERALLY, ANIMALS.
WANNA BET THE INTERNATIONAL ULTRAMARINE CORPS CAN WRAP THIS LITTLE INSURRECTION UP IN...WHAT?
LET'S GIVE IT TEN MINUTES?
WHO NEEDS THE JUSTICE LEAGUE?
ISLAND OF THE MIGHTY
SHOCK AND AWE, GENTLE-MEN.

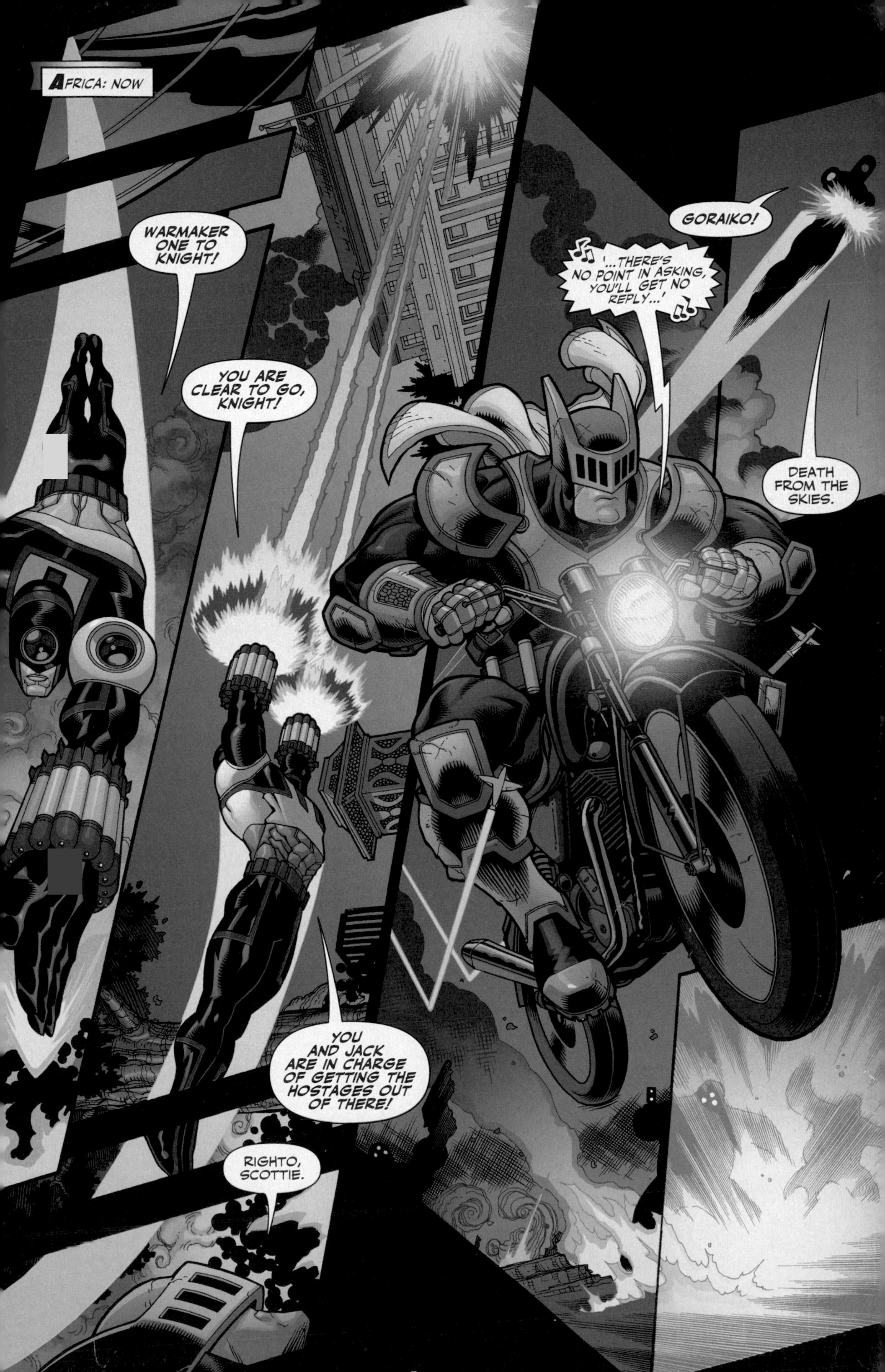
AFRICA: NOW
WARMAKER ONE TO KNIGHT!
YOU ARE CLEAR TO GO, KNIGHT!
YOU AND JACK ARE IN CHARGE OF GETTING THE HOSTAGES OUT OF THERE!
RIGHTO, SCOTTIE.
'...THERE'S NO POINT IN ASKING, YOU'LL GET NO REPLY...'
GORAIKO!
DEATH FROM THE SKIES.

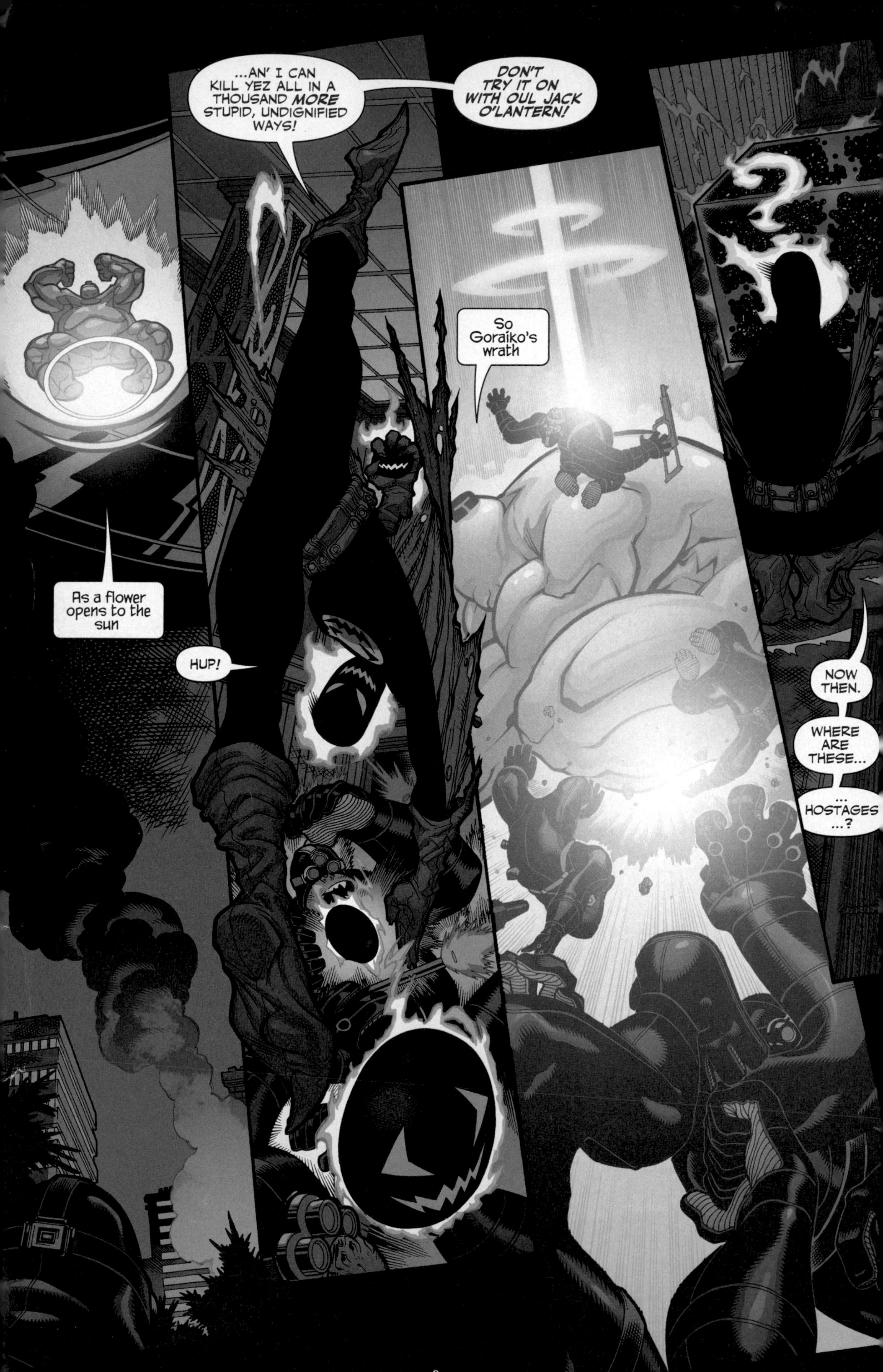

...AN' I CAN KILL YEZ ALL IN A THOUSAND MORE STUPID, UNDIGNIFIED WAYS!
DON'T TRY IT ON WITH OUL JACK O'LANTERN!
As a flower opens to the sun
HUP!
So Goraiko's wrath
NOW THEN.
WHERE ARE THESE...
...HOSTAGES ...?

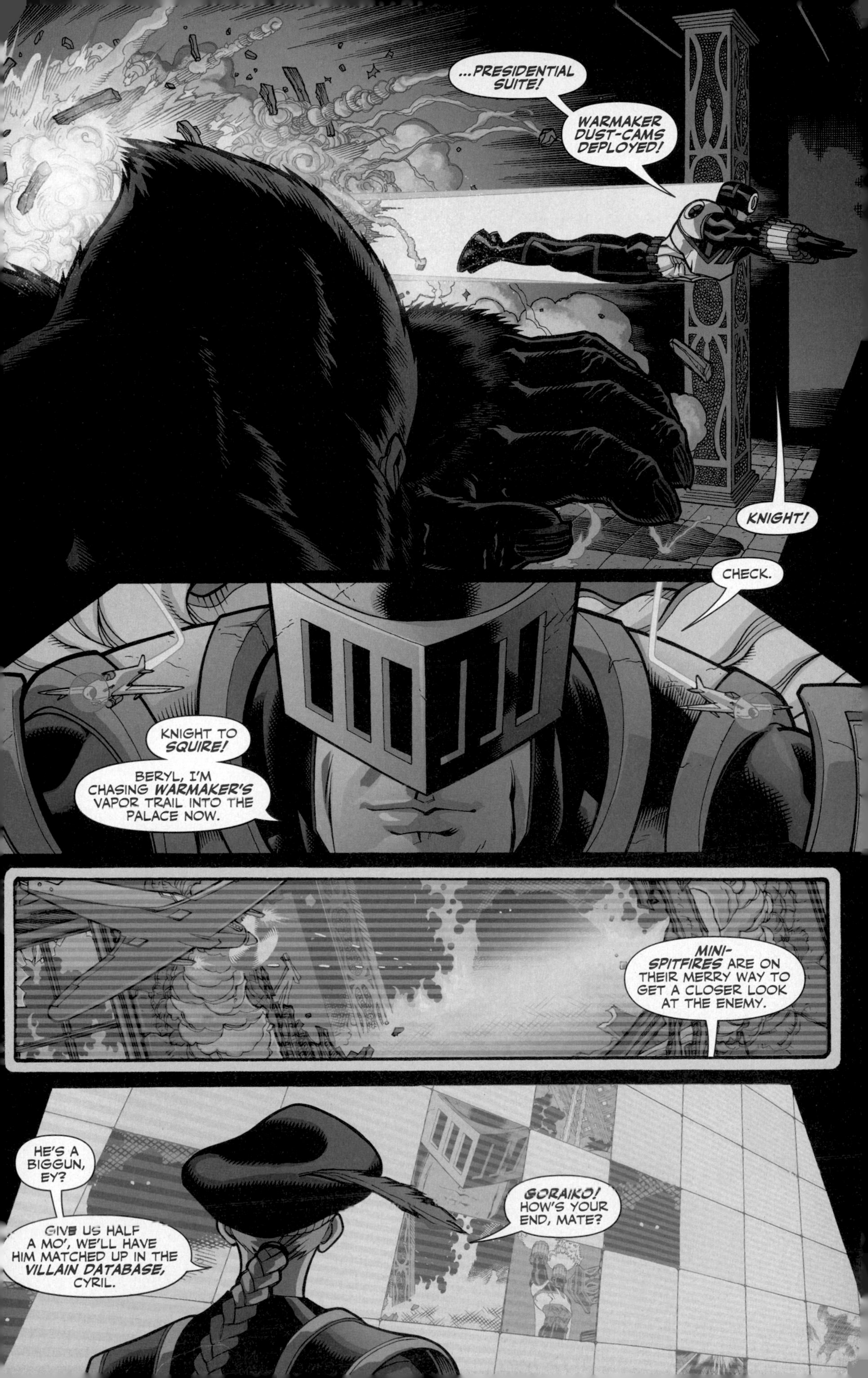
...PRESIDENTIAL SUITE!
WARMAKER DUST-CAMS DEPLOYED!
KNIGHT!
CHECK.
KNIGHT TO SQUIRE!
BERYL, I'M CHASING WARMAKER'S VAPOR TRAIL INTO THE PALACE NOW.
MINI-SPITFIRES ARE ON THEIR MERRY WAY TO GET A CLOSER LOOK AT THE ENEMY.
HE'S A BIGGUN, EY?
GIVE US HALF A MO', WE'LL HAVE HIM MATCHED UP IN THE VILLAIN DATABASE, CYRIL.
GORAIKO! HOW'S YOUR END, MATE?

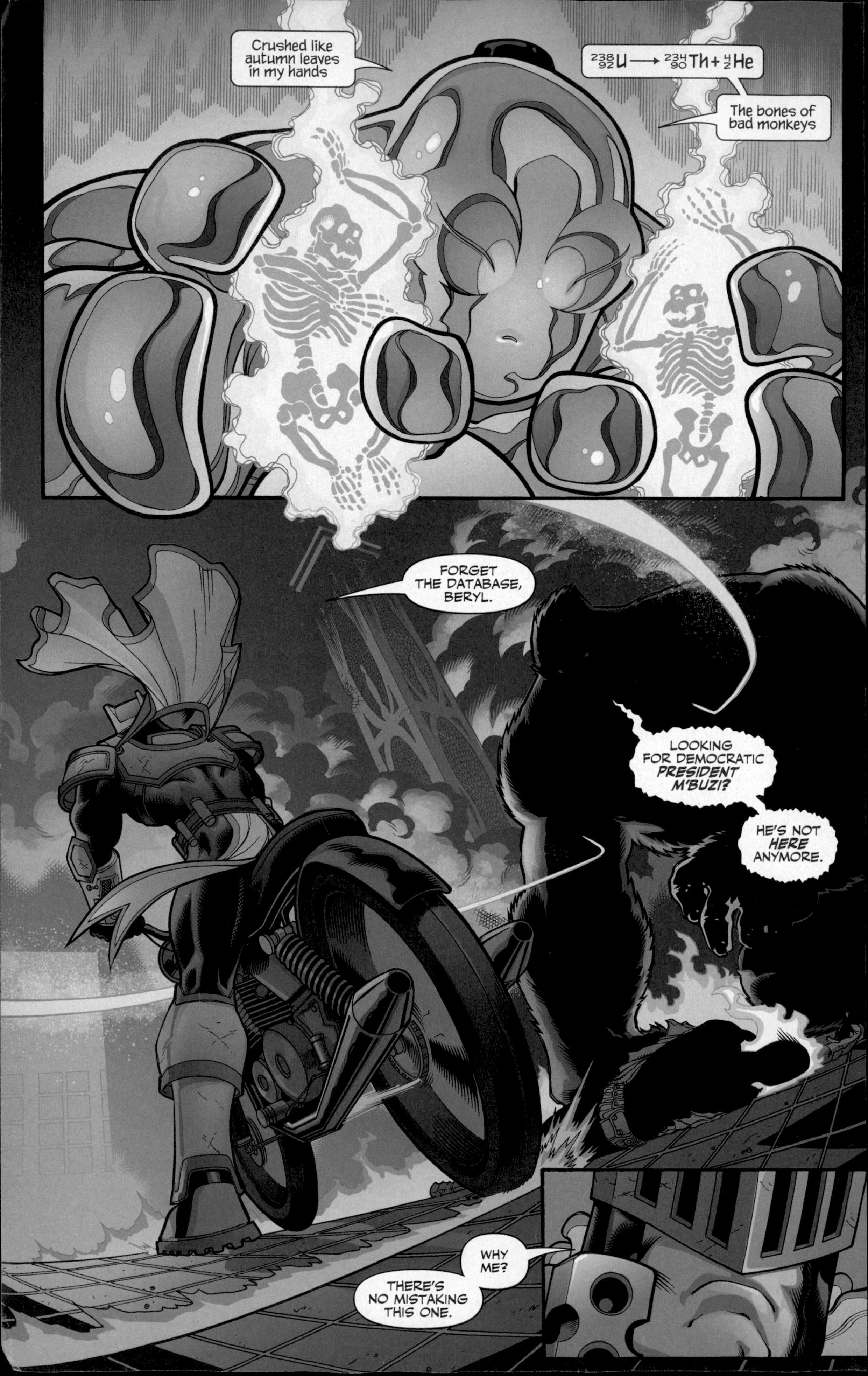
Crushed like autumn leaves in my hands
$^{238}_{92}U \longrightarrow ^{234}_{90}Th + ^{4}_{2}He$
The bones of bad monkeys
FORGET THE DATABASE, BERYL.
LOOKING FOR DEMOCRATIC *PRESIDENT M'BUZI?*
HE'S NOT *HERE* ANYMORE.
WHY ME?
THERE'S NO MISTAKING THIS ONE.

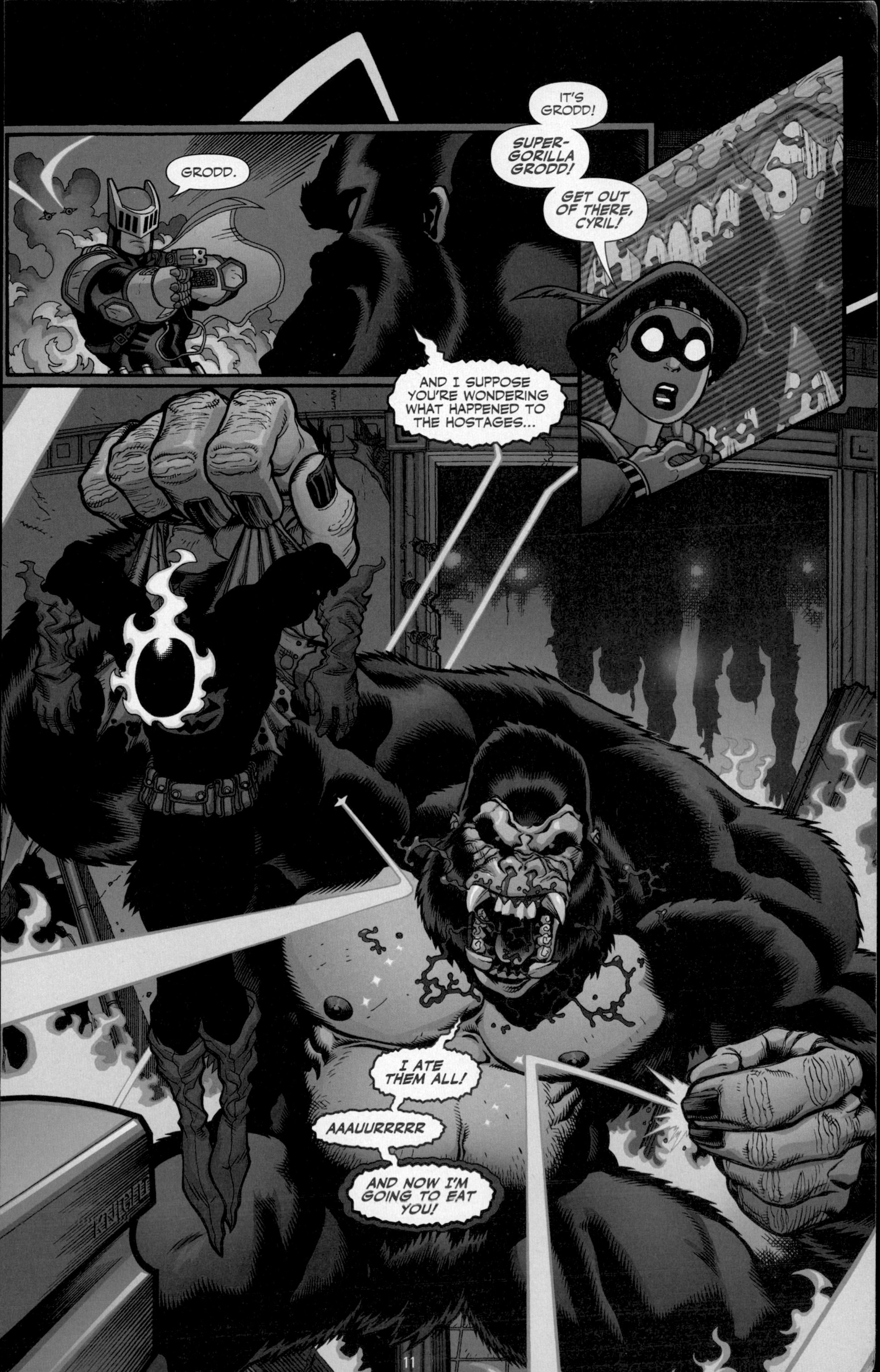
GRODD.
IT'S GRODD!
SUPER-GORILLA GRODD!
GET OUT OF THERE, CYRIL!
AND I SUPPOSE YOU'RE WONDERING WHAT HAPPENED TO THE HOSTAGES...
I ATE THEM ALL!
AAAUURRRRR
AND NOW I'M GOING TO EAT YOU!

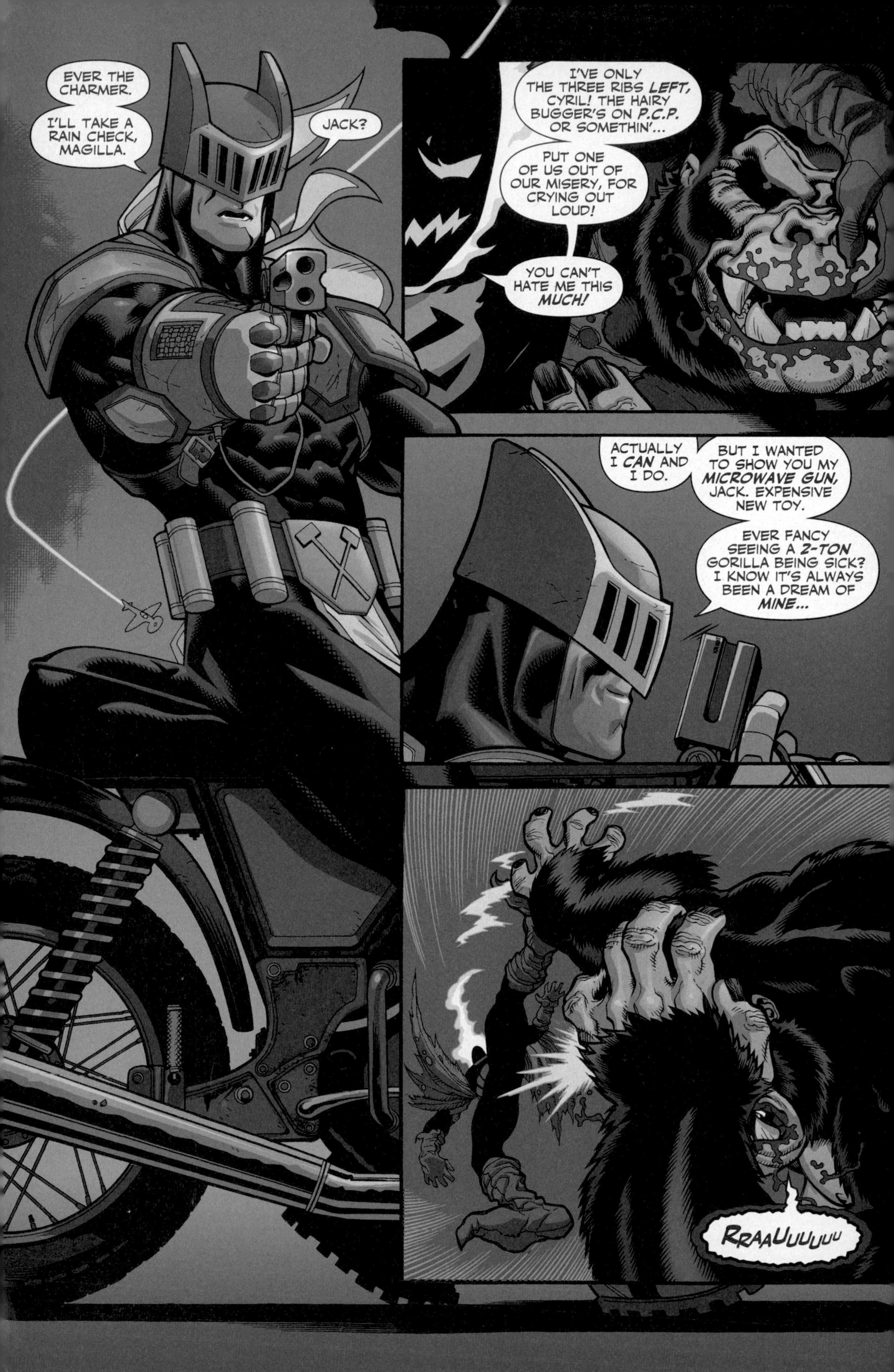
EVER THE CHARMER.
I'LL TAKE A RAIN CHECK, MAGILLA.
JACK?
I'VE ONLY THE THREE RIBS LEFT, CYRIL! THE HAIRY BUGGER'S ON P.C.P. OR SOMETHIN'...
PUT ONE OF US OUT OF OUR MISERY, FOR CRYING OUT LOUD!
YOU CAN'T HATE ME THIS MUCH!
ACTUALLY I CAN AND I DO.
BUT I WANTED TO SHOW YOU MY MICROWAVE GUN, JACK. EXPENSIVE NEW TOY.
EVER FANCY SEEING A 2-TON GORILLA BEING SICK? I KNOW IT'S ALWAYS BEEN A DREAM OF MINE...
RRAAUUUUUU

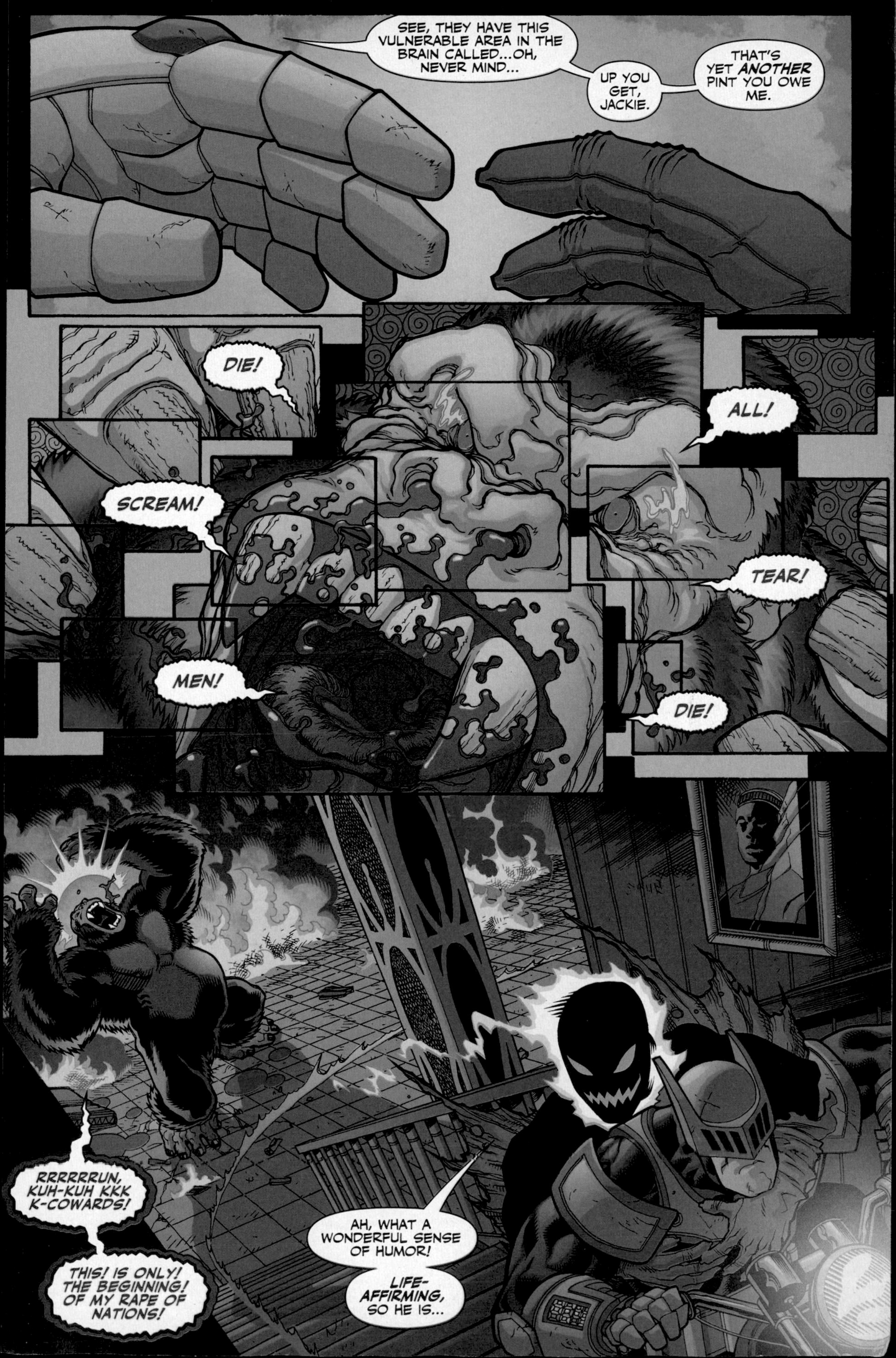
SEE, THEY HAVE THIS VULNERABLE AREA IN THE BRAIN CALLED...OH, NEVER MIND...
UP YOU GET, JACKIE.
THAT'S YET ANOTHER PINT YOU OWE ME.
DIE!
ALL!
SCREAM!
TEAR!
MEN!
DIE!
RRRRRRUN, KUH-KUH KKK K-COWARDS!
THIS! IS ONLY! THE BEGINNING! OF MY RAPE OF NATIONS!
AH, WHAT A WONDERFUL SENSE OF HUMOR!
LIFE-AFFIRMING, SO HE IS...

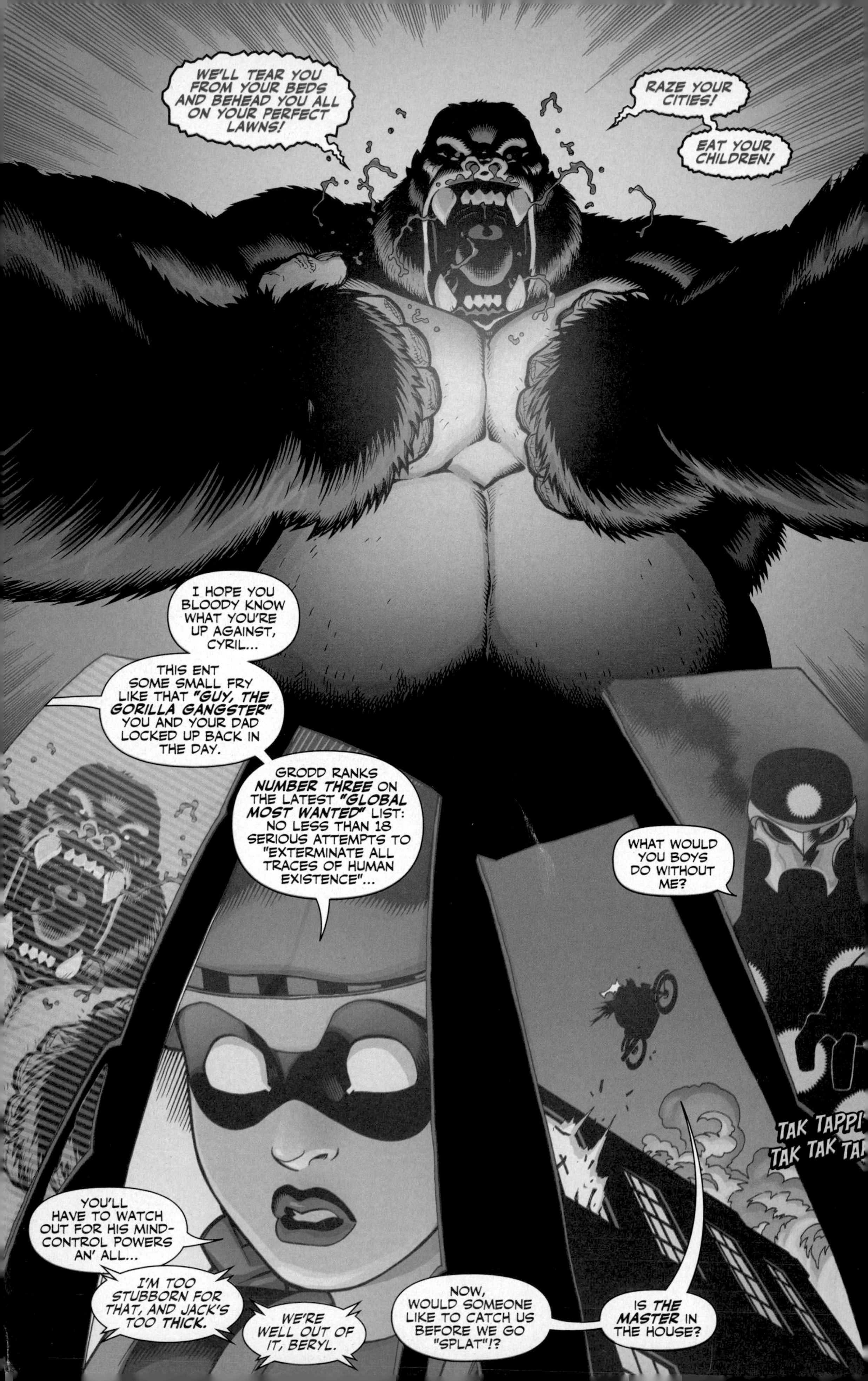
WE'LL TEAR YOU FROM YOUR BEDS AND BEHEAD YOU ALL ON YOUR PERFECT LAWNS!
RAZE YOUR CITIES!
EAT YOUR CHILDREN!
I HOPE YOU BLOODY KNOW WHAT YOU'RE UP AGAINST, CYRIL...
THIS ENT SOME SMALL FRY LIKE THAT "GUY, THE GORILLA GANGSTER" YOU AND YOUR DAD LOCKED UP BACK IN THE DAY.
GRODD RANKS NUMBER THREE ON THE LATEST "GLOBAL MOST WANTED" LIST: NO LESS THAN 18 SERIOUS ATTEMPTS TO "EXTERMINATE ALL TRACES OF HUMAN EXISTENCE"...
WHAT WOULD YOU BOYS DO WITHOUT ME?
TAK TAPPI TAK TAK TA
YOU'LL HAVE TO WATCH OUT FOR HIS MIND-CONTROL POWERS AN' ALL...
I'M TOO STUBBORN FOR THAT, AND JACK'S TOO THICK.
WE'RE WELL OUT OF IT, BERYL.
NOW, WOULD SOMEONE LIKE TO CATCH US BEFORE WE GO "SPLAT"!?
IS THE MASTER IN THE HOUSE?

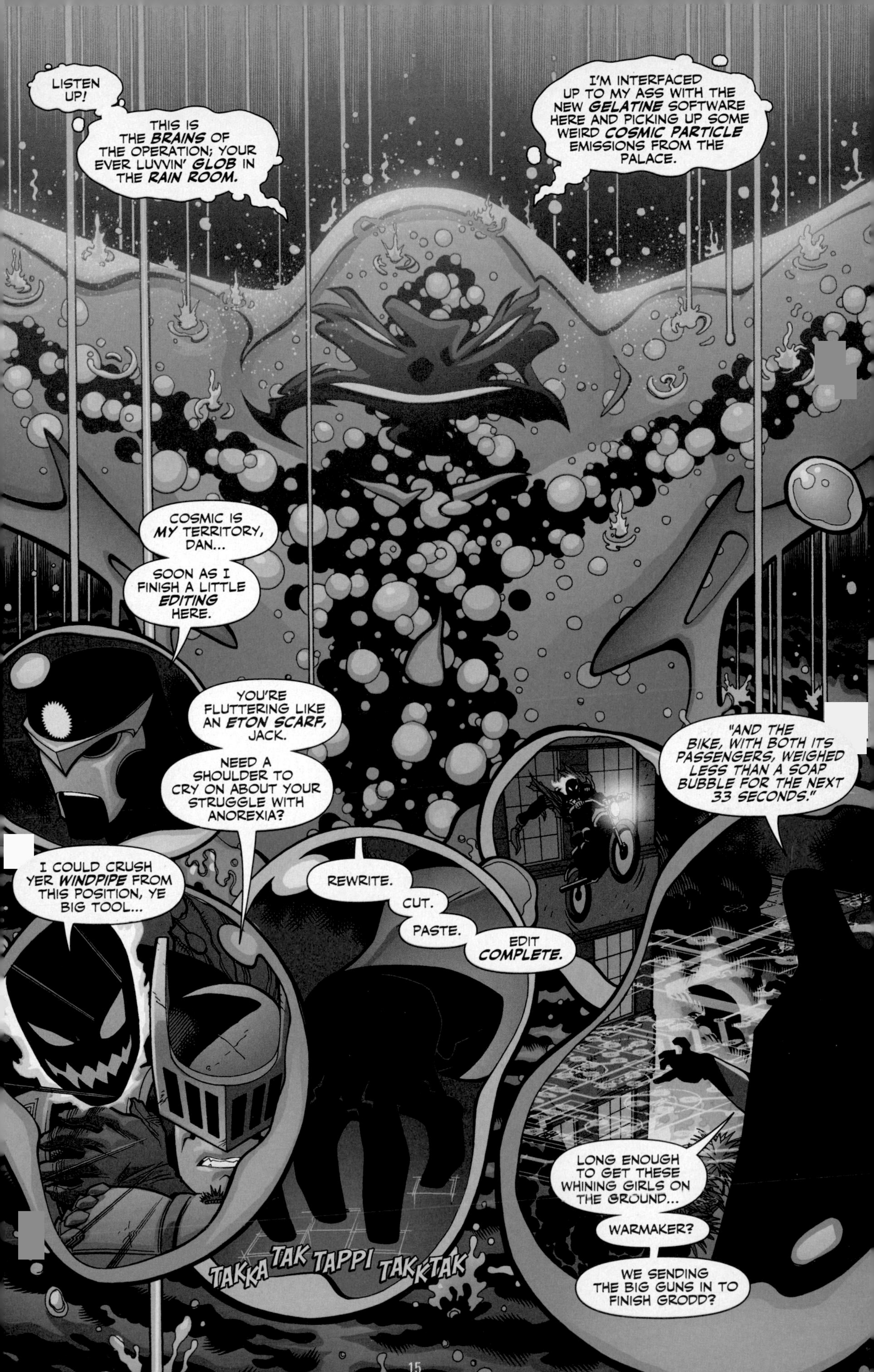
LISTEN UP!
THIS IS THE BRAINS OF THE OPERATION; YOUR EVER LUVVIN' GLOB IN THE RAIN ROOM.
I'M INTERFACED UP TO MY ASS WITH THE NEW GELATINE SOFTWARE HERE AND PICKING UP SOME WEIRD COSMIC PARTICLE EMISSIONS FROM THE PALACE.
COSMIC IS MY TERRITORY, DAN...
SOON AS I FINISH A LITTLE EDITING HERE.
YOU'RE FLUTTERING LIKE AN ETON SCARF, JACK.
NEED A SHOULDER TO CRY ON ABOUT YOUR STRUGGLE WITH ANOREXIA?
I COULD CRUSH YER WINDPIPE FROM THIS POSITION, YE BIG TOOL...
REWRITE.
CUT.
PASTE.
EDIT COMPLETE.
"AND THE BIKE, WITH BOTH ITS PASSENGERS, WEIGHED LESS THAN A SOAP BUBBLE FOR THE NEXT 33 SECONDS."
LONG ENOUGH TO GET THESE WHINING GIRLS ON THE GROUND...
WARMAKER?
WE SENDING THE BIG GUNS IN TO FINISH GRODD?
TAKKA TAK TAPPI TAKKTAK

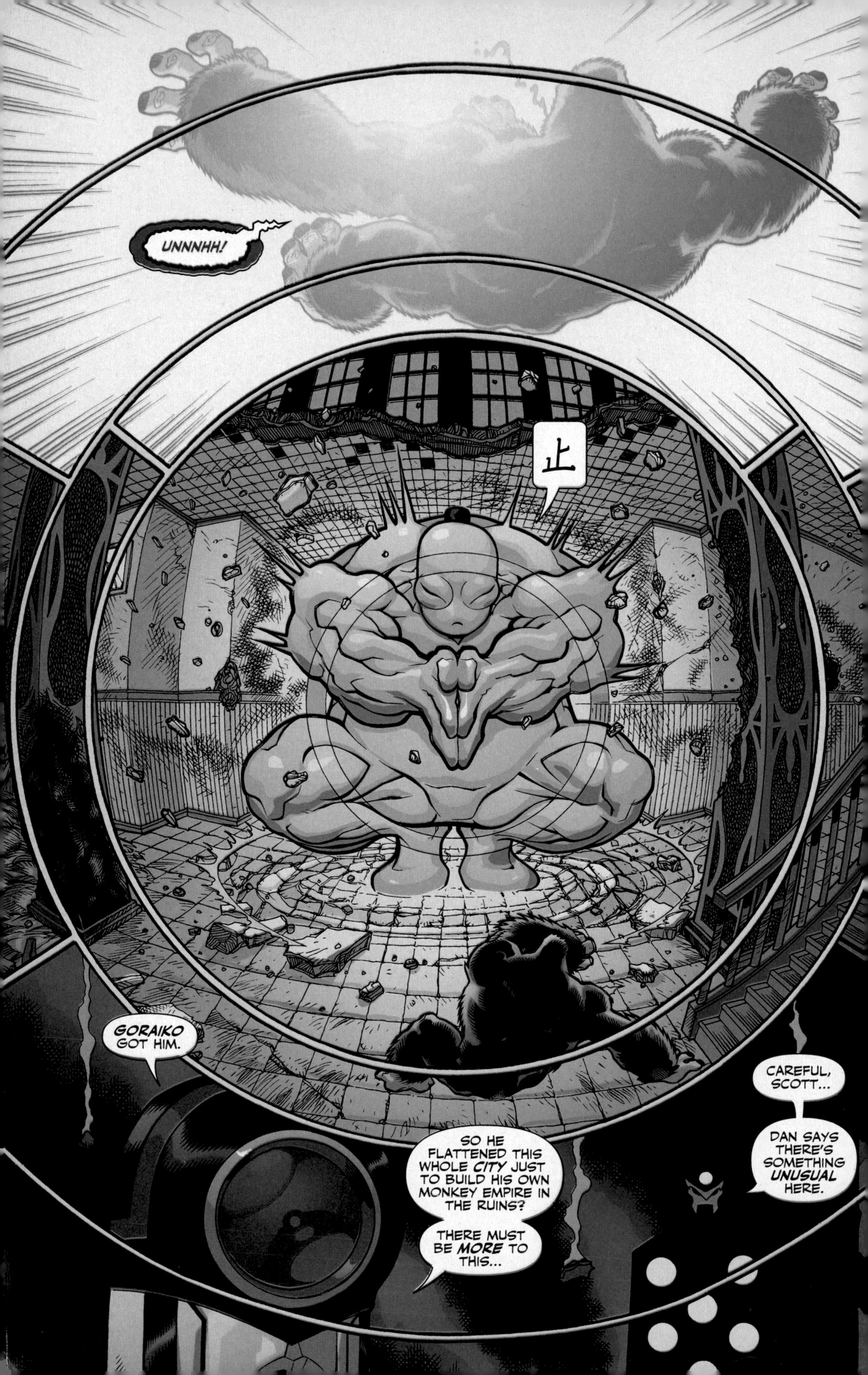
UNNNHH!
止
GORAIKO GOT HIM.
CAREFUL, SCOTT...
DAN SAYS THERE'S SOMETHING UNUSUAL HERE.
SO HE FLATTENED THIS WHOLE CITY JUST TO BUILD HIS OWN MONKEY EMPIRE IN THE RUINS?
THERE MUST BE MORE TO THIS...

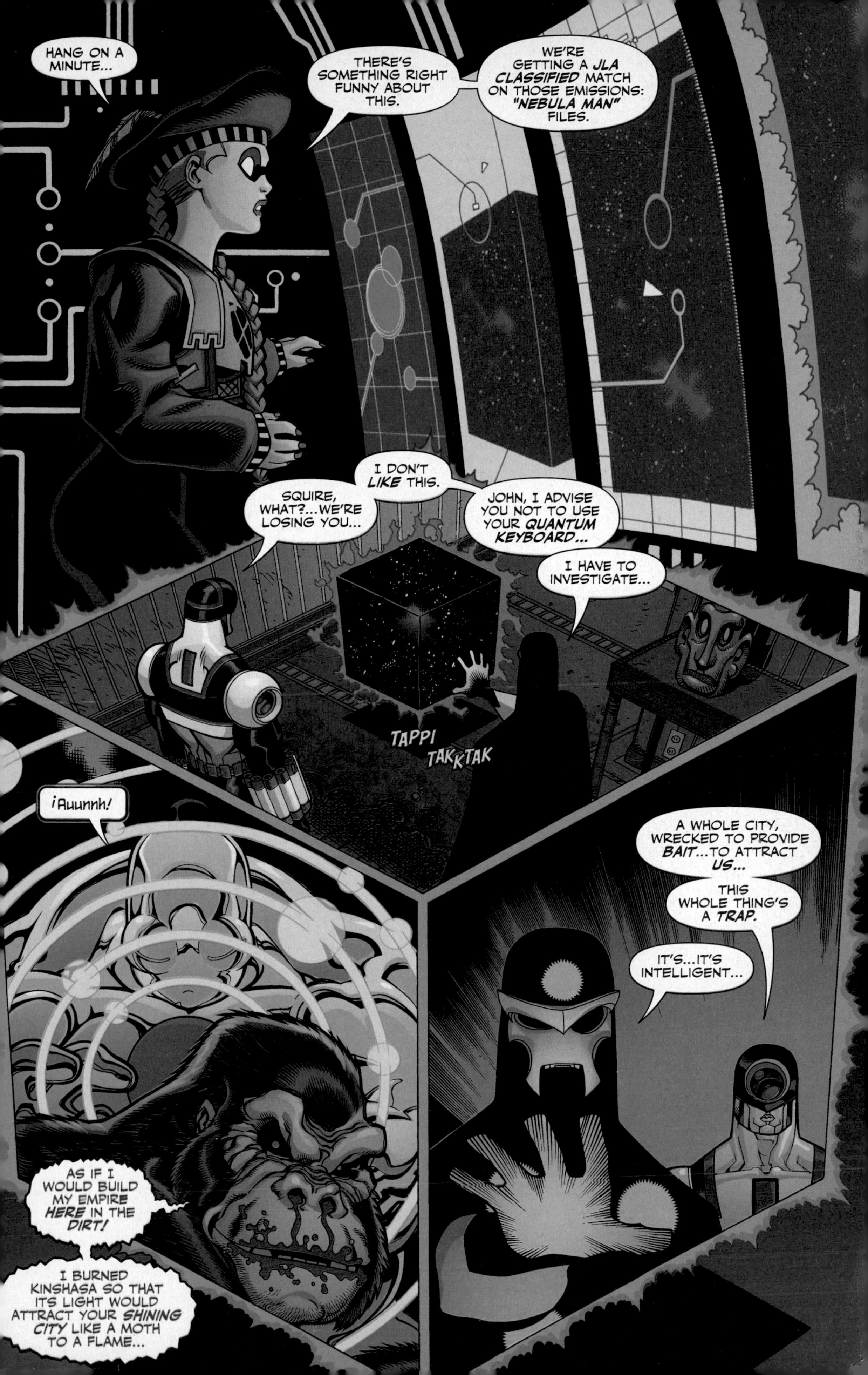
HANG ON A MINUTE...
THERE'S SOMETHING RIGHT FUNNY ABOUT THIS.
WE'RE GETTING A JLA CLASSIFIED MATCH ON THOSE EMISSIONS: "NEBULA MAN" FILES.
I DON'T LIKE THIS.
SQUIRE, WHAT?...WE'RE LOSING YOU...
JOHN, I ADVISE YOU NOT TO USE YOUR QUANTUM KEYBOARD...
I HAVE TO INVESTIGATE...
TAPPI
TAKKTAK
¡Auunnh!
A WHOLE CITY, WRECKED TO PROVIDE BAIT...TO ATTRACT US...
THIS WHOLE THING'S A TRAP.
IT'S...IT'S INTELLIGENT...
AS IF I WOULD BUILD MY EMPIRE HERE IN THE DIRT!
I BURNED KINSHASA SO THAT ITS LIGHT WOULD ATTRACT YOUR SHINING CITY LIKE A MOTH TO A FLAME...

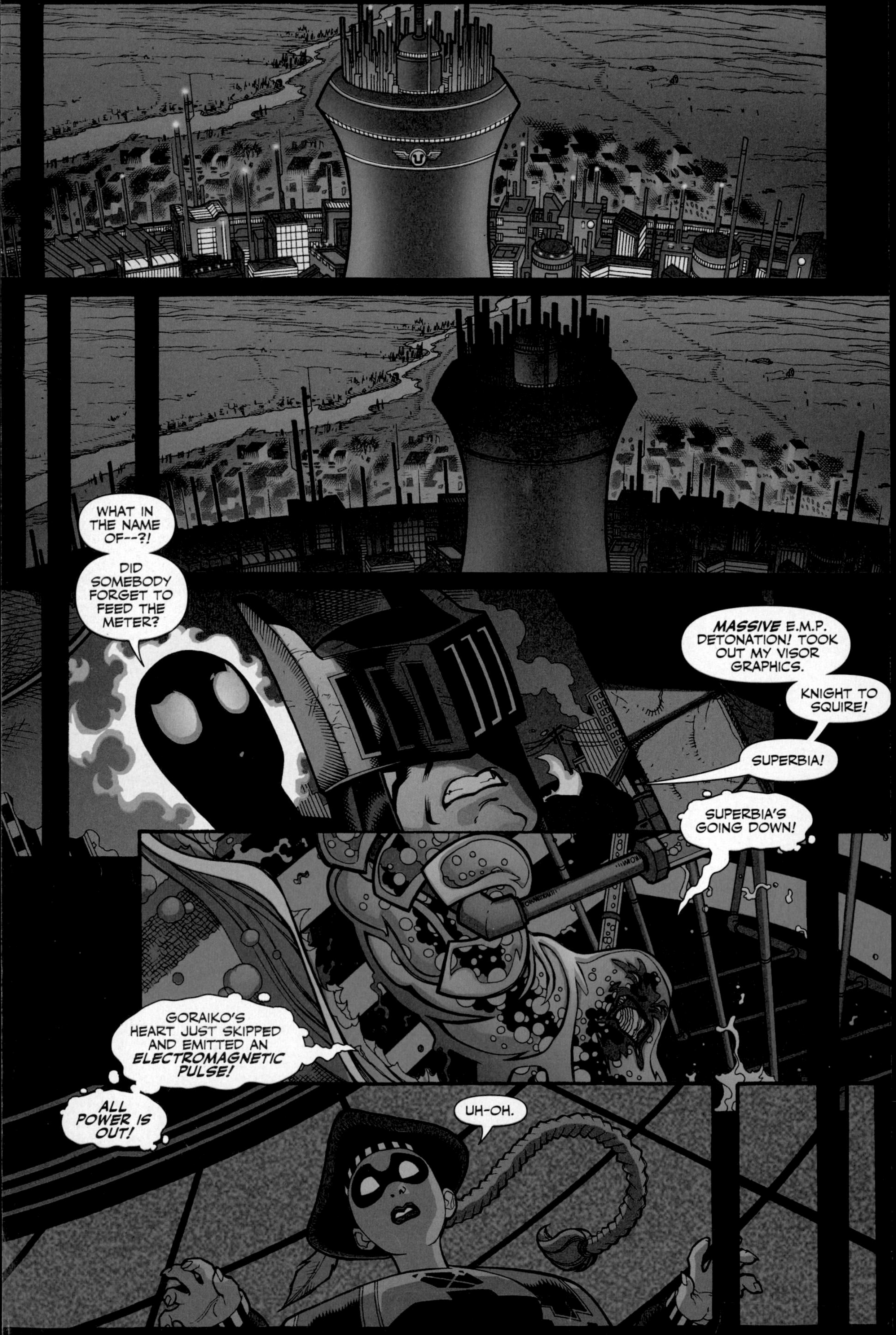
WHAT IN THE NAME OF--?!
DID SOMEBODY FORGET TO FEED THE METER?
MASSIVE E.M.P. DETONATION! TOOK OUT MY VISOR GRAPHICS.
KNIGHT TO SQUIRE!
SUPERBIA!
SUPERBIA'S GOING DOWN!
GORAIKO'S HEART JUST SKIPPED AND EMITTED AN ELECTROMAGNETIC PULSE!
ALL POWER IS OUT!
UH-OH.

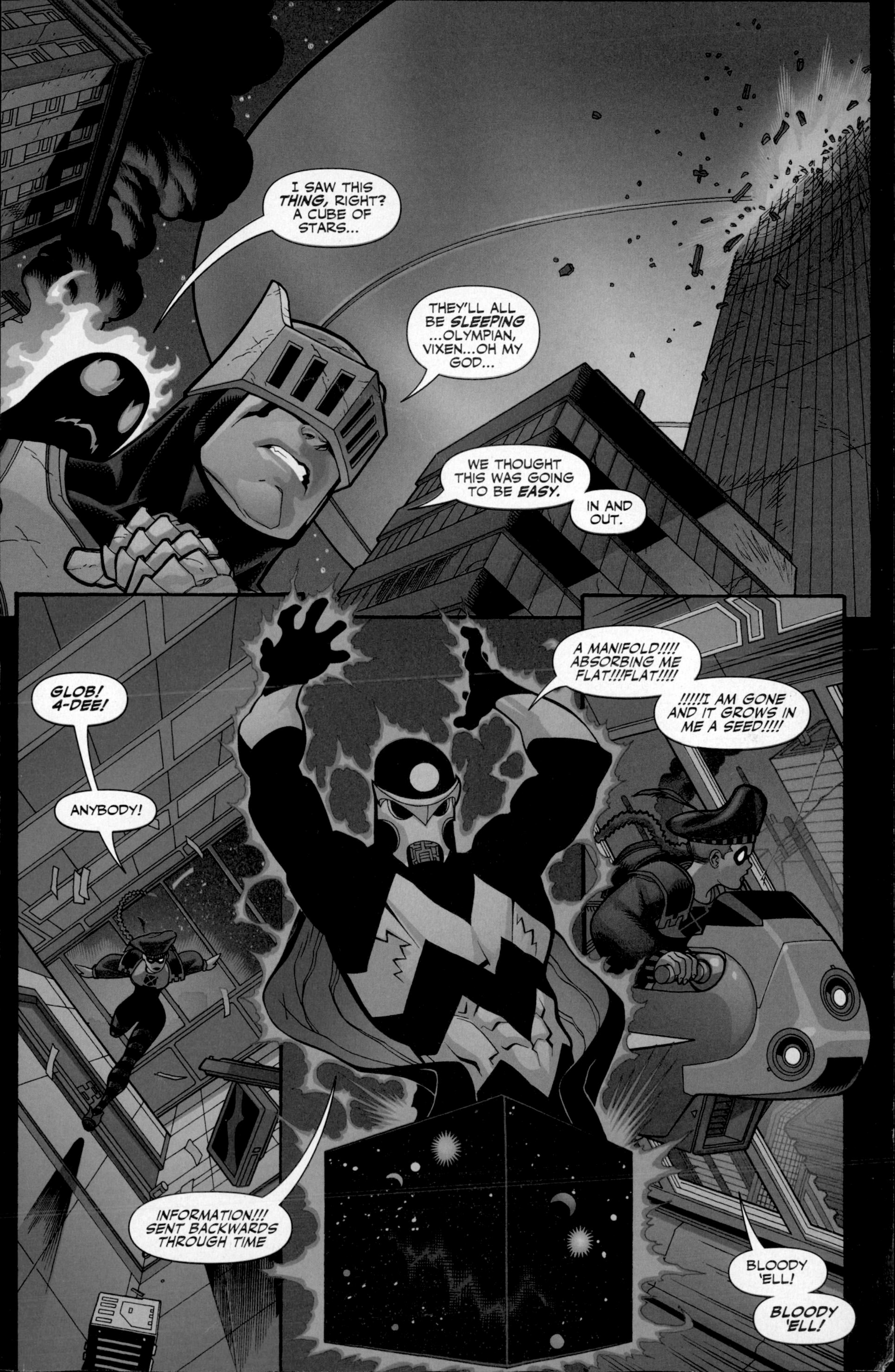
I SAW THIS THING, RIGHT? A CUBE OF STARS...
THEY'LL ALL BE SLEEPING ...OLYMPIAN, VIXEN...OH MY GOD...
WE THOUGHT THIS WAS GOING TO BE EASY.
IN AND OUT.
GLOB! 4-DEE!
ANYBODY!
A MANIFOLD!!!! ABSORBING ME FLAT!!!FLAT!!!!
!!!!!I AM GONE AND IT GROWS IN ME A SEED!!!!
INFORMATION!!! SENT BACKWARDS THROUGH TIME
BLOODY 'ELL!
BLOODY 'ELL!

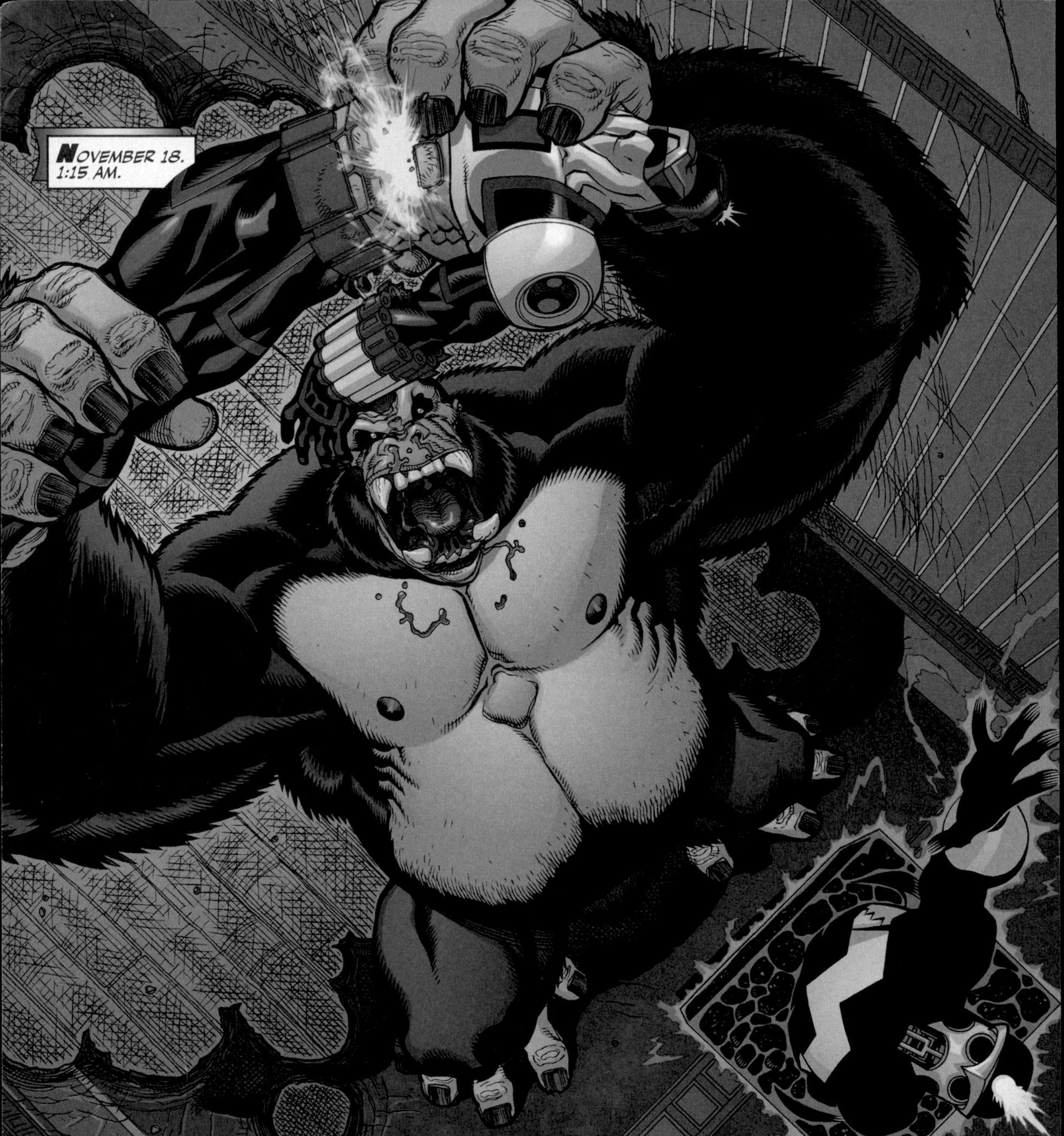
NOVEMBER 18.
1:15 AM.
SAVAGERY IS
CROWNED KING.

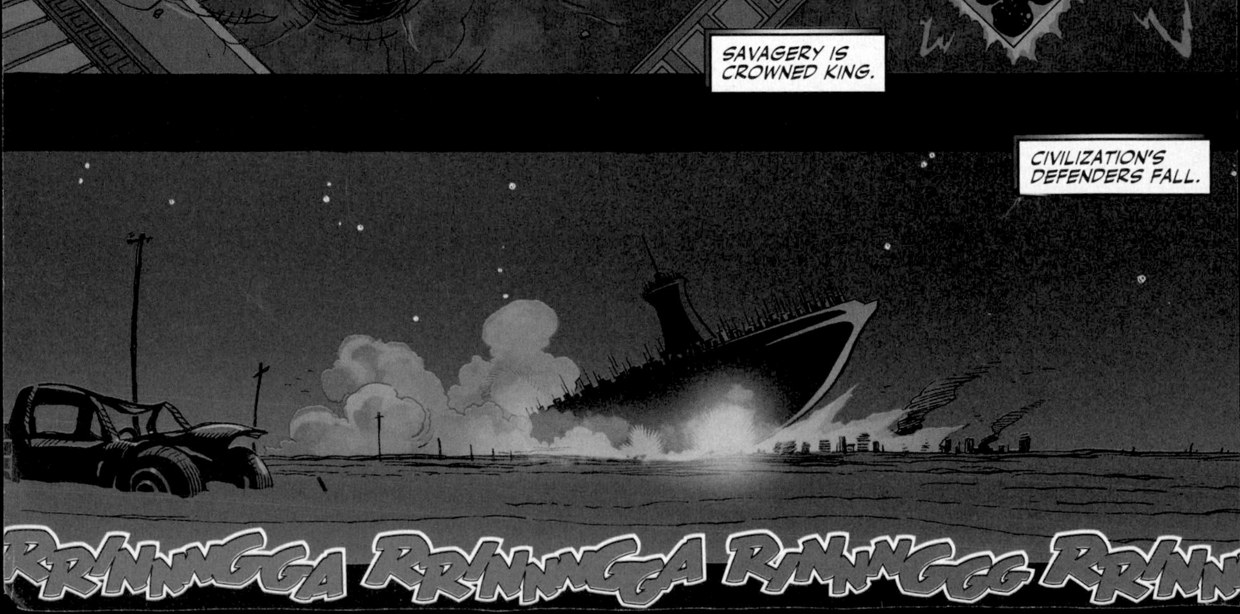
CIVILIZATION'S
DEFENDERS FALL.
RRINNNGGA RRINNNGGA RRINNGGG RRINN

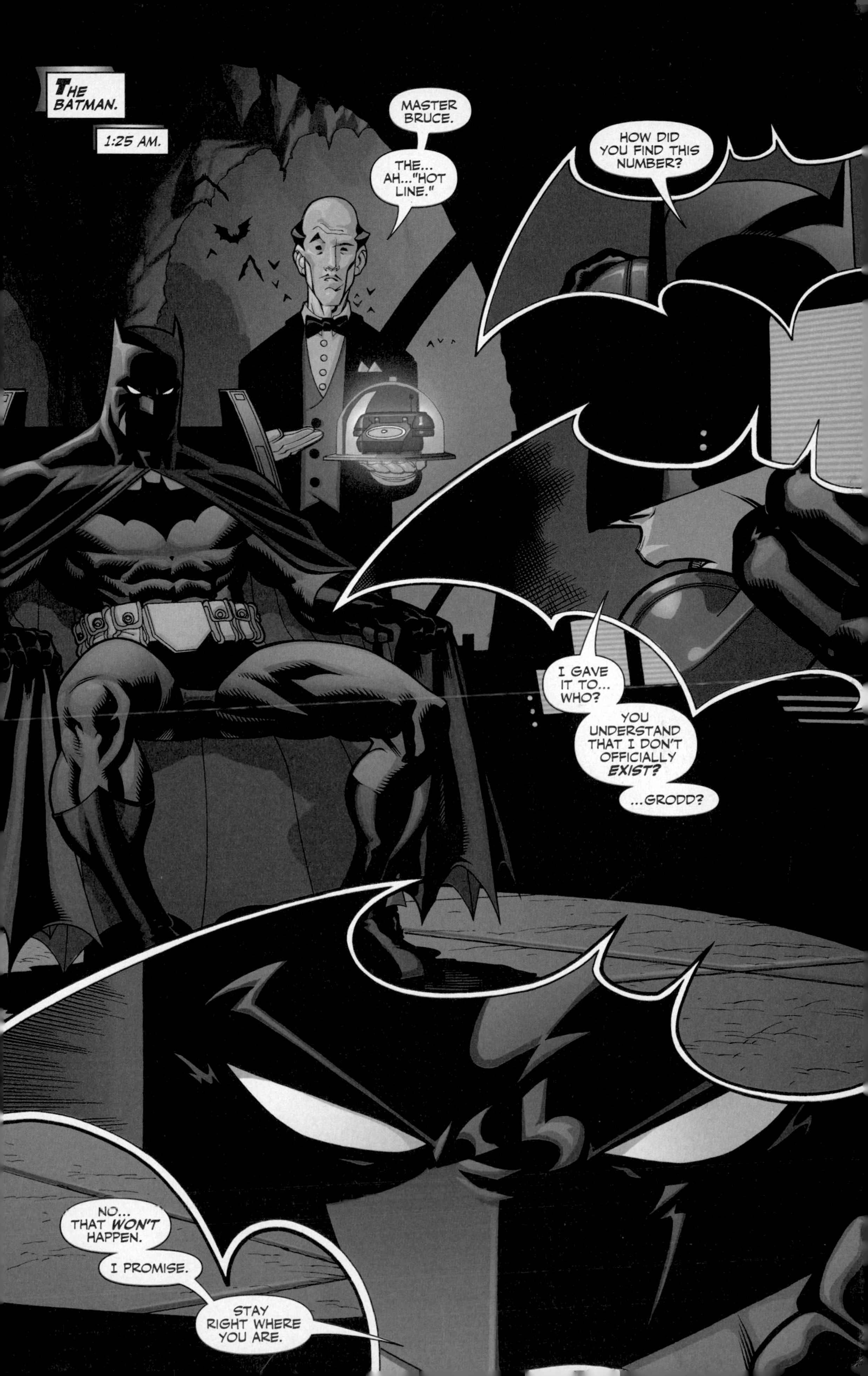
THE BATMAN.
1:25 AM.
MASTER BRUCE.
THE... AH..."HOT LINE."
HOW DID YOU FIND THIS NUMBER?
I GAVE IT TO... WHO?
YOU UNDERSTAND THAT I DON'T OFFICIALLY EXIST?
...GRODD?
NO... THAT WON'T HAPPEN.
I PROMISE.
STAY RIGHT WHERE YOU ARE.

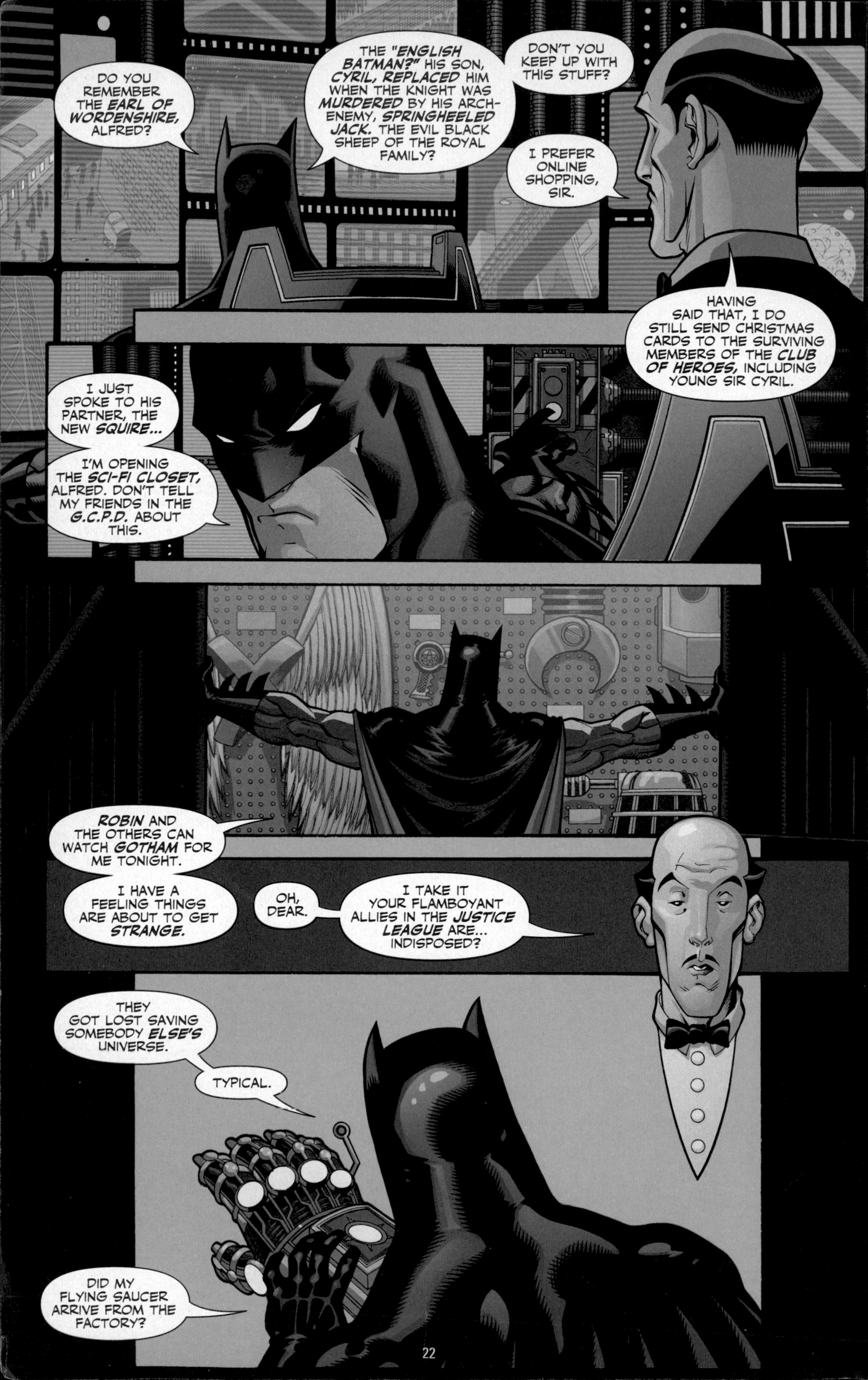
DO YOU REMEMBER THE EARL OF WORDENSHIRE, ALFRED?
THE "ENGLISH BATMAN?" HIS SON, CYRIL, REPLACED HIM WHEN THE KNIGHT WAS MURDERED BY HIS ARCH-ENEMY, SPRINGHEELED JACK. THE EVIL BLACK SHEEP OF THE ROYAL FAMILY?
DON'T YOU KEEP UP WITH THIS STUFF?
I PREFER ONLINE SHOPPING, SIR.
HAVING SAID THAT, I DO STILL SEND CHRISTMAS CARDS TO THE SURVIVING MEMBERS OF THE CLUB OF HEROES, INCLUDING YOUNG SIR CYRIL.
I JUST SPOKE TO HIS PARTNER, THE NEW SQUIRE...
I'M OPENING THE SCI-FI CLOSET, ALFRED. DON'T TELL MY FRIENDS IN THE G.C.P.D. ABOUT THIS.
ROBIN AND THE OTHERS CAN WATCH GOTHAM FOR ME TONIGHT.
I HAVE A FEELING THINGS ARE ABOUT TO GET STRANGE.
OH, DEAR.
I TAKE IT YOUR FLAMBOYANT ALLIES IN THE JUSTICE LEAGUE ARE... INDISPOSED?
THEY GOT LOST SAVING SOMEBODY ELSE'S UNIVERSE.
TYPICAL.
DID MY FLYING SAUCER ARRIVE FROM THE FACTORY?

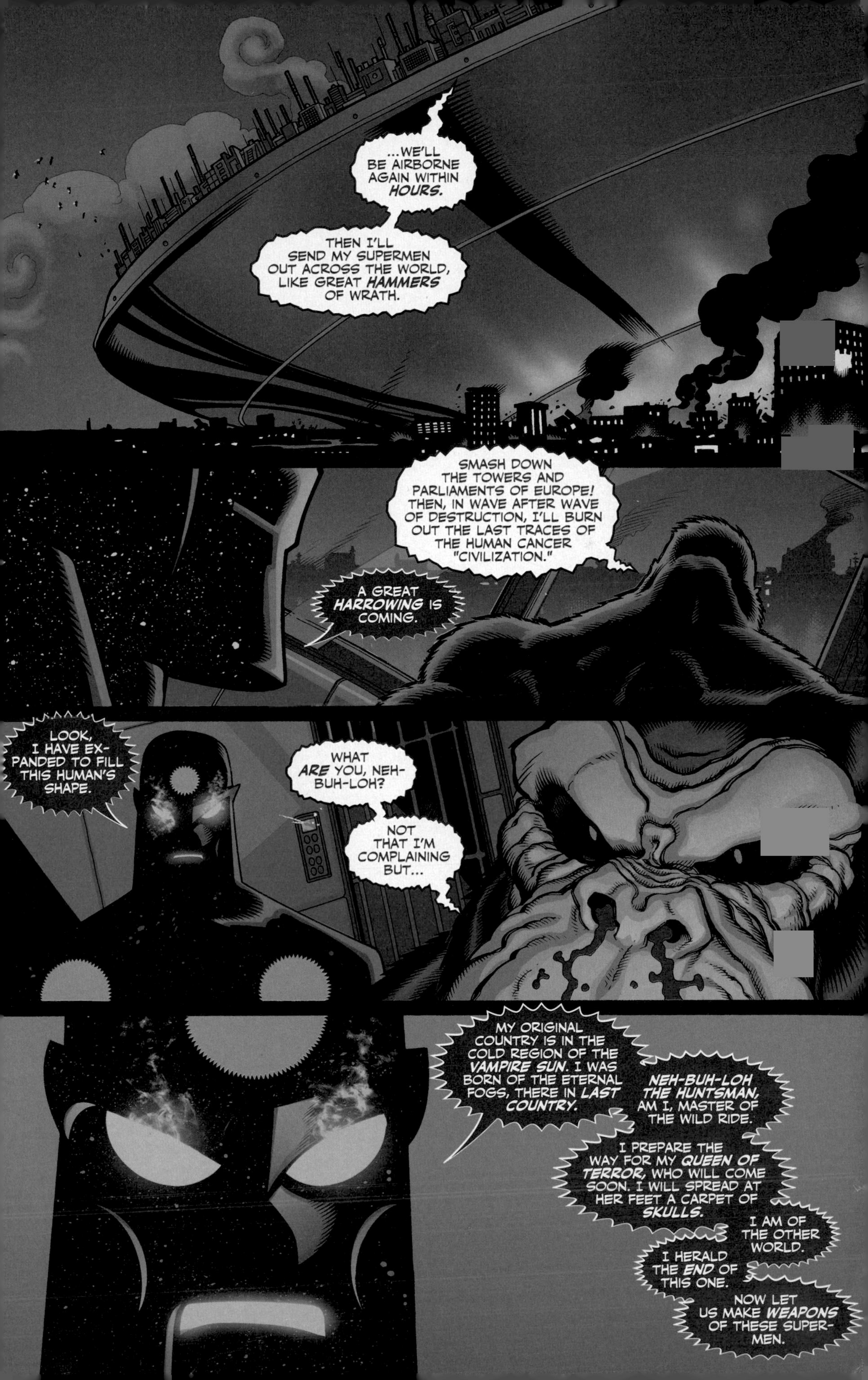
...WE'LL BE AIRBORNE AGAIN WITHIN HOURS.
THEN I'LL SEND MY SUPERMEN OUT ACROSS THE WORLD, LIKE GREAT HAMMERS OF WRATH.
SMASH DOWN THE TOWERS AND PARLIAMENTS OF EUROPE! THEN, IN WAVE AFTER WAVE OF DESTRUCTION, I'LL BURN OUT THE LAST TRACES OF THE HUMAN CANCER "CIVILIZATION."
A GREAT HARROWING IS COMING.
LOOK, I HAVE EX- PANDED TO FILL THIS HUMAN'S SHAPE.
WHAT ARE YOU, NEH- BUH-LOH?
NOT THAT I'M COMPLAINING BUT...
MY ORIGINAL COUNTRY IS IN THE COLD REGION OF THE VAMPIRE SUN. I WAS BORN OF THE ETERNAL FOGS, THERE IN LAST COUNTRY.
NEH-BUH-LOH THE HUNTSMAN, AM I, MASTER OF THE WILD RIDE.
I PREPARE THE WAY FOR MY QUEEN OF TERROR, WHO WILL COME SOON. I WILL SPREAD AT HER FEET A CARPET OF SKULLS.
I AM OF THE OTHER WORLD.
I HERALD THE END OF THIS ONE.
NOW LET US MAKE WEAPONS OF THESE SUPER- MEN.

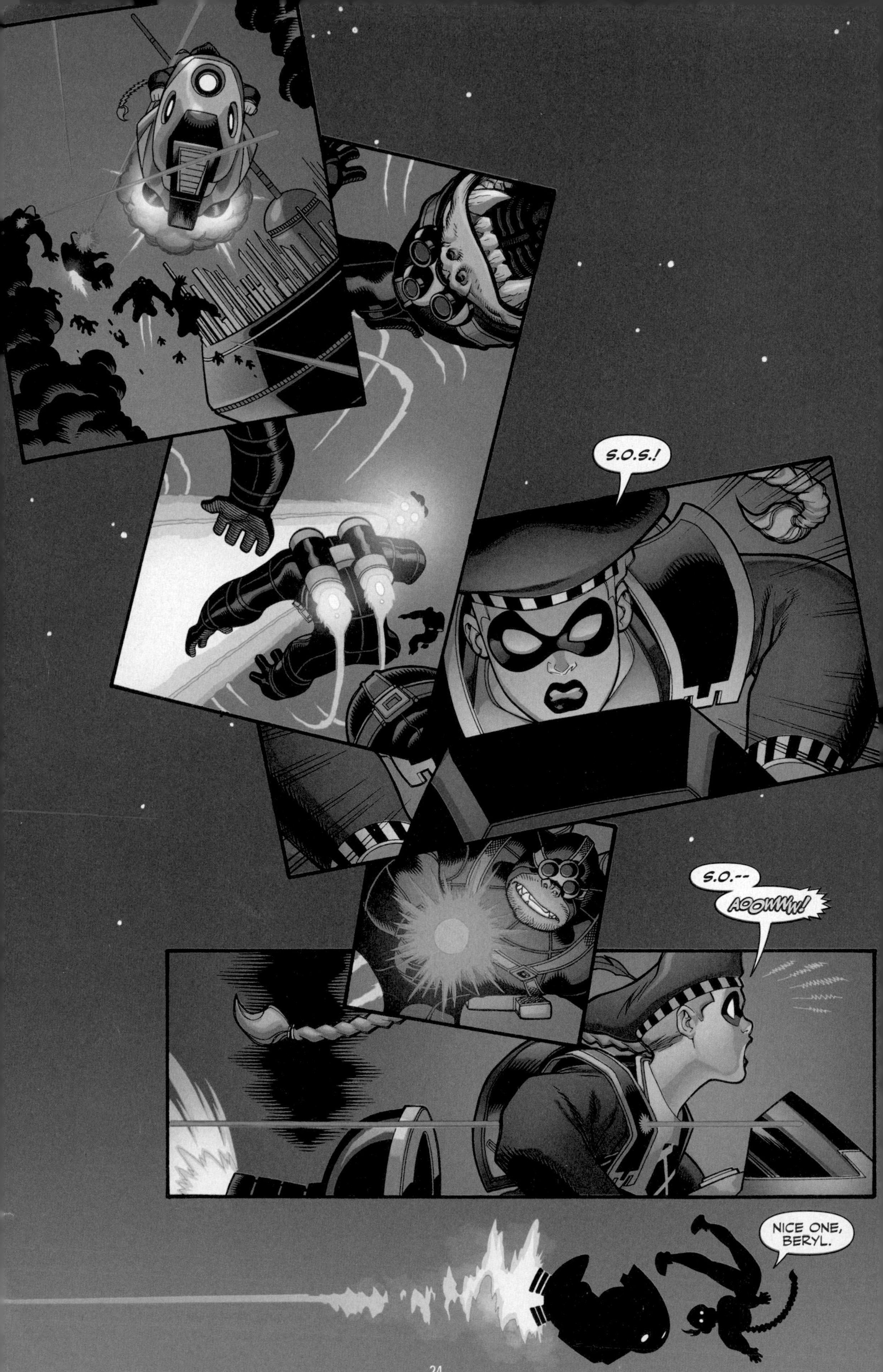
S.O.S.!
S.O.--
AOOWWW!
NICE ONE, BERYL.

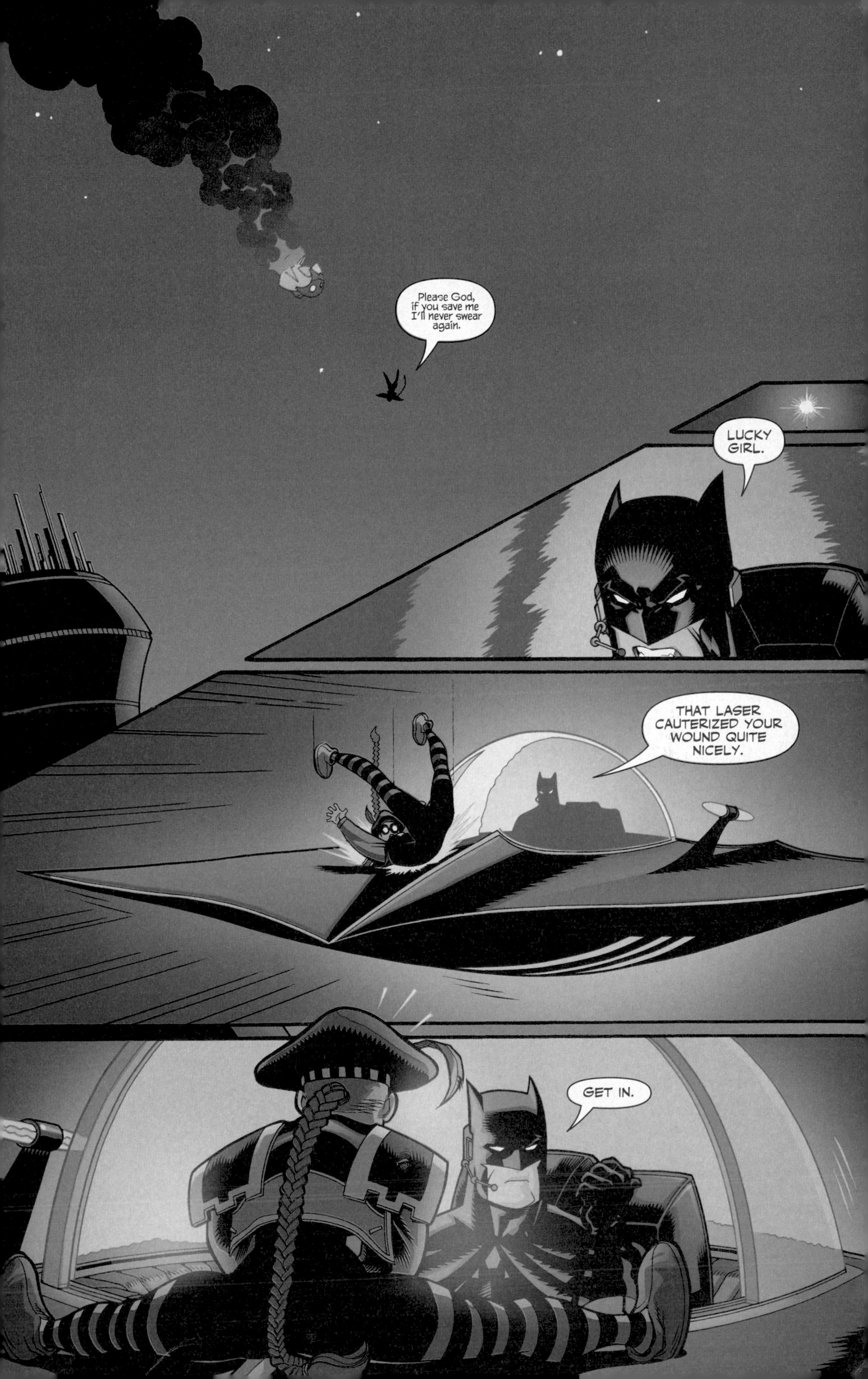
Please God, if you save me I'll never swear again.
LUCKY GIRL.
THAT LASER CAUTERIZED YOUR WOUND QUITE NICELY.
GET IN.

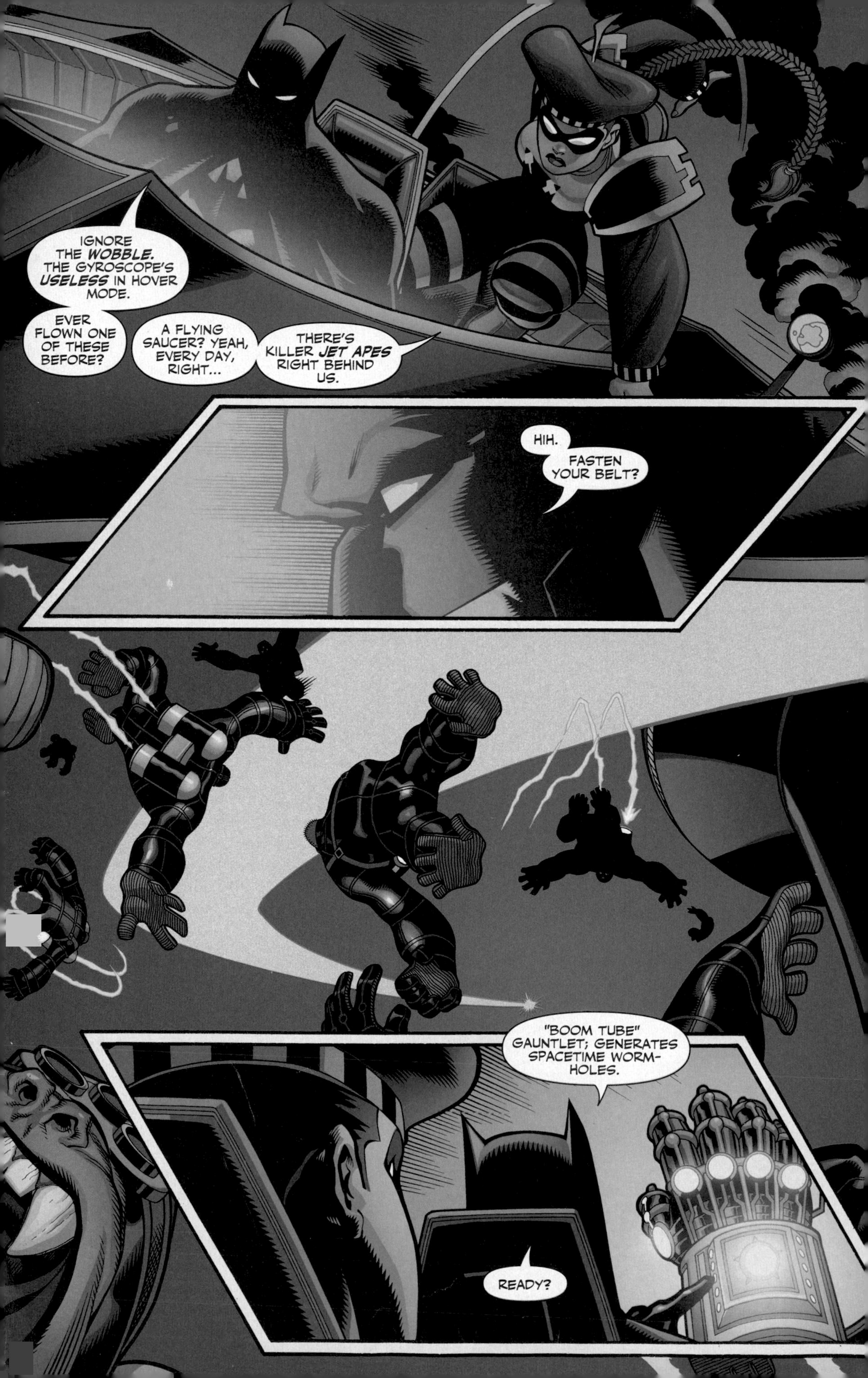

IGNORE THE WOBBLE. THE GYROSCOPE'S USELESS IN HOVER MODE.
EVER FLOWN ONE OF THESE BEFORE?
A FLYING SAUCER? YEAH, EVERY DAY, RIGHT...
THERE'S KILLER JET APES RIGHT BEHIND US.
HIH.
FASTEN YOUR BELT?
"BOOM TUBE" GAUNTLET; GENERATES SPACETIME WORM-HOLES.
READY?

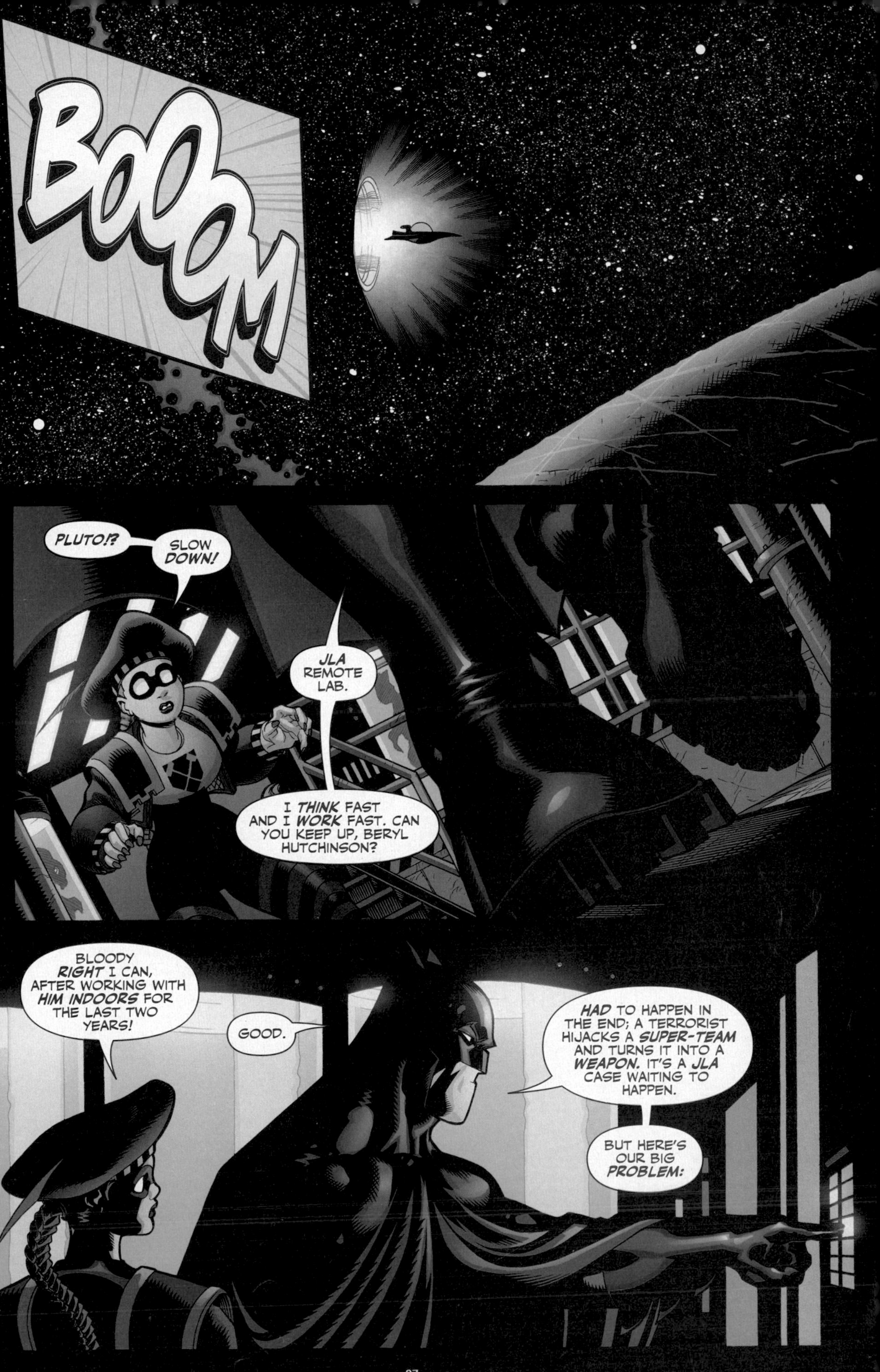
BOOOM
PLUTO!?
SLOW DOWN!
JLA REMOTE LAB.
I THINK FAST AND I WORK FAST. CAN YOU KEEP UP, BERYL HUTCHINSON?
BLOODY RIGHT I CAN, AFTER WORKING WITH HIM INDOORS FOR THE LAST TWO YEARS!
GOOD.
HAD TO HAPPEN IN THE END; A TERRORIST HIJACKS A SUPER-TEAM AND TURNS IT INTO A WEAPON. IT'S A JLA CASE WAITING TO HAPPEN.
BUT HERE'S OUR BIG PROBLEM:

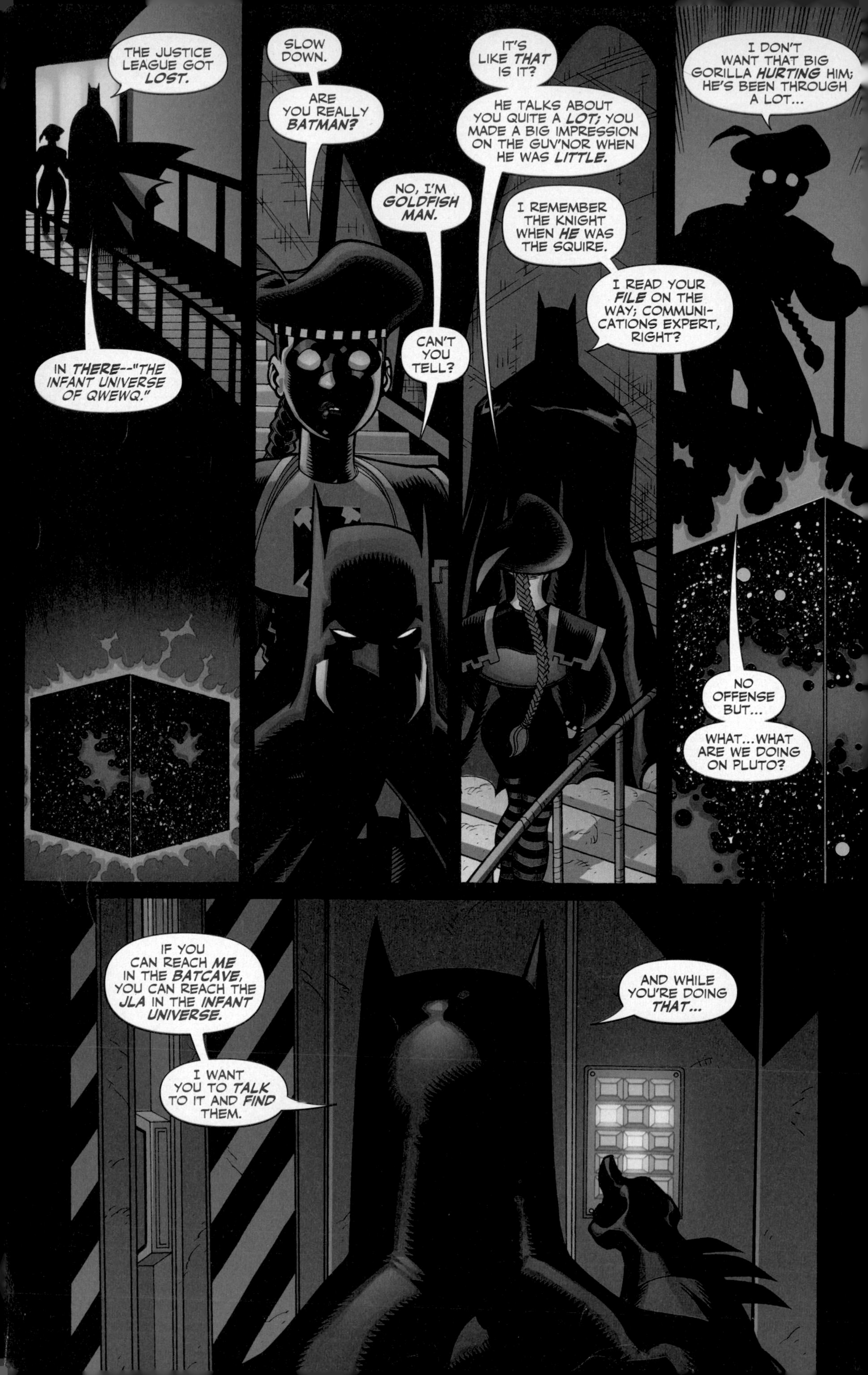
THE JUSTICE LEAGUE GOT *LOST.*
IN *THERE*--"THE INFANT UNIVERSE OF QWEWQ."
SLOW DOWN.
ARE YOU REALLY *BATMAN?*
NO, I'M *GOLDFISH MAN.*
CAN'T YOU TELL?
IT'S LIKE *THAT* IS IT?
HE TALKS ABOUT YOU QUITE A *LOT;* YOU MADE A BIG IMPRESSION ON THE GUV'NOR WHEN HE WAS *LITTLE.*
I REMEMBER THE KNIGHT WHEN *HE* WAS THE SQUIRE.
I READ YOUR *FILE* ON THE WAY; COMMUNICATIONS EXPERT, RIGHT?
I DON'T WANT THAT BIG GORILLA *HURTING* HIM; HE'S BEEN THROUGH A LOT...
NO OFFENSE BUT...
WHAT...WHAT ARE WE DOING ON PLUTO?
IF YOU CAN REACH *ME* IN THE *BATCAVE,* YOU CAN REACH THE *JLA* IN THE *INFANT UNIVERSE.*
I WANT YOU TO *TALK* TO IT AND *FIND* THEM.
AND WHILE YOU'RE DOING *THAT...*

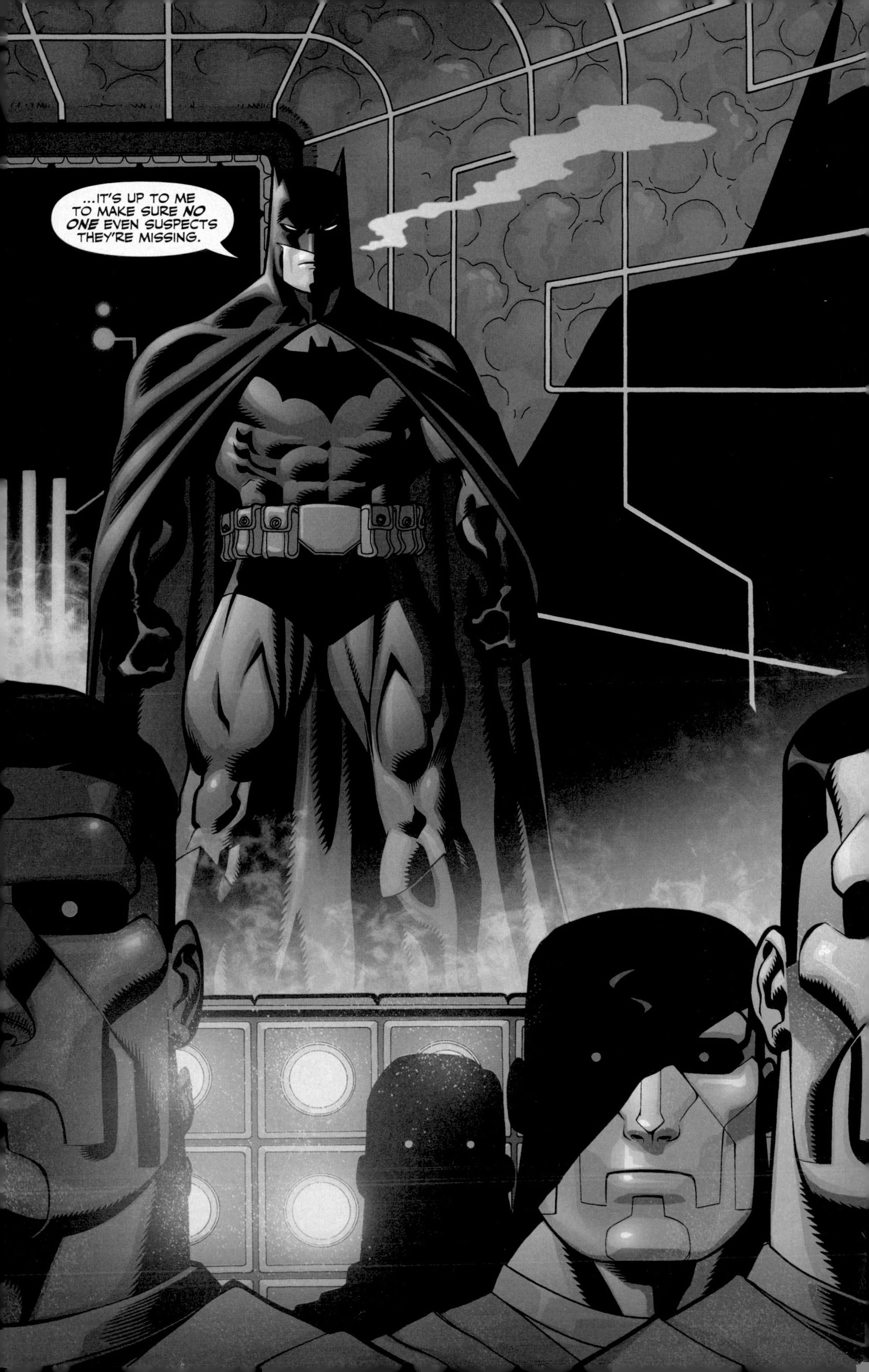
...IT'S UP TO ME TO MAKE SURE *NO ONE* EVEN SUSPECTS THEY'RE MISSING.

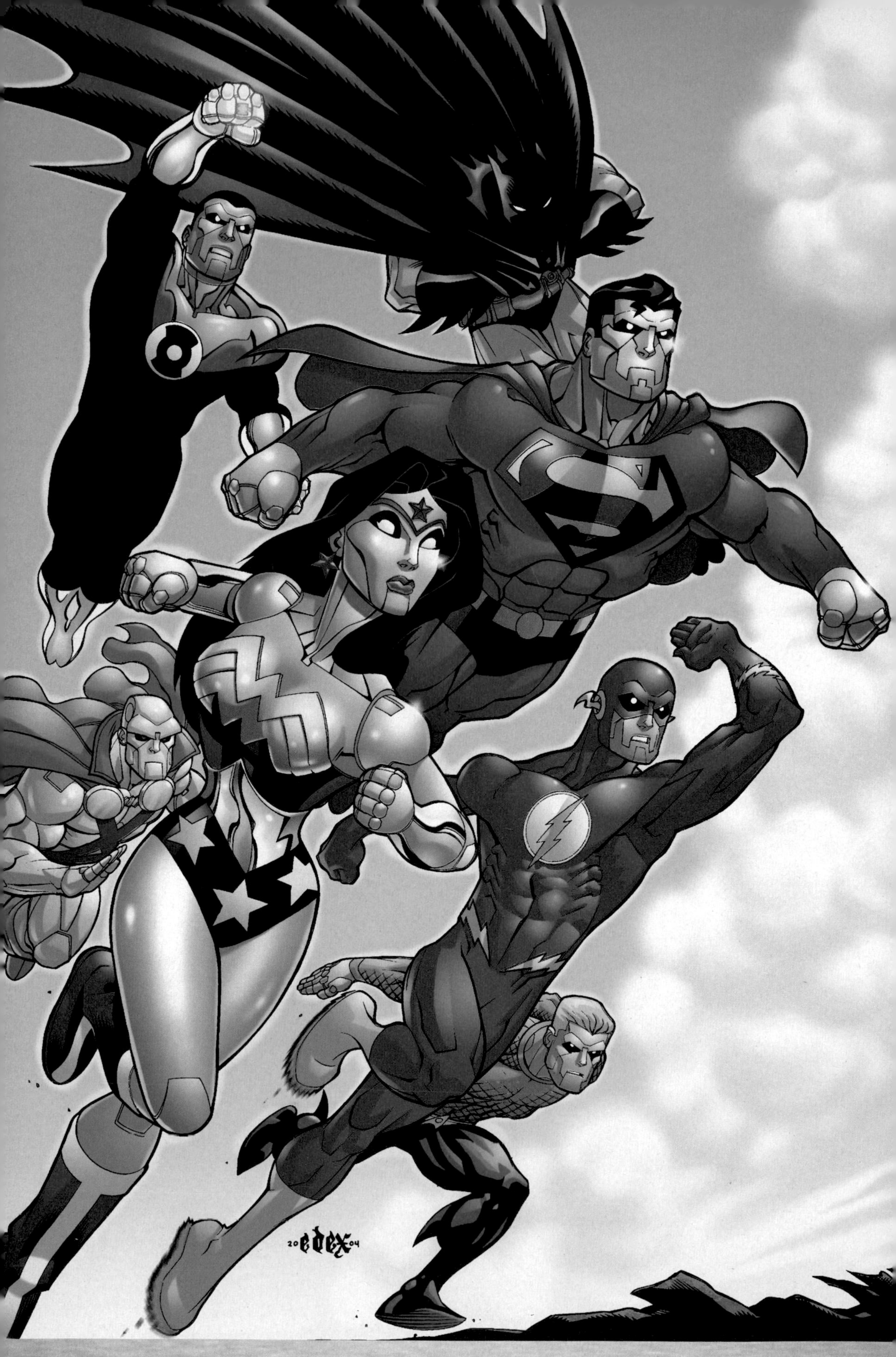
20 edex 04

JLA CLASSIFIED #2

...A SPOKESMAN FOR MICHAEL JACKSON'S LAWYERS...

...MEMBERS OF A PEACE-KEEPING FORCE WERE KILLED OUTSIDE THE TOWN OF...

...TODAY, WHEN THE PRESIDENT GOT TO GRIPS...

I DON'T BELIEVE IT.

THEY MAY AS WELL GIVE MONKEYS THE VOTE.

I'VE NEVER BEEN ABLE TO KEEP A DIARY BEFORE.

⟩HNN!⟨

I'VE NEVER TO KEEP A NO MICROSCOPIC MEN THE WEAVE OF MY X-RAY EYES PROBING

BEEN ABLE DIARY BEFORE. HIDDEN IN TIE, NO ME.

NO ONE PRYING THROUGH MY THOUGHTS. I COULD STAY HERE FOREVER. I LOVE THIS PLACE.

WOULD YOU MIND?

I'LL BE RIGHT BACK FOR IT.

SWEET.

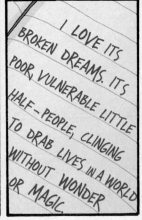

I LOVE ITS BROKEN DREAMS. ITS POOR, VULNERABLE LITTLE HALF-PEOPLE, CLINGING TO DRAB LIVES IN A WORLD WITHOUT WONDER OR MAGIC.

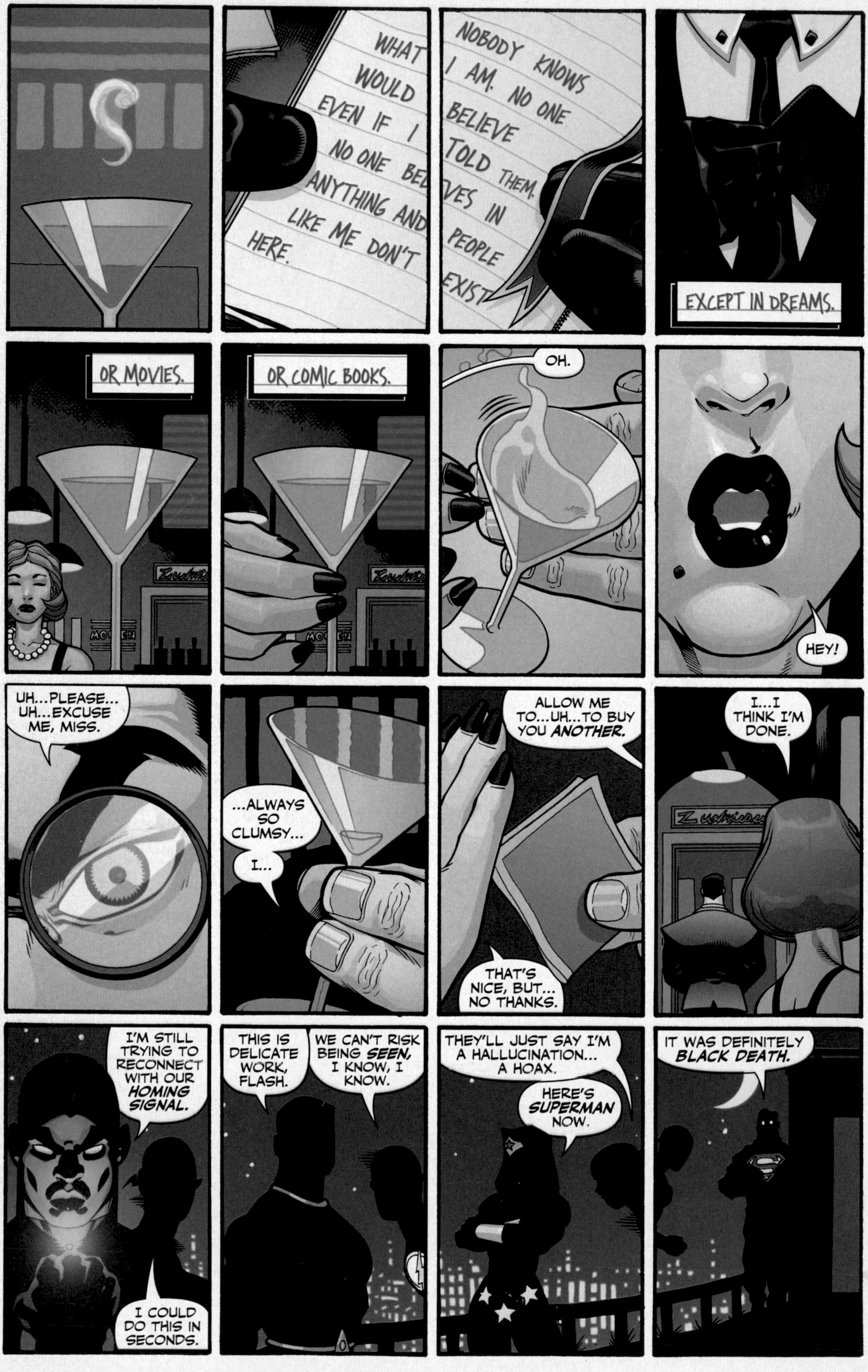
WHAT WOULD EVEN IF I NO ONE BELIEVES ANYTHING AND LIKE ME DON'T HERE.
NOBODY KNOWS I AM. NO ONE BELIEVE TOLD THEM. IN PEOPLE EXIST
EXCEPT IN DREAMS.
OR MOVIES.
OR COMIC BOOKS.
OH.
HEY!
UH...PLEASE... UH...EXCUSE ME, MISS.
...ALWAYS SO CLUMSY...
I...
ALLOW ME TO...UH...TO BUY YOU ANOTHER.
THAT'S NICE, BUT... NO THANKS.
I...I THINK I'M DONE.
I'M STILL TRYING TO RECONNECT WITH OUR HOMING SIGNAL.
I COULD DO THIS IN SECONDS.
THIS IS DELICATE WORK, FLASH.
WE CAN'T RISK BEING SEEN, I KNOW, I KNOW.
THEY'LL JUST SAY I'M A HALLUCINATION... A HOAX.
HERE'S SUPERMAN NOW.
IT WAS DEFINITELY BLACK DEATH.

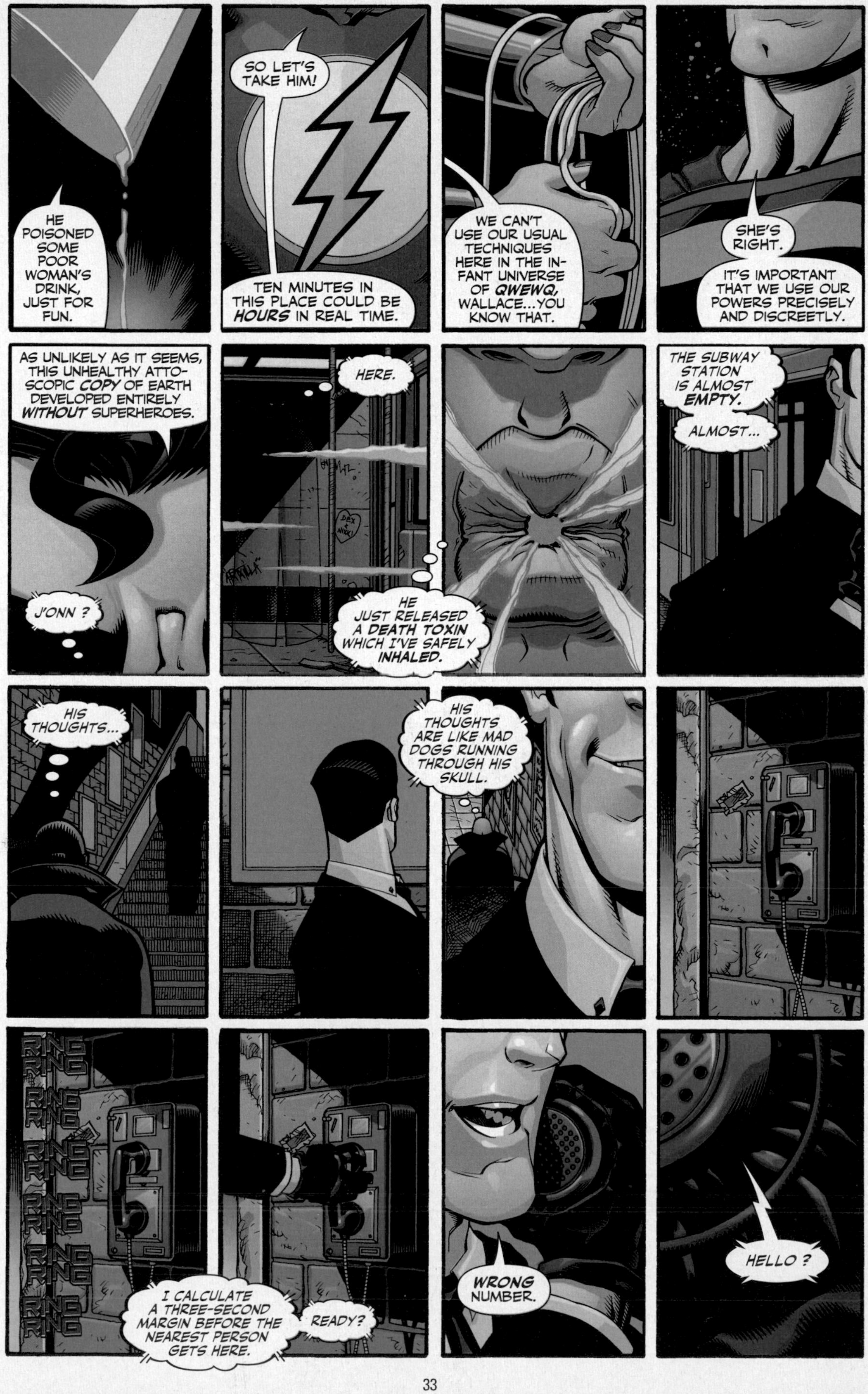
HE POISONED SOME POOR WOMAN'S DRINK, JUST FOR FUN.
SO LET'S TAKE HIM!
TEN MINUTES IN THIS PLACE COULD BE HOURS IN REAL TIME.
WE CAN'T USE OUR USUAL TECHNIQUES HERE IN THE INFANT UNIVERSE OF QWEWQ, WALLACE...YOU KNOW THAT.
SHE'S RIGHT.
IT'S IMPORTANT THAT WE USE OUR POWERS PRECISELY AND DISCREETLY.
AS UNLIKELY AS IT SEEMS, THIS UNHEALTHY ATTO-SCOPIC COPY OF EARTH DEVELOPED ENTIRELY WITHOUT SUPERHEROES.
J'ONN ?
HERE.
HE JUST RELEASED A DEATH TOXIN WHICH I'VE SAFELY INHALED.
THE SUBWAY STATION IS ALMOST EMPTY.
ALMOST...
HIS THOUGHTS...
HIS THOUGHTS ARE LIKE MAD DOGS RUNNING THROUGH HIS SKULL.
RING RING RING RING RING RING RING RING RING RING
I CALCULATE A THREE-SECOND MARGIN BEFORE THE NEAREST PERSON GETS HERE.
READY?
WRONG NUMBER.
HELLO ?

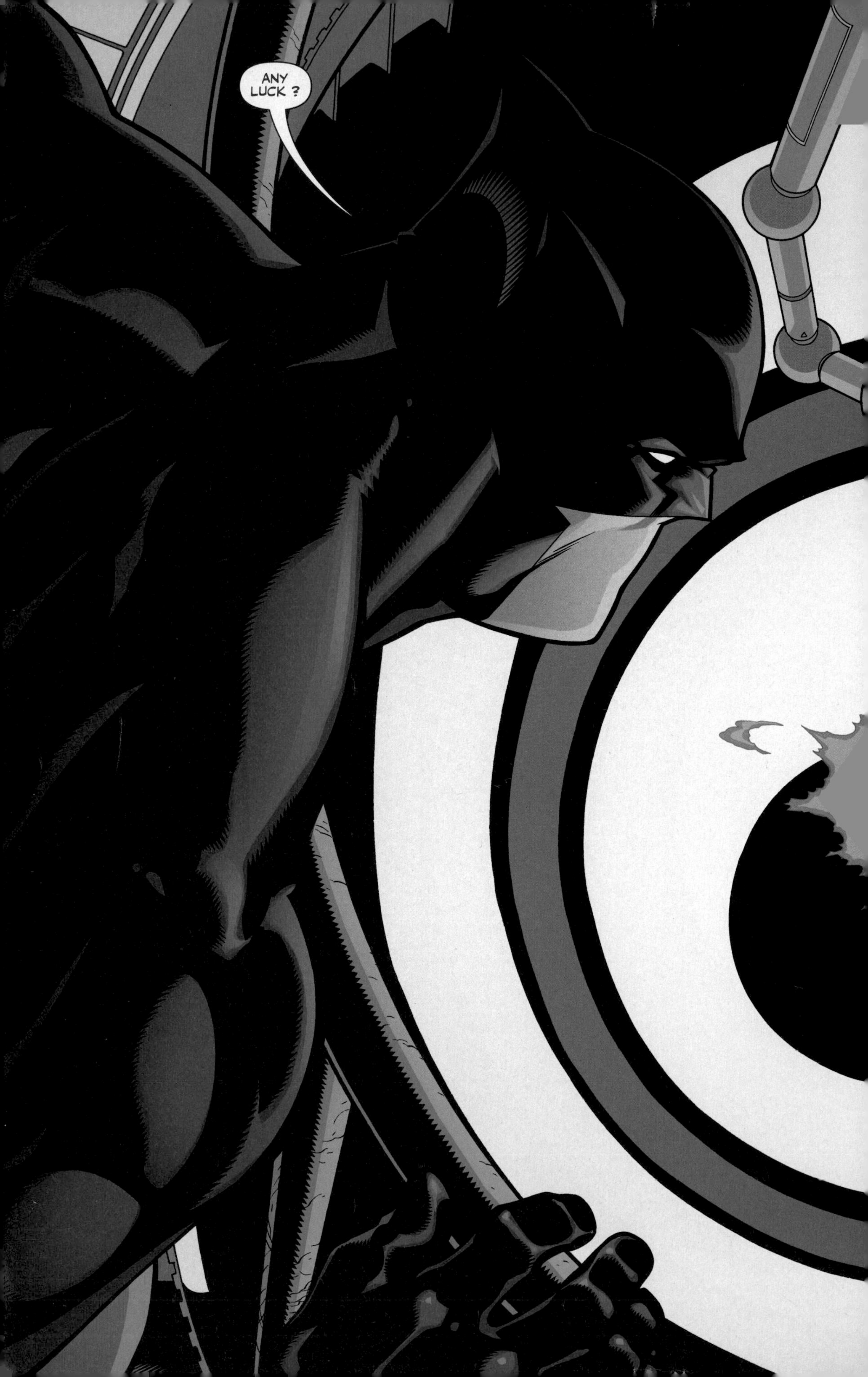
ANY LUCK ?

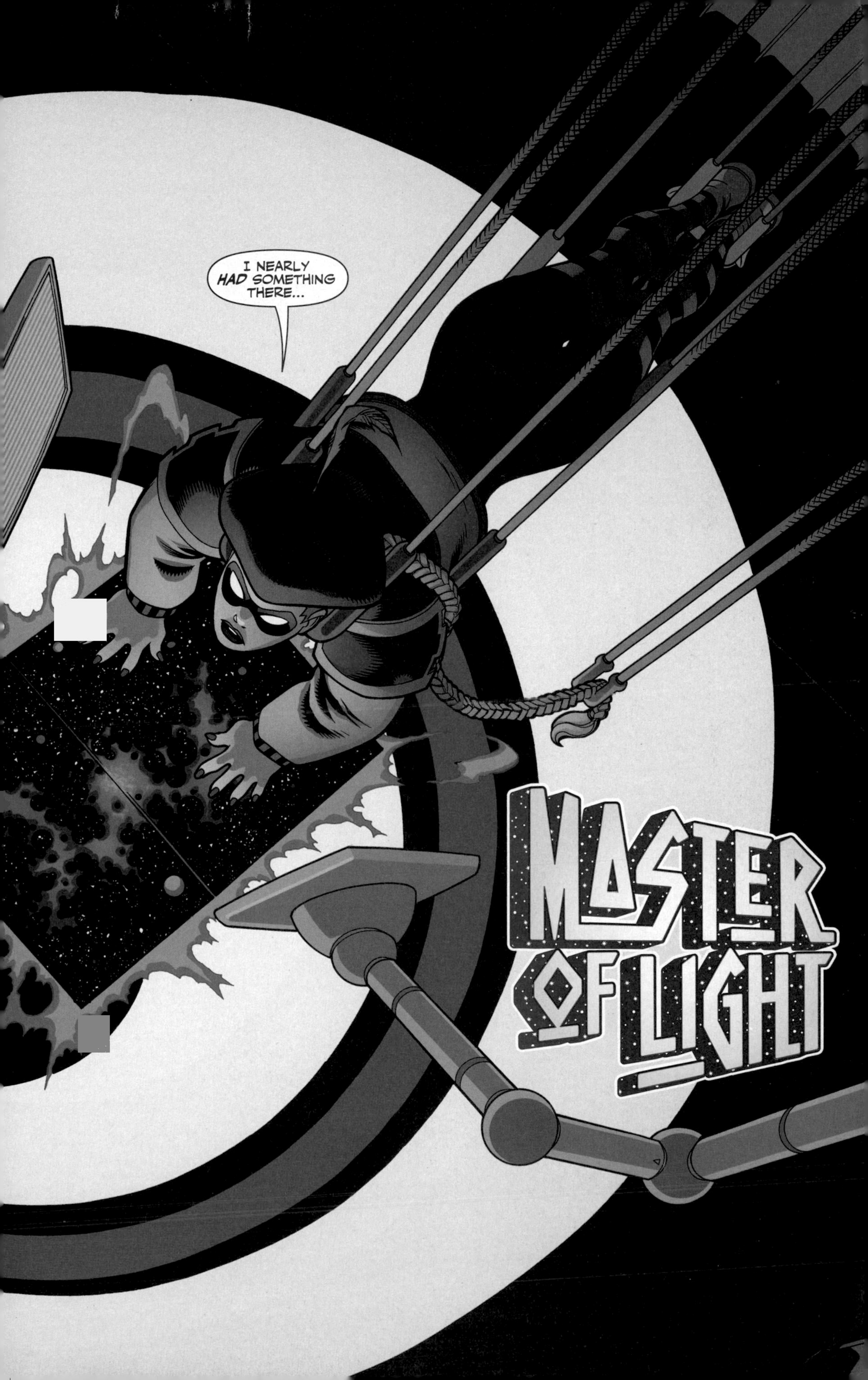
I NEARLY HAD SOMETHING THERE...
MASTER OF LIGHT

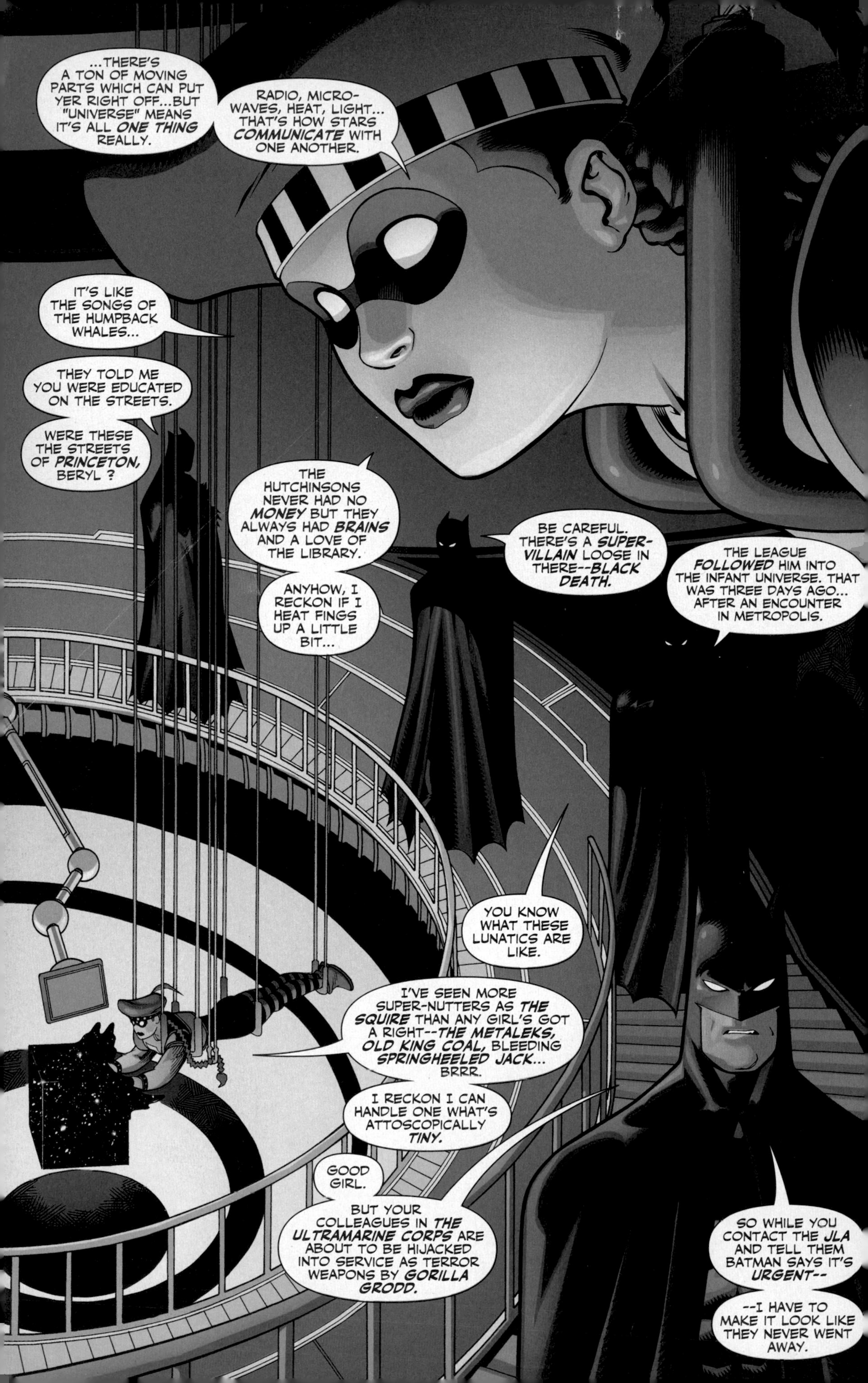
...THERE'S A TON OF MOVING PARTS WHICH CAN PUT YER RIGHT OFF...BUT "UNIVERSE" MEANS IT'S ALL ONE THING REALLY.
RADIO, MICRO-WAVES, HEAT, LIGHT... THAT'S HOW STARS COMMUNICATE WITH ONE ANOTHER.
IT'S LIKE THE SONGS OF THE HUMPBACK WHALES...
THEY TOLD ME YOU WERE EDUCATED ON THE STREETS.
WERE THESE THE STREETS OF PRINCETON, BERYL ?
THE HUTCHINSONS NEVER HAD NO MONEY BUT THEY ALWAYS HAD BRAINS AND A LOVE OF THE LIBRARY.
ANYHOW, I RECKON IF I HEAT FINGS UP A LITTLE BIT...
BE CAREFUL. THERE'S A SUPER-VILLAIN LOOSE IN THERE--BLACK DEATH.
THE LEAGUE FOLLOWED HIM INTO THE INFANT UNIVERSE. THAT WAS THREE DAYS AGO... AFTER AN ENCOUNTER IN METROPOLIS.
YOU KNOW WHAT THESE LUNATICS ARE LIKE.
I'VE SEEN MORE SUPER-NUTTERS AS THE SQUIRE THAN ANY GIRL'S GOT A RIGHT--THE METALEKS, OLD KING COAL, BLEEDING SPRINGHEELED JACK... BRRR.
I RECKON I CAN HANDLE ONE WHAT'S ATTOSCOPICALLY TINY.
GOOD GIRL.
BUT YOUR COLLEAGUES IN THE ULTRAMARINE CORPS ARE ABOUT TO BE HIJACKED INTO SERVICE AS TERROR WEAPONS BY GORILLA GRODD.
SO WHILE YOU CONTACT THE JLA AND TELL THEM BATMAN SAYS IT'S URGENT--
--I HAVE TO MAKE IT LOOK LIKE THEY NEVER WENT AWAY.

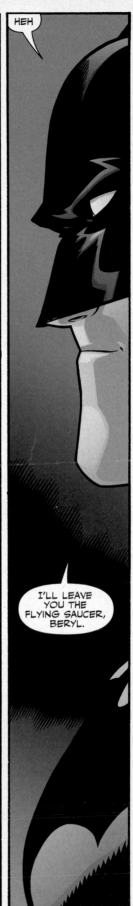

Look after yourself, Batman.

HEH

I'LL LEAVE YOU THE FLYING SAUCER, BERYL.

BOOM TUBE ENGAGE.

YOU'VE GOT MY *NUMBER* IF YOU NEED IT.

"KNIGHT TO PAWNS 1 THROUGH 5."

FOLLOW ME.

POWERS ONLINE.

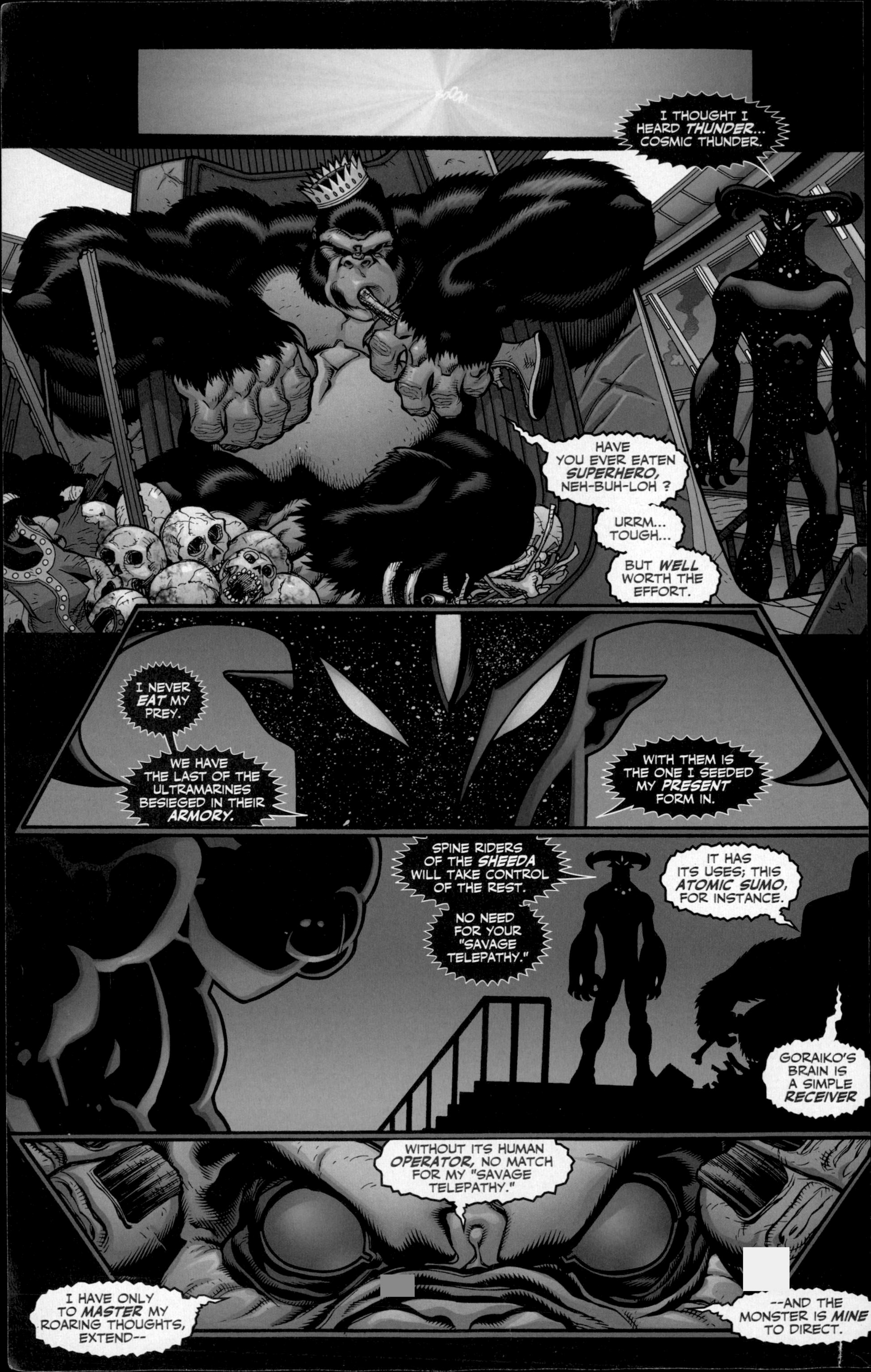
I THOUGHT I HEARD THUNDER... COSMIC THUNDER.
HAVE YOU EVER EATEN SUPERHERO, NEH-BUH-LOH ?
URRM... TOUGH...
BUT WELL WORTH THE EFFORT.
I NEVER EAT MY PREY.
WE HAVE THE LAST OF THE ULTRAMARINES BESIEGED IN THEIR ARMORY.
WITH THEM IS THE ONE I SEEDED MY PRESENT FORM IN.
SPINE RIDERS OF THE SHEEDA WILL TAKE CONTROL OF THE REST.
NO NEED FOR YOUR "SAVAGE TELEPATHY."
IT HAS ITS USES; THIS ATOMIC SUMO, FOR INSTANCE.
GORAIKO'S BRAIN IS A SIMPLE RECEIVER
WITHOUT ITS HUMAN OPERATOR, NO MATCH FOR MY "SAVAGE TELEPATHY."
I HAVE ONLY TO MASTER MY ROARING THOUGHTS, EXTEND--
--AND THE MONSTER IS MINE TO DIRECT.

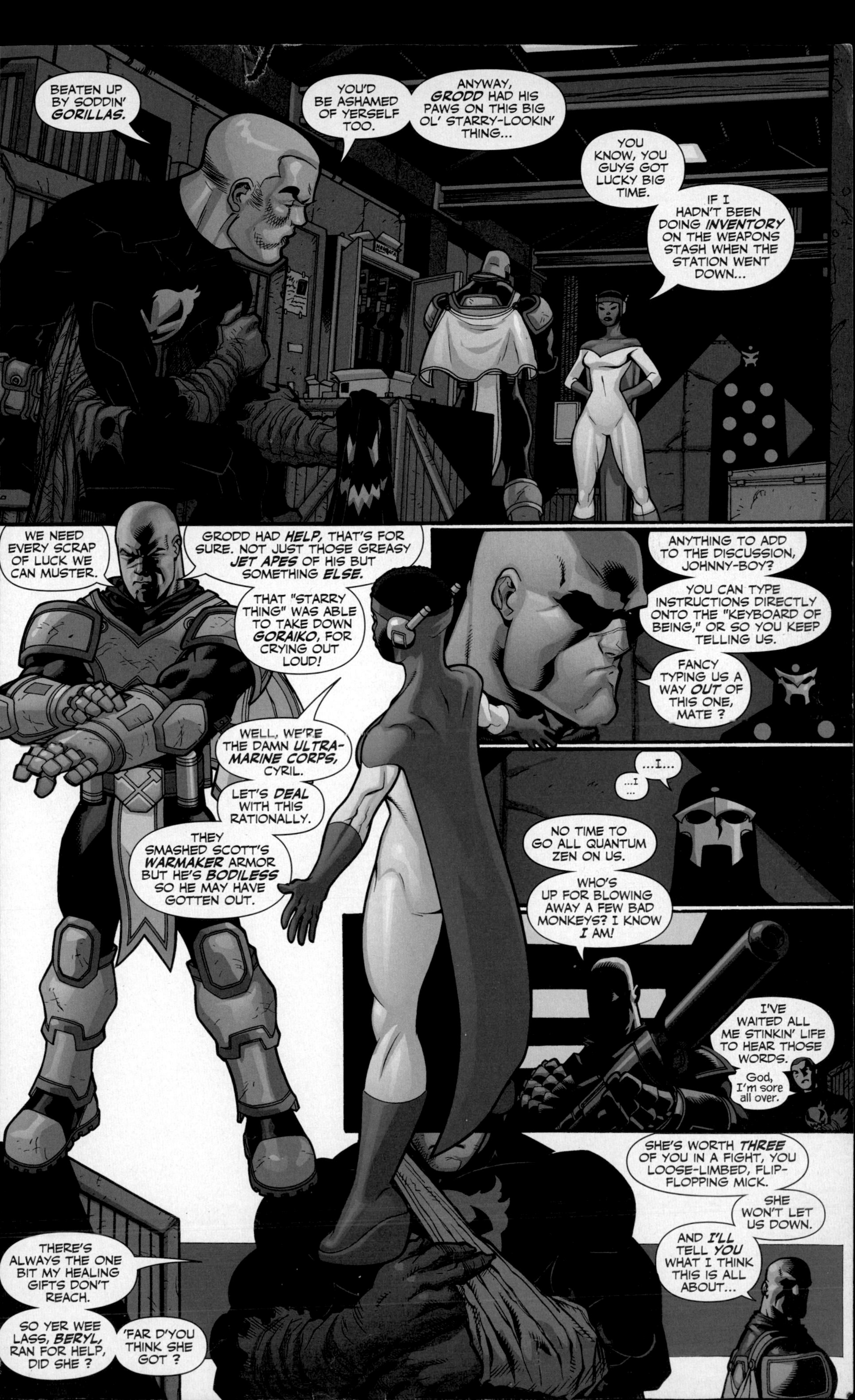

BEATEN UP BY SODDIN' GORILLAS.
YOU'D BE ASHAMED OF YERSELF TOO.
ANYWAY, GRODD HAD HIS PAWS ON THIS BIG OL' STARRY-LOOKIN' THING...
YOU KNOW, YOU GUYS GOT LUCKY BIG TIME.
IF I HADN'T BEEN DOING INVENTORY ON THE WEAPONS STASH WHEN THE STATION WENT DOWN...
WE NEED EVERY SCRAP OF LUCK WE CAN MUSTER.
GRODD HAD HELP, THAT'S FOR SURE. NOT JUST THOSE GREASY JET APES OF HIS BUT SOMETHING ELSE.
THAT "STARRY THING" WAS ABLE TO TAKE DOWN GORAIKO, FOR CRYING OUT LOUD!
WELL, WE'RE THE DAMN ULTRA-MARINE CORPS, CYRIL.
LET'S DEAL WITH THIS RATIONALLY.
THEY SMASHED SCOTT'S WARMAKER ARMOR BUT HE'S BODILESS SO HE MAY HAVE GOTTEN OUT.
ANYTHING TO ADD TO THE DISCUSSION, JOHNNY-BOY?
YOU CAN TYPE INSTRUCTIONS DIRECTLY ONTO THE "KEYBOARD OF BEING," OR SO YOU KEEP TELLING US.
FANCY TYPING US A WAY OUT OF THIS ONE, MATE ?
...I...
...I ...
NO TIME TO GO ALL QUANTUM ZEN ON US.
WHO'S UP FOR BLOWING AWAY A FEW BAD MONKEYS? I KNOW I AM!
I'VE WAITED ALL ME STINKIN' LIFE TO HEAR THOSE WORDS.
God, I'm sore all over.
THERE'S ALWAYS THE ONE BIT MY HEALING GIFTS DON'T REACH.
SO YER WEE LASS, BERYL, RAN FOR HELP, DID SHE ?
'FAR D'YOU THINK SHE GOT ?
SHE'S WORTH THREE OF YOU IN A FIGHT, YOU LOOSE-LIMBED, FLIP-FLOPPING MICK.
SHE WON'T LET US DOWN.
AND I'LL TELL YOU WHAT I THINK THIS IS ALL ABOUT...

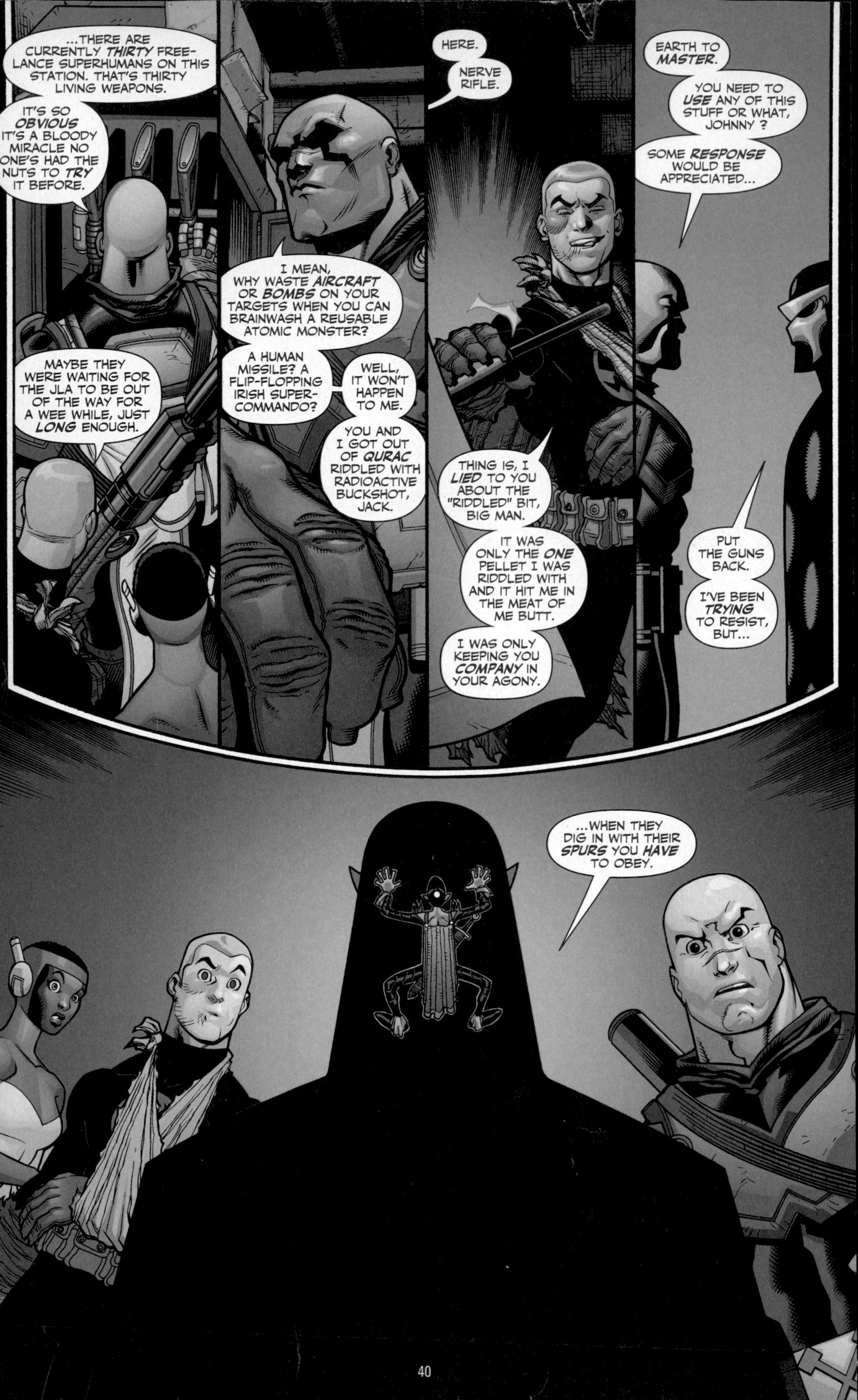

...THERE ARE CURRENTLY THIRTY FREE-LANCE SUPERHUMANS ON THIS STATION. THAT'S THIRTY LIVING WEAPONS.
IT'S SO OBVIOUS IT'S A BLOODY MIRACLE NO ONE'S HAD THE NUTS TO TRY IT BEFORE.
MAYBE THEY WERE WAITING FOR THE JLA TO BE OUT OF THE WAY FOR A WEE WHILE, JUST LONG ENOUGH.
I MEAN, WHY WASTE AIRCRAFT OR BOMBS ON YOUR TARGETS WHEN YOU CAN BRAINWASH A REUSABLE ATOMIC MONSTER?
A HUMAN MISSILE? A FLIP-FLOPPING IRISH SUPER-COMMANDO?
WELL, IT WON'T HAPPEN TO ME.
YOU AND I GOT OUT OF QURAC RIDDLED WITH RADIOACTIVE BUCKSHOT, JACK.
HERE.
NERVE RIFLE.
THING IS, I LIED TO YOU ABOUT THE "RIDDLED" BIT, BIG MAN.
IT WAS ONLY THE ONE PELLET I WAS RIDDLED WITH AND IT HIT ME IN THE MEAT OF ME BUTT.
I WAS ONLY KEEPING YOU COMPANY IN YOUR AGONY.
EARTH TO MASTER.
YOU NEED TO USE ANY OF THIS STUFF OR WHAT, JOHNNY ?
SOME RESPONSE WOULD BE APPRECIATED...
PUT THE GUNS BACK.
I'VE BEEN TRYING TO RESIST, BUT...
...WHEN THEY DIG IN WITH THEIR SPURS YOU HAVE TO OBEY.

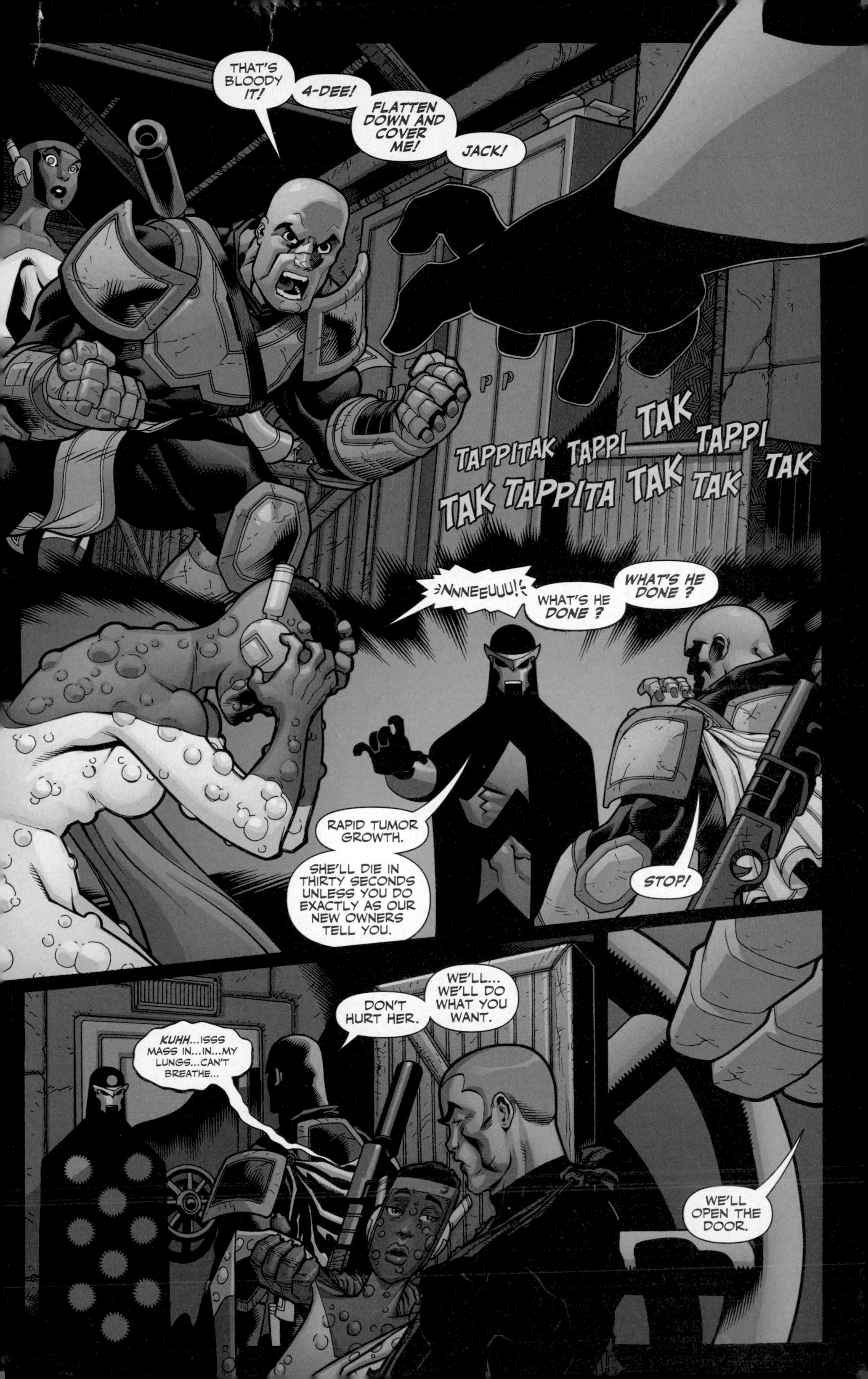
THAT'S BLOODY IT!
4-DEE!
FLATTEN DOWN AND COVER ME!
JACK!
TAPPITAK TAPPI TAK TAPPI TAK TAPPITA TAK TAK TAK
NNNEEUUU!
WHAT'S HE DONE?
WHAT'S HE DONE?
RAPID TUMOR GROWTH.
SHE'LL DIE IN THIRTY SECONDS UNLESS YOU DO EXACTLY AS OUR NEW OWNERS TELL YOU.
STOP!
KUHH...ISSS MASS IN...IN...MY LUNGS...CAN'T BREATHE...
DON'T HURT HER.
WE'LL... WE'LL DO WHAT YOU WANT.
WE'LL OPEN THE DOOR.

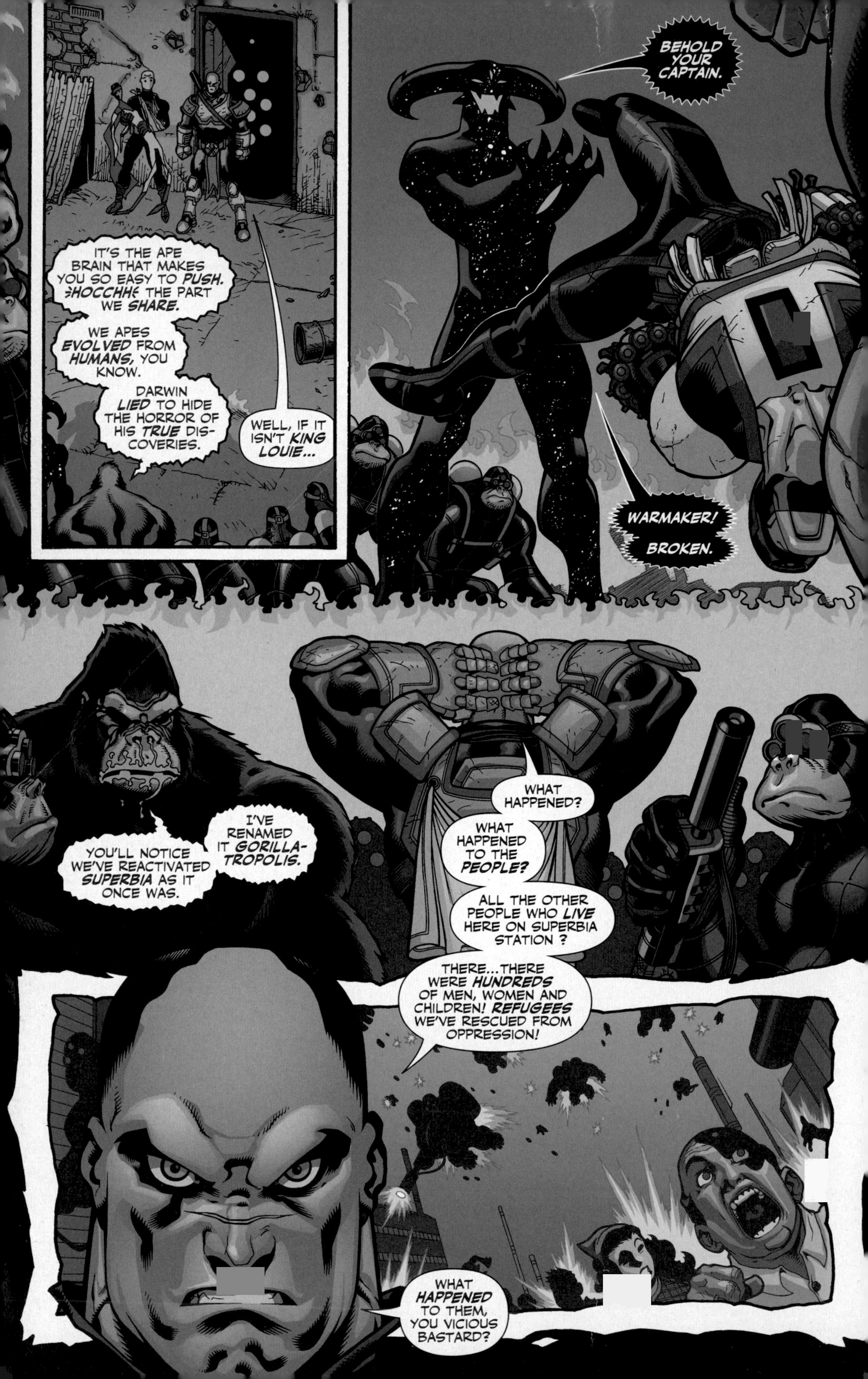
IT'S THE APE BRAIN THAT MAKES YOU SO EASY TO PUSH. HOCCHH THE PART WE SHARE.
WE APES EVOLVED FROM HUMANS, YOU KNOW.
DARWIN LIED TO HIDE THE HORROR OF HIS TRUE DISCOVERIES.
WELL, IF IT ISN'T KING LOUIE...
BEHOLD YOUR CAPTAIN.
WARMAKER!
BROKEN.
YOU'LL NOTICE WE'VE REACTIVATED SUPERBIA AS IT ONCE WAS.
I'VE RENAMED IT GORILLA-TROPOLIS.
WHAT HAPPENED?
WHAT HAPPENED TO THE PEOPLE?
ALL THE OTHER PEOPLE WHO LIVE HERE ON SUPERBIA STATION ?
THERE...THERE WERE HUNDREDS OF MEN, WOMEN AND CHILDREN! REFUGEES WE'VE RESCUED FROM OPPRESSION!
WHAT HAPPENED TO THEM, YOU VICIOUS BASTARD?

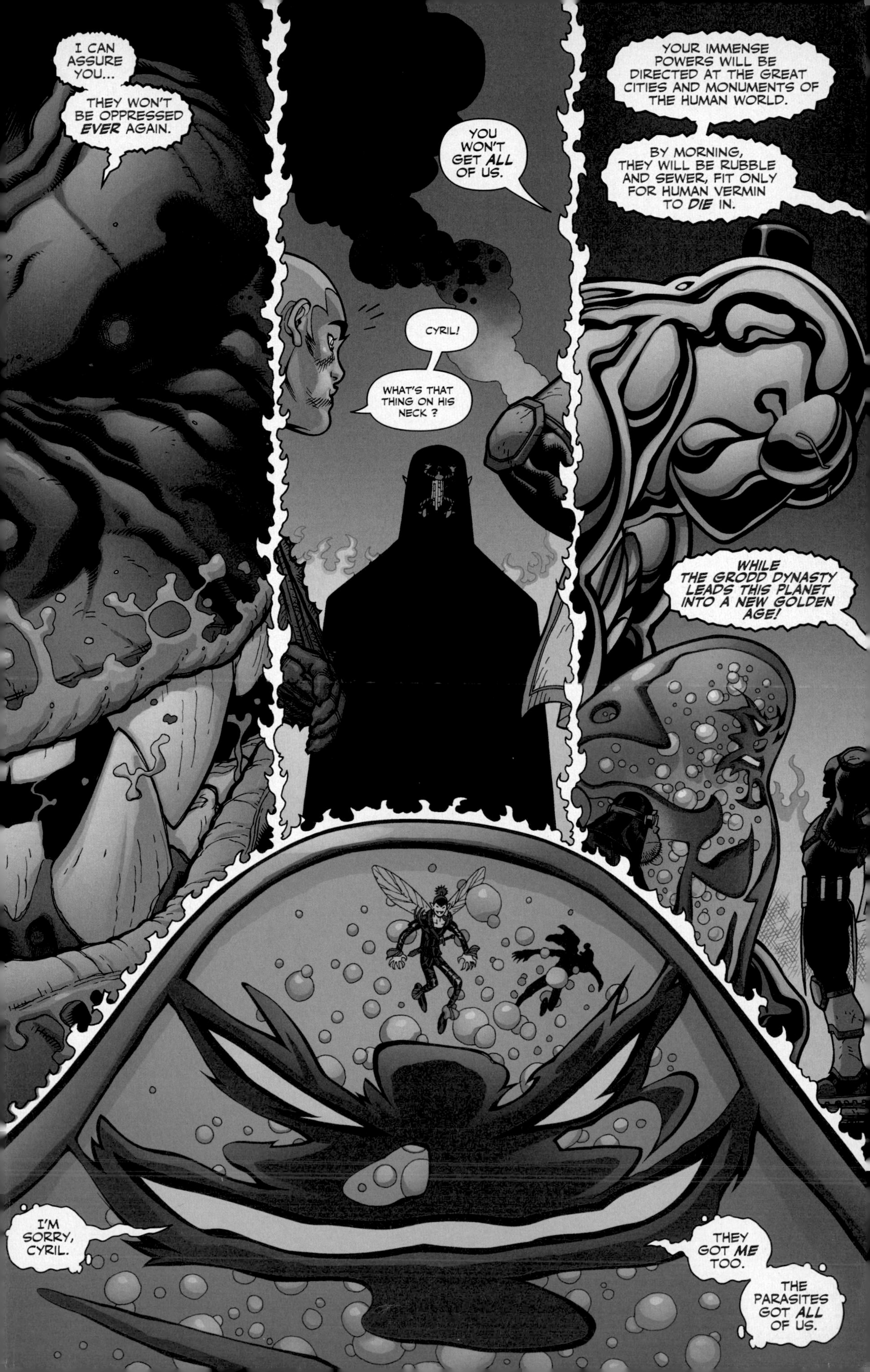
I CAN ASSURE YOU...
THEY WON'T BE OPPRESSED EVER AGAIN.
YOU WON'T GET ALL OF US.
CYRIL!
WHAT'S THAT THING ON HIS NECK ?
YOUR IMMENSE POWERS WILL BE DIRECTED AT THE GREAT CITIES AND MONUMENTS OF THE HUMAN WORLD.
BY MORNING, THEY WILL BE RUBBLE AND SEWER, FIT ONLY FOR HUMAN VERMIN TO DIE IN.
WHILE THE GRODD DYNASTY LEADS THIS PLANET INTO A NEW GOLDEN AGE!
I'M SORRY, CYRIL.
THEY GOT ME TOO.
THE PARASITES GOT ALL OF US.

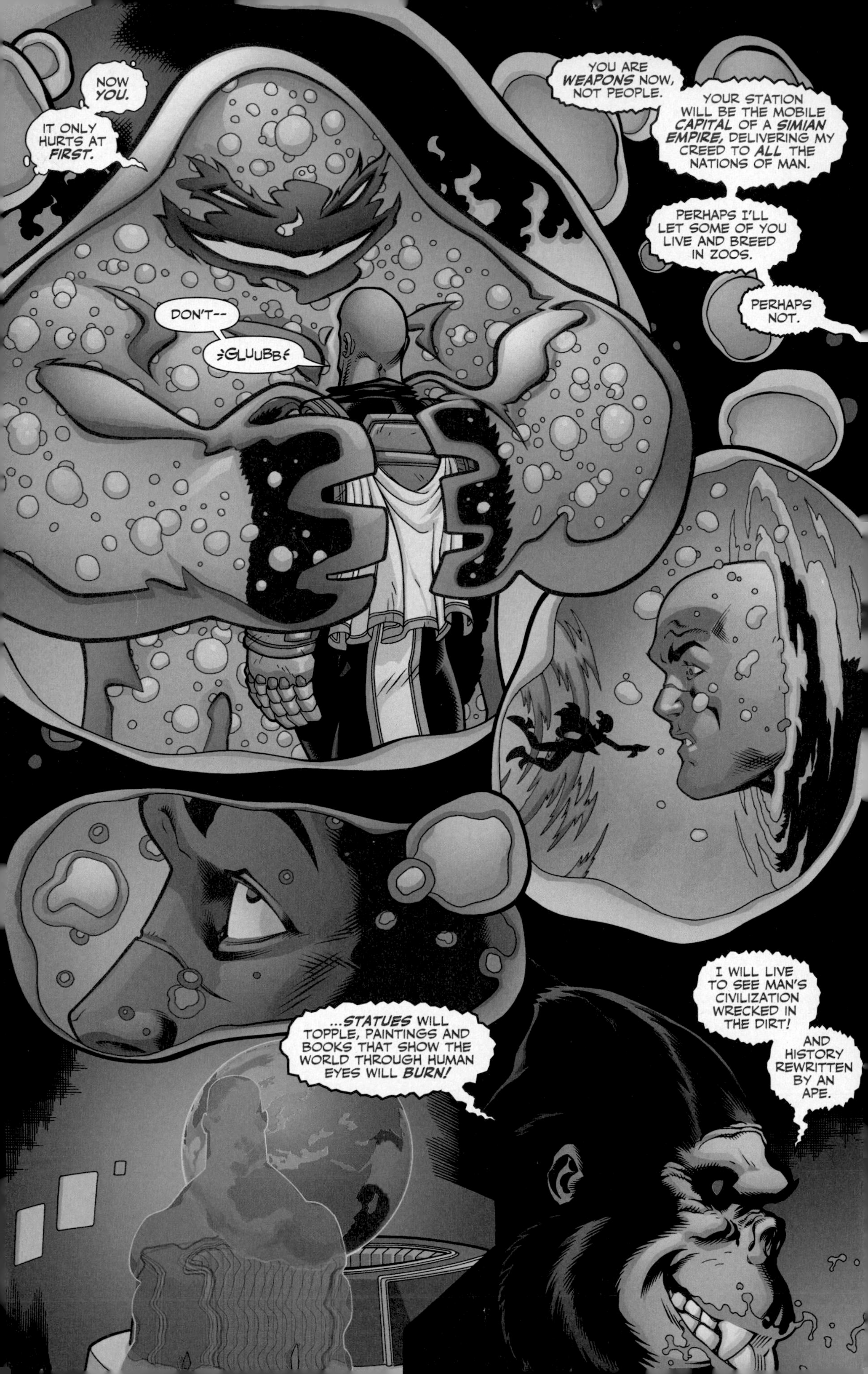
NOW YOU.
IT ONLY HURTS AT FIRST.
YOU ARE WEAPONS NOW, NOT PEOPLE.
YOUR STATION WILL BE THE MOBILE CAPITAL OF A SIMIAN EMPIRE, DELIVERING MY CREED TO ALL THE NATIONS OF MAN.
PERHAPS I'LL LET SOME OF YOU LIVE AND BREED IN ZOOS.
PERHAPS NOT.
DON'T--
GLUUBB
...STATUES WILL TOPPLE, PAINTINGS AND BOOKS THAT SHOW THE WORLD THROUGH HUMAN EYES WILL BURN!
I WILL LIVE TO SEE MAN'S CIVILIZATION WRECKED IN THE DIRT!
AND HISTORY REWRITTEN BY AN APE.

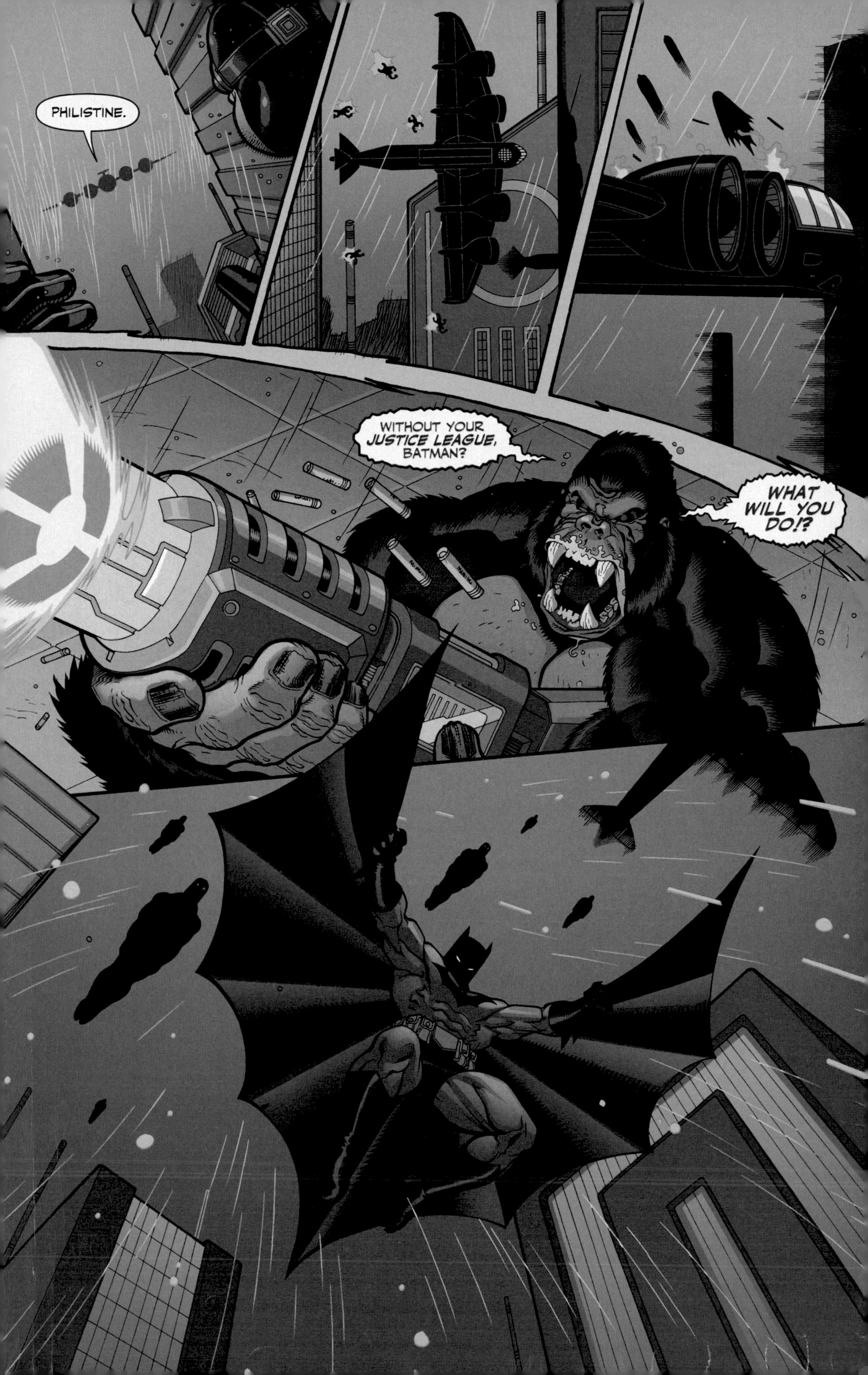

PHILISTINE.
WITHOUT YOUR *JUSTICE LEAGUE,* BATMAN?
WHAT WILL YOU DO!?

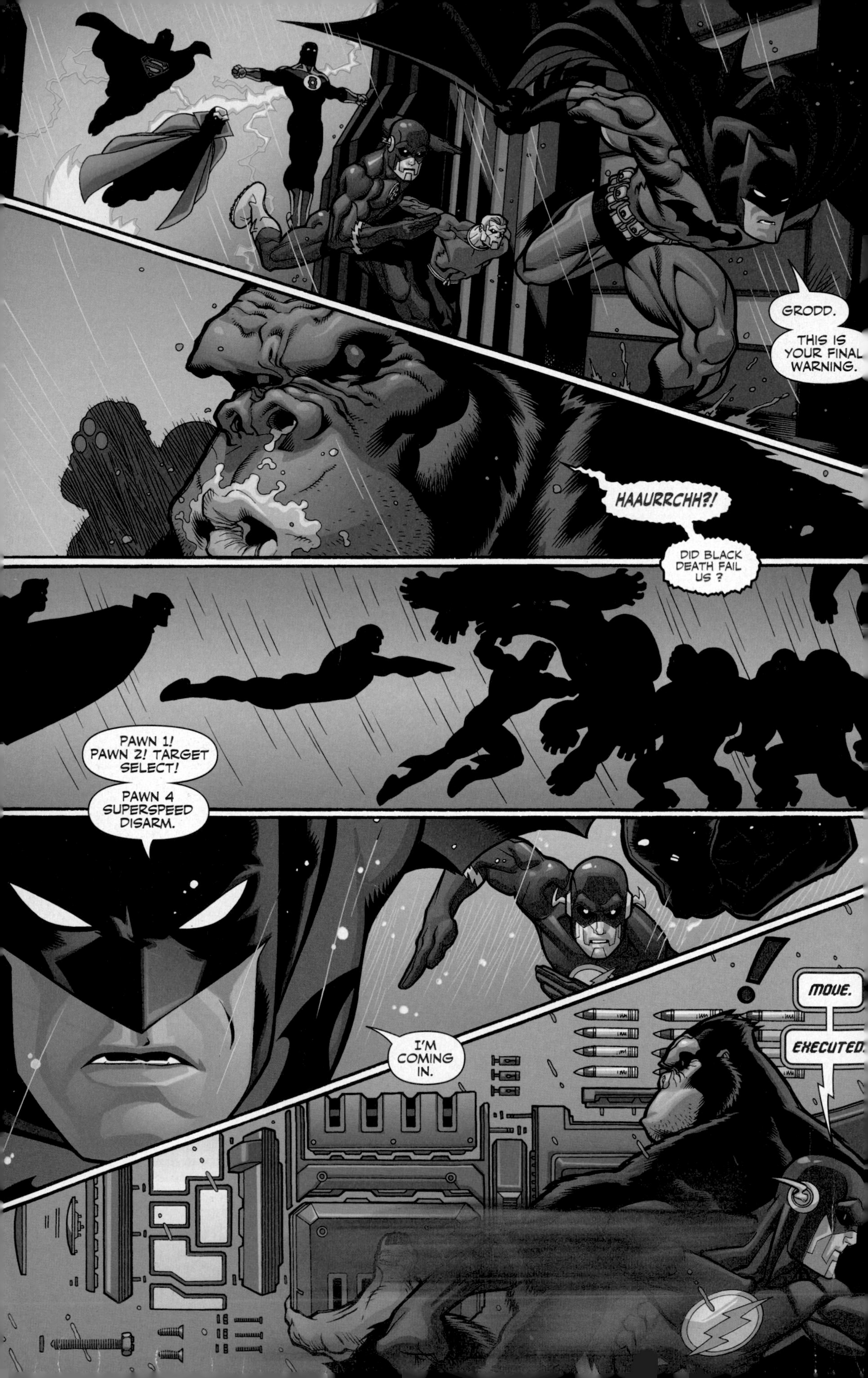
GRODD.
THIS IS YOUR FINAL WARNING.
HAAURRCHH?!
DID BLACK DEATH FAIL US ?
PAWN 1! PAWN 2! TARGET SELECT!
PAWN 4 SUPERSPEED DISARM.
I'M COMING IN.
!
MOVE.
EXECUTED.

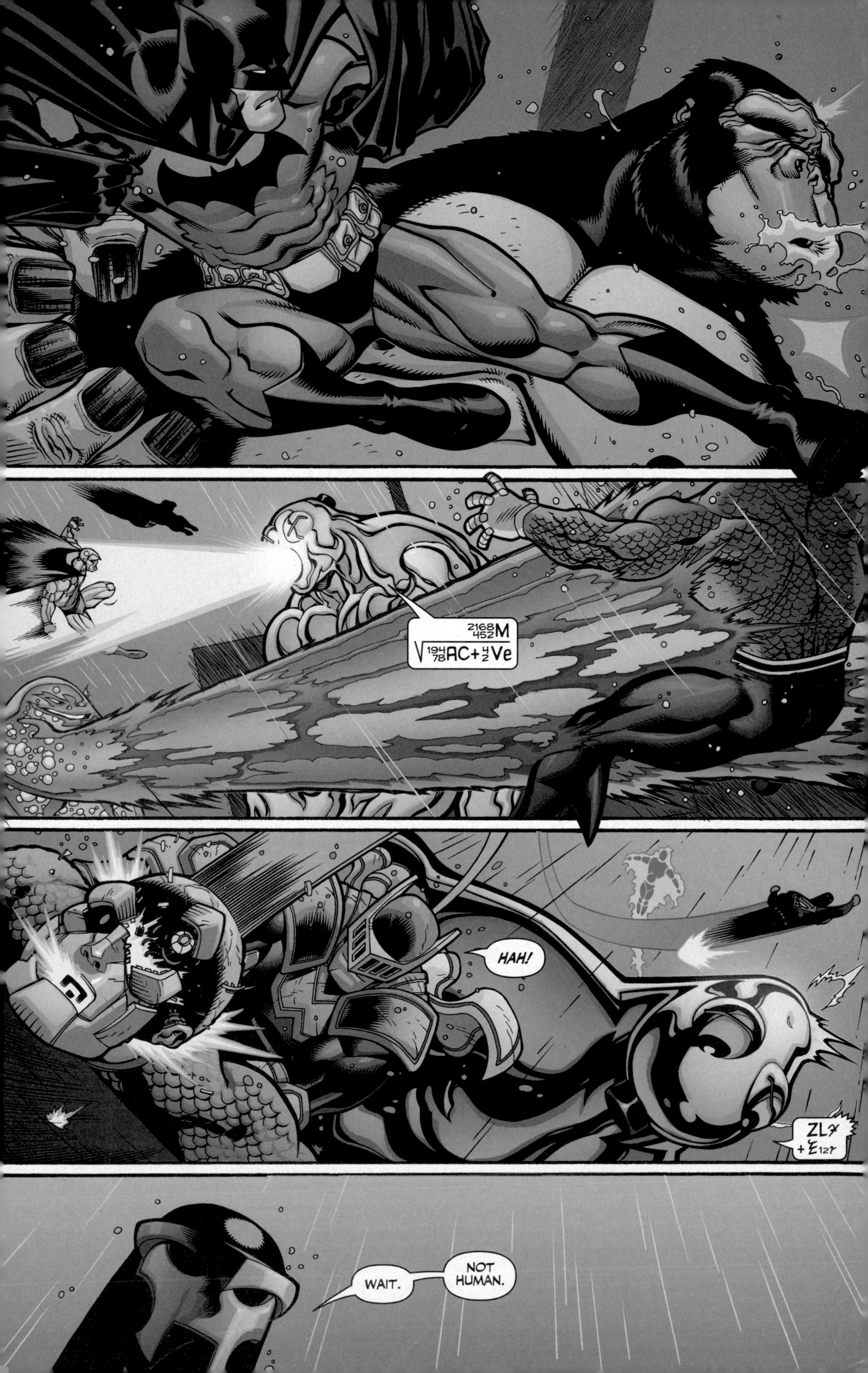

$\frac{^{2168}_{452}M}{\sqrt{^{194}_{78}AC+^{4}_{2}Ve}}$
HAH!
WAIT.
NOT HUMAN.

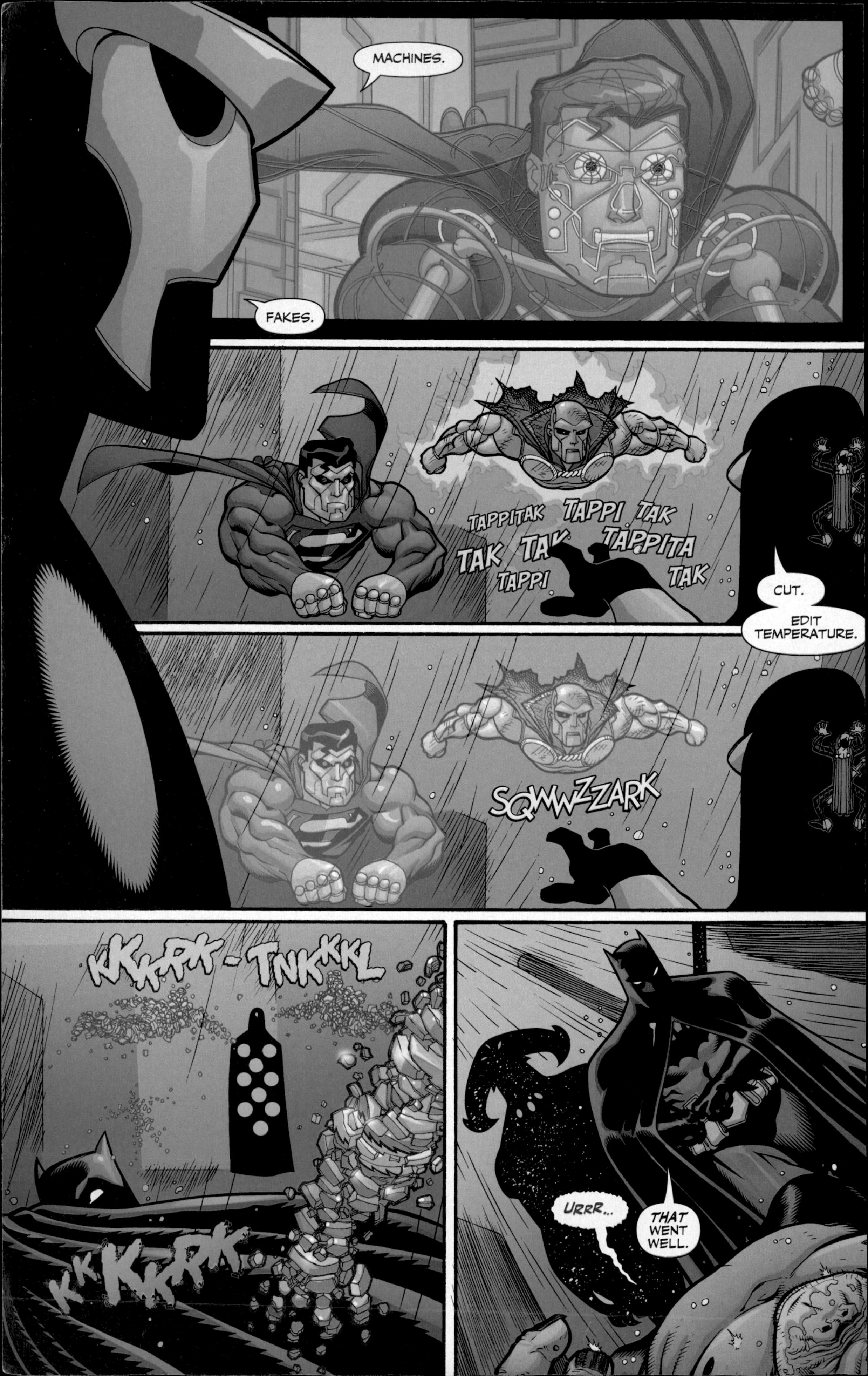
MACHINES.
FAKES.
TAPPITAK TAPPI TAK
TAK TAK TAPPITA
TAPPI TAK
CUT.
EDIT TEMPERATURE.
SQWWZZARK
KKKRK - TNKKKL
KKKKRK
URRR...
THAT WENT WELL.

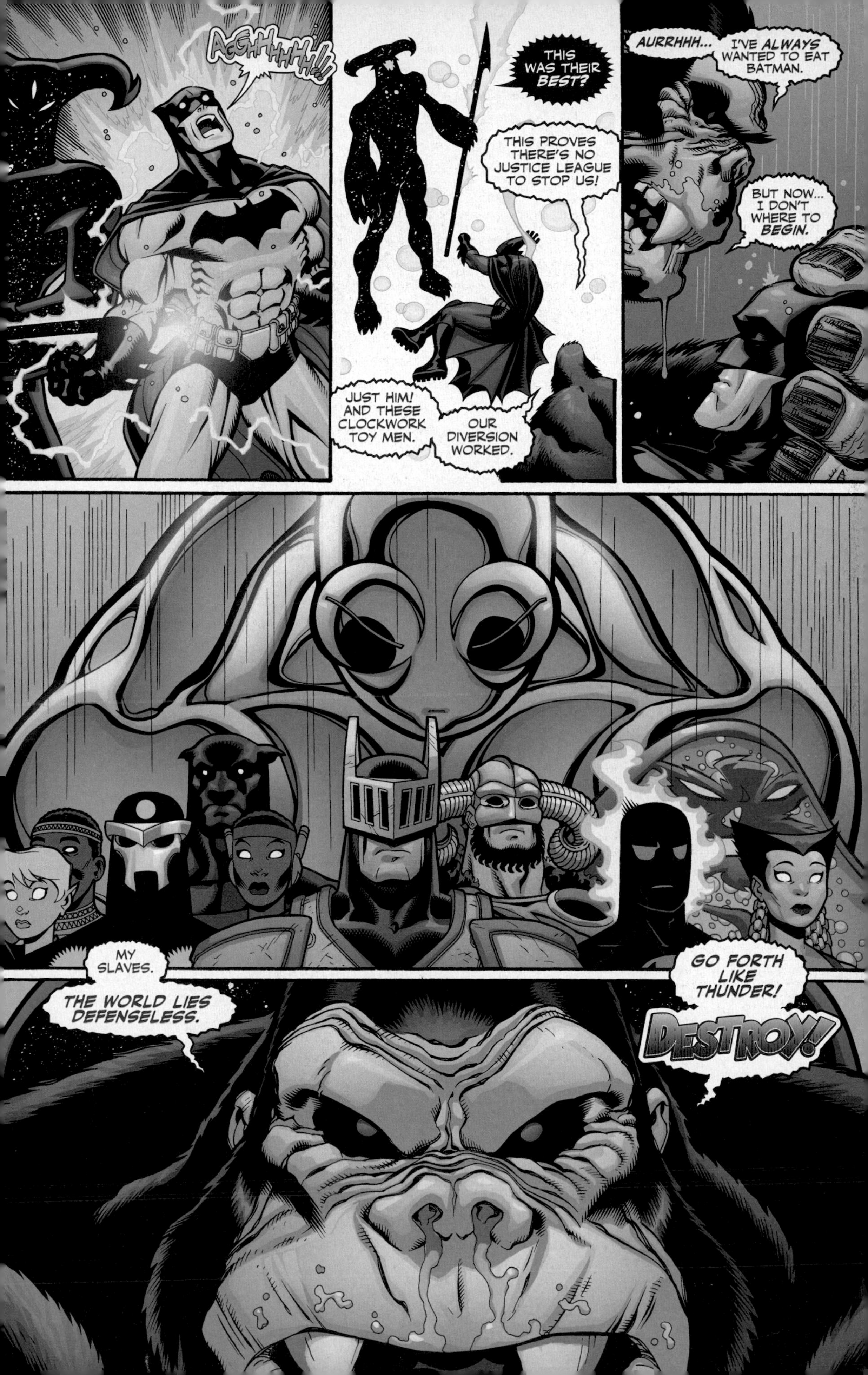
AGGHHHHH!!
THIS WAS THEIR BEST?
THIS PROVES THERE'S NO JUSTICE LEAGUE TO STOP US!
JUST HIM! AND THESE CLOCKWORK TOY MEN.
OUR DIVERSION WORKED.
AURRHHH...
I'VE ALWAYS WANTED TO EAT BATMAN.
BUT NOW... I DON'T WHERE TO BEGIN.
MY SLAVES.
THE WORLD LIES DEFENSELESS.
GO FORTH LIKE THUNDER!
DESTROY!

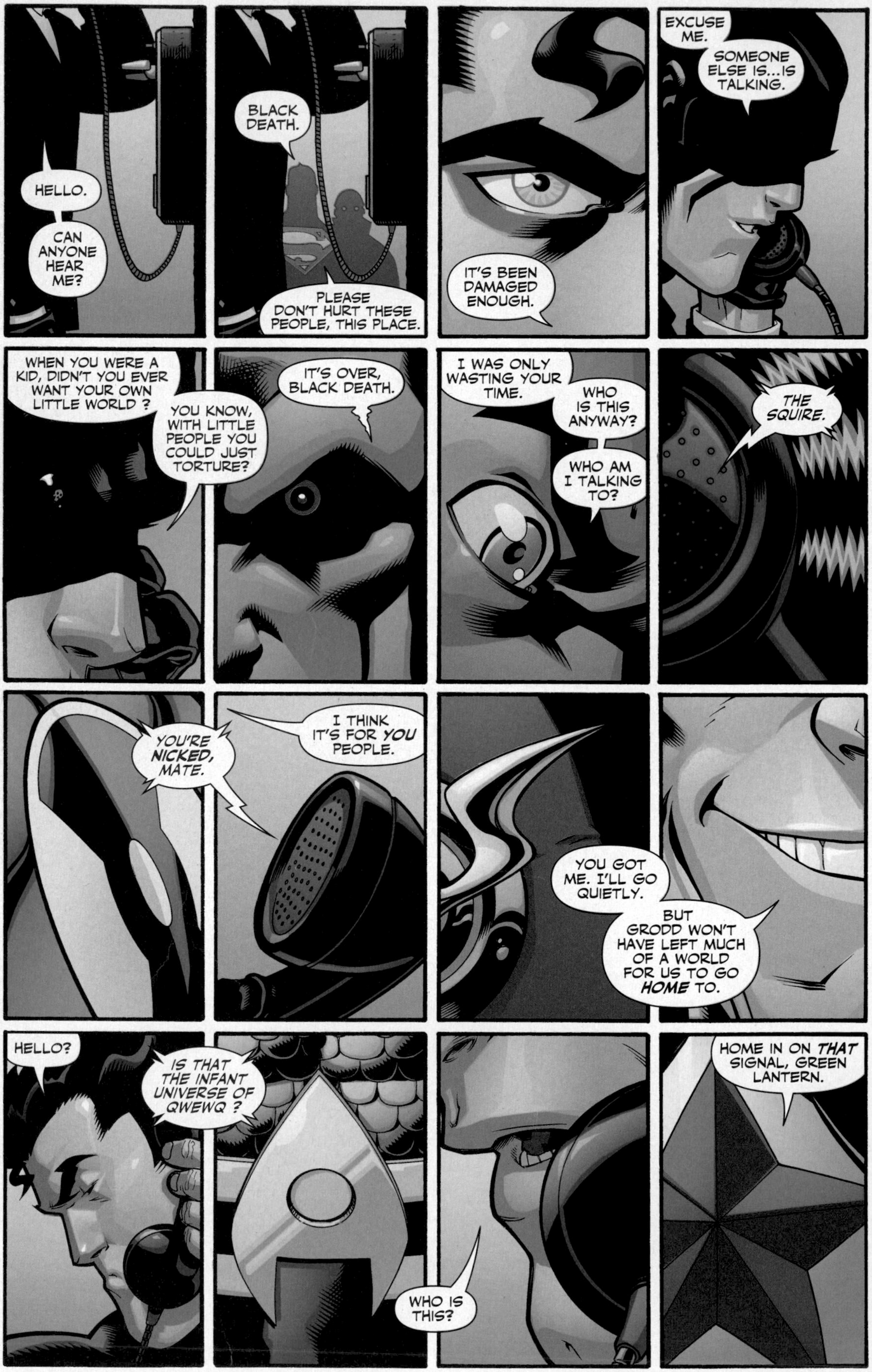
HELLO.
CAN ANYONE HEAR ME?
BLACK DEATH.
PLEASE DON'T HURT THESE PEOPLE, THIS PLACE.
IT'S BEEN DAMAGED ENOUGH.
EXCUSE ME.
SOMEONE ELSE IS...IS TALKING.
WHEN YOU WERE A KID, DIDN'T YOU EVER WANT YOUR OWN LITTLE WORLD ?
YOU KNOW, WITH LITTLE PEOPLE YOU COULD JUST TORTURE?
IT'S OVER, BLACK DEATH.
I WAS ONLY WASTING YOUR TIME.
WHO IS THIS ANYWAY?
WHO AM I TALKING TO?
THE SQUIRE.
YOU'RE NICKED, MATE.
I THINK IT'S FOR YOU PEOPLE.
YOU GOT ME. I'LL GO QUIETLY.
BUT GRODD WON'T HAVE LEFT MUCH OF A WORLD FOR US TO GO HOME TO.
HELLO?
IS THAT THE INFANT UNIVERSE OF QWEWQ ?
WHO IS THIS?
HOME IN ON THAT SIGNAL, GREEN LANTERN.

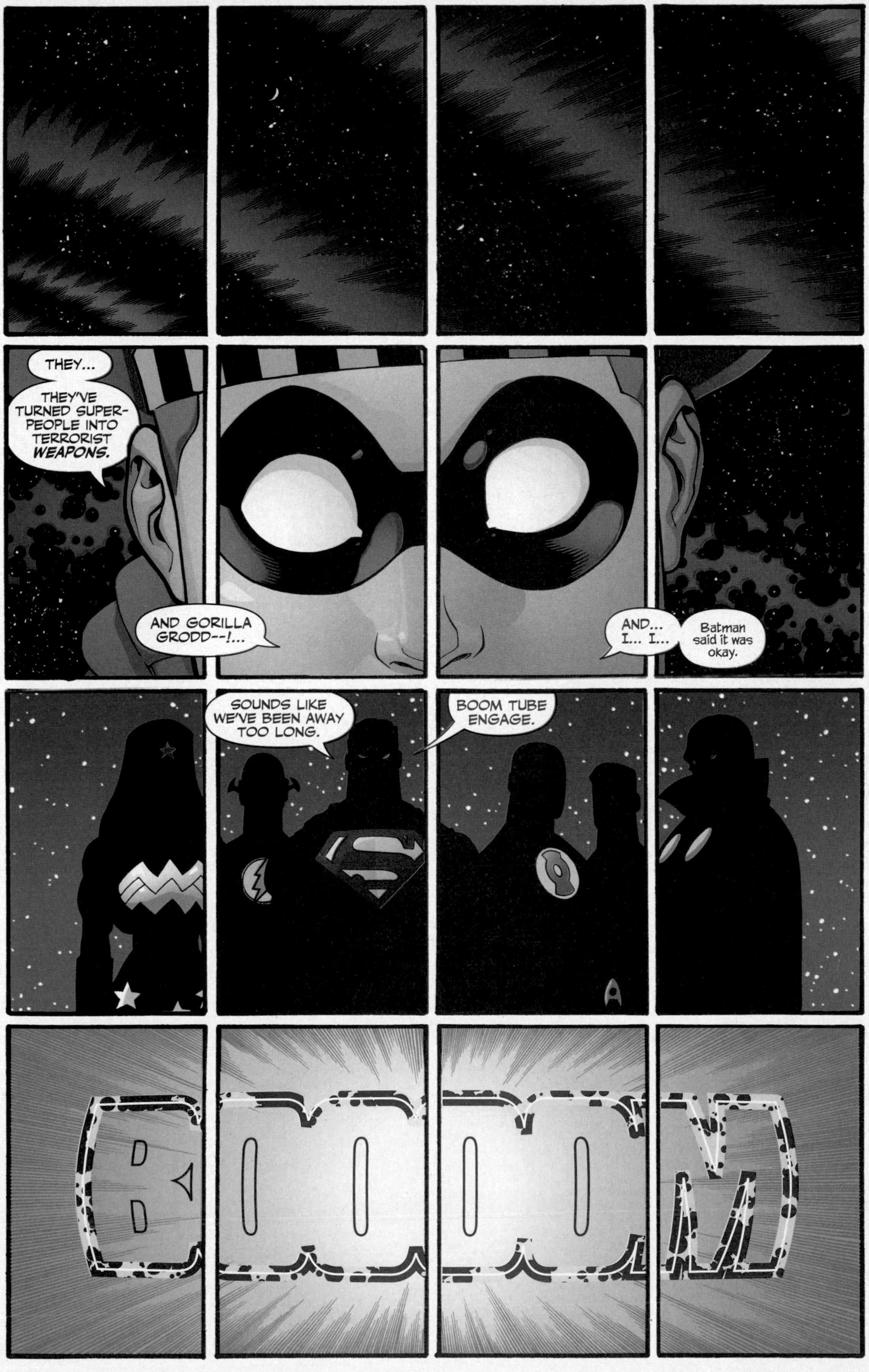
THEY...
THEY'VE TURNED SUPER-PEOPLE INTO TERRORIST *WEAPONS.*
AND GORILLA GRODD--!...
AND... I... I...
Batman said it was okay.
SOUNDS LIKE WE'VE BEEN AWAY TOO LONG.
BOOM TUBE ENGAGE.
BOOOM

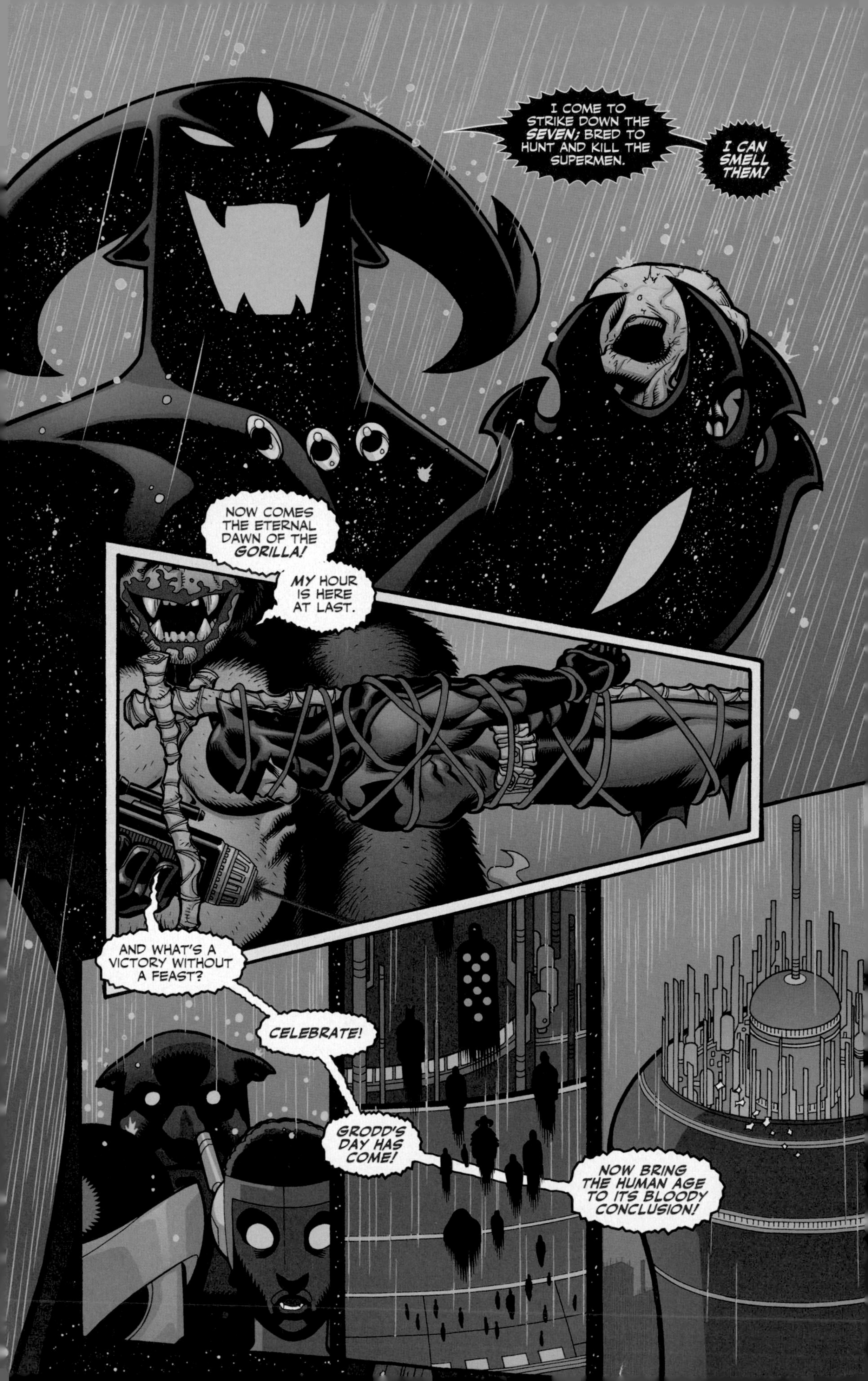
I COME TO STRIKE DOWN THE SEVEN; BRED TO HUNT AND KILL THE SUPERMEN.
I CAN SMELL THEM!
NOW COMES THE ETERNAL DAWN OF THE GORILLA!
MY HOUR IS HERE AT LAST.
AND WHAT'S A VICTORY WITHOUT A FEAST?
CELEBRATE!
GRODD'S DAY HAS COME!
NOW BRING THE HUMAN AGE TO ITS BLOODY CONCLUSION!

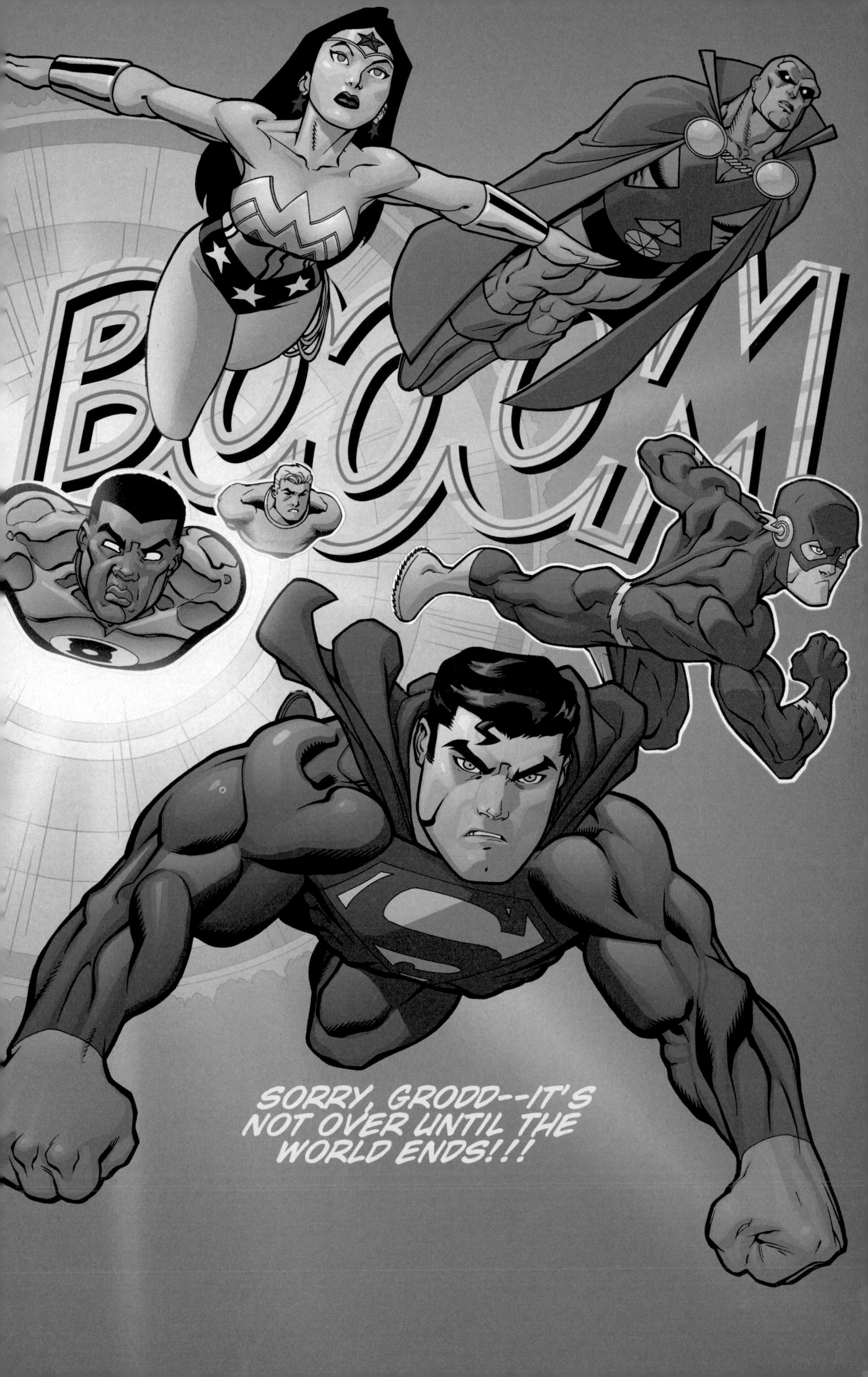
BOOM
SORRY, GRODD--IT'S NOT OVER UNTIL THE WORLD ENDS!!!

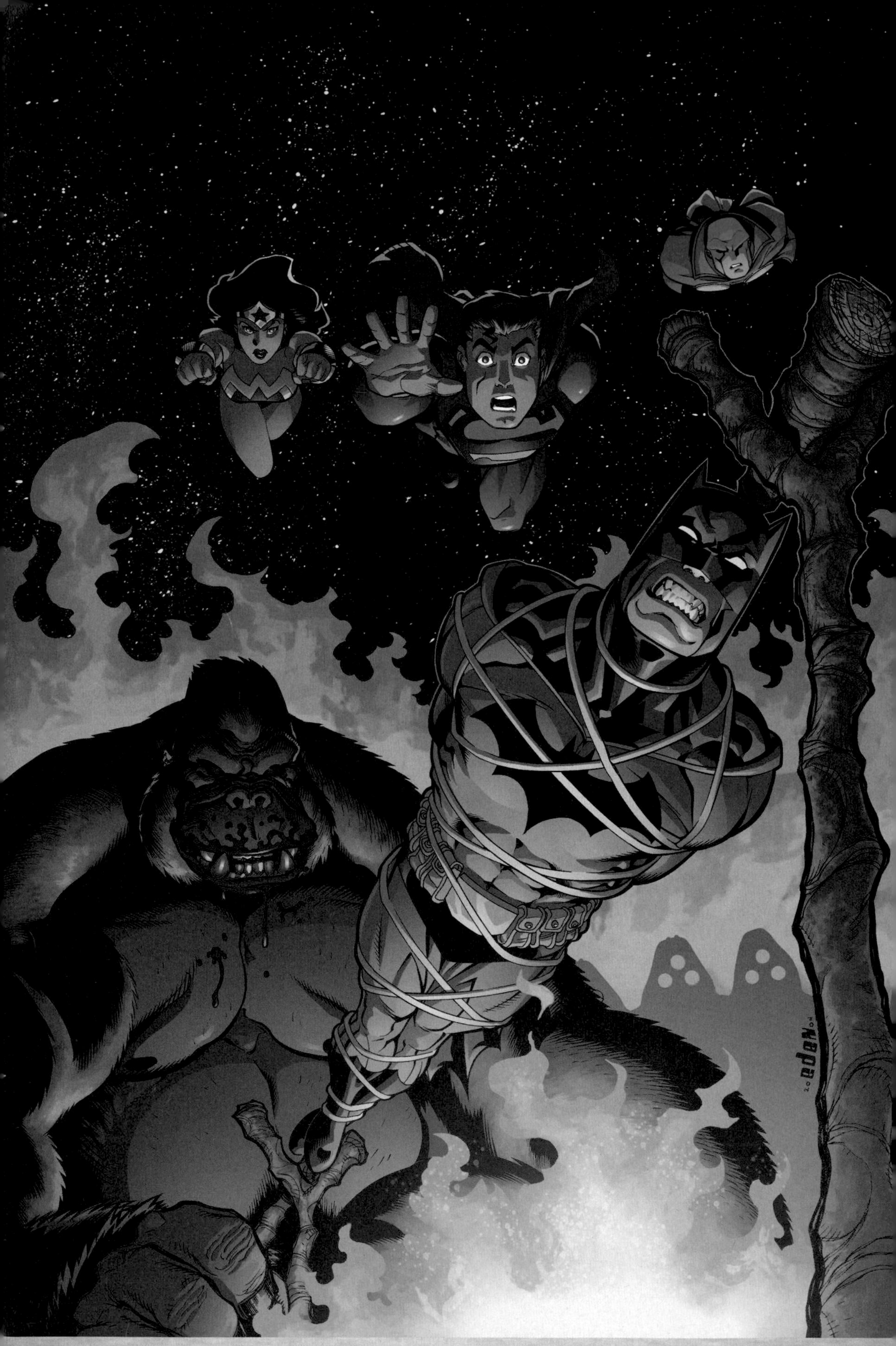

JLA CLASSIFIED #3

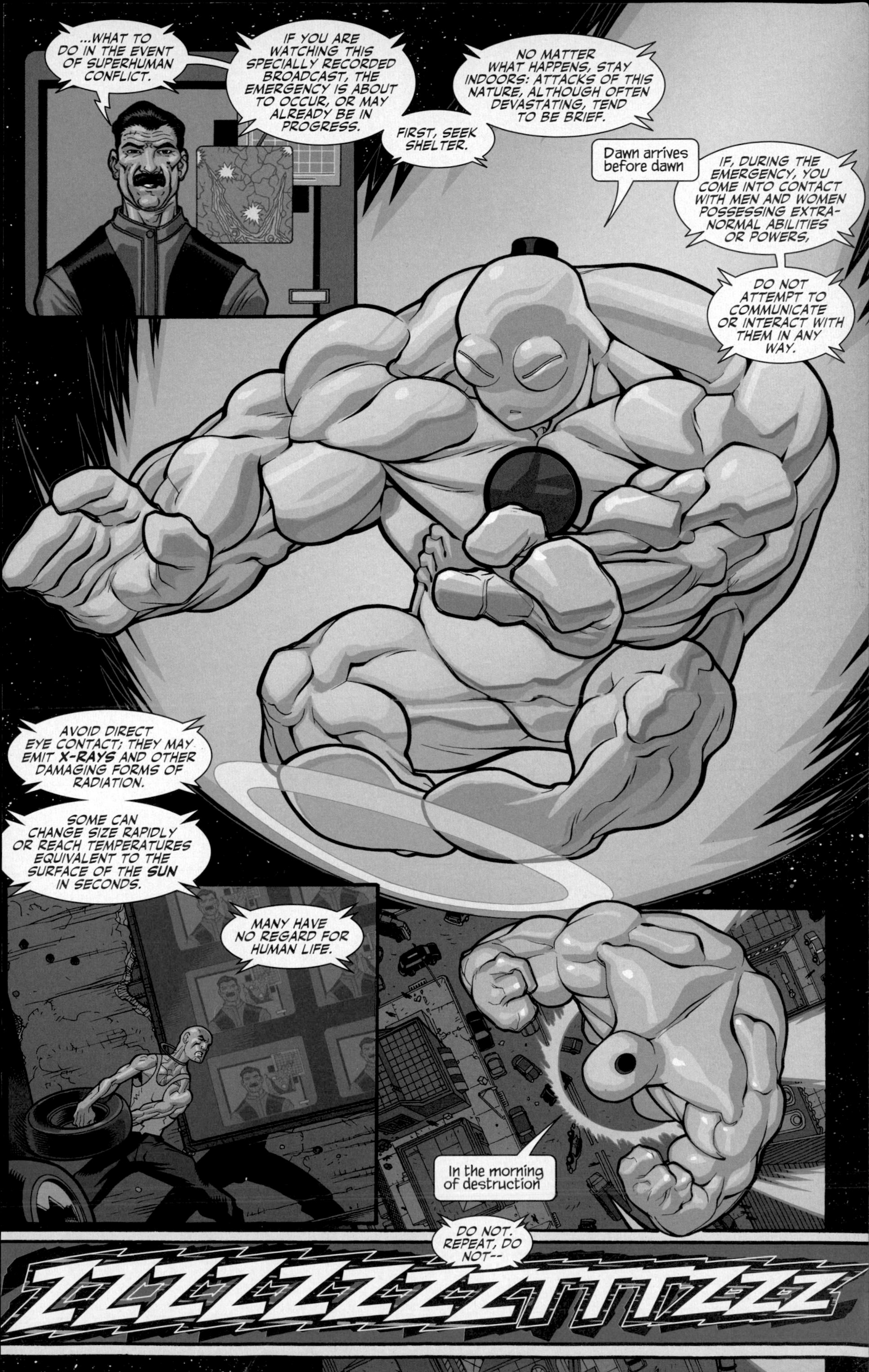
...WHAT TO DO IN THE EVENT OF SUPERHUMAN CONFLICT.
IF YOU ARE WATCHING THIS SPECIALLY RECORDED BROADCAST, THE EMERGENCY IS ABOUT TO OCCUR, OR MAY ALREADY BE IN PROGRESS.
FIRST, SEEK SHELTER.
NO MATTER WHAT HAPPENS, STAY INDOORS: ATTACKS OF THIS NATURE, ALTHOUGH OFTEN DEVASTATING, TEND TO BE BRIEF.
Dawn arrives before dawn
IF, DURING THE EMERGENCY, YOU COME INTO CONTACT WITH MEN AND WOMEN POSSESSING EXTRA-NORMAL ABILITIES OR POWERS,
DO NOT ATTEMPT TO COMMUNICATE OR INTERACT WITH THEM IN ANY WAY.
AVOID DIRECT EYE CONTACT; THEY MAY EMIT X-RAYS AND OTHER DAMAGING FORMS OF RADIATION.
SOME CAN CHANGE SIZE RAPIDLY OR REACH TEMPERATURES EQUIVALENT TO THE SURFACE OF THE SUN IN SECONDS.
MANY HAVE NO REGARD FOR HUMAN LIFE.
In the morning of destruction
DO NOT. REPEAT, DO NOT--
ZZZZZZZZZTTTTZZZ

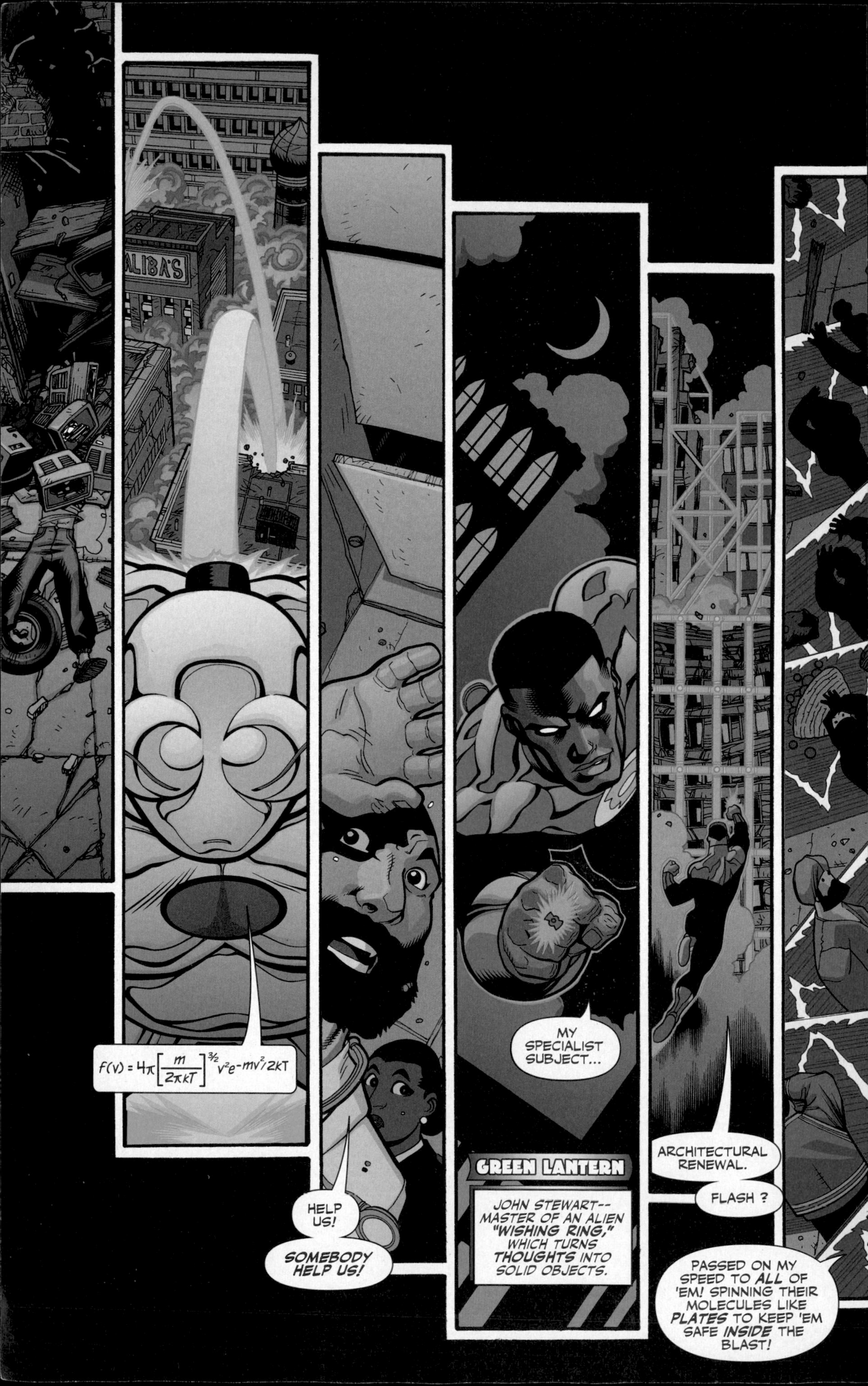
ALIBA'S
$f(v) = 4\pi\left[\frac{m}{2\pi kT}\right]^{3/2} v^2 e^{-mv^2/2kT}$
HELP US!
SOMEBODY HELP US!
MY SPECIALIST SUBJECT...
GREEN LANTERN
JOHN STEWART-- MASTER OF AN ALIEN "WISHING RING," WHICH TURNS THOUGHTS INTO SOLID OBJECTS.
ARCHITECTURAL RENEWAL.
FLASH ?
PASSED ON MY SPEED TO ALL OF 'EM! SPINNING THEIR MOLECULES LIKE PLATES TO KEEP 'EM SAFE INSIDE THE BLAST!

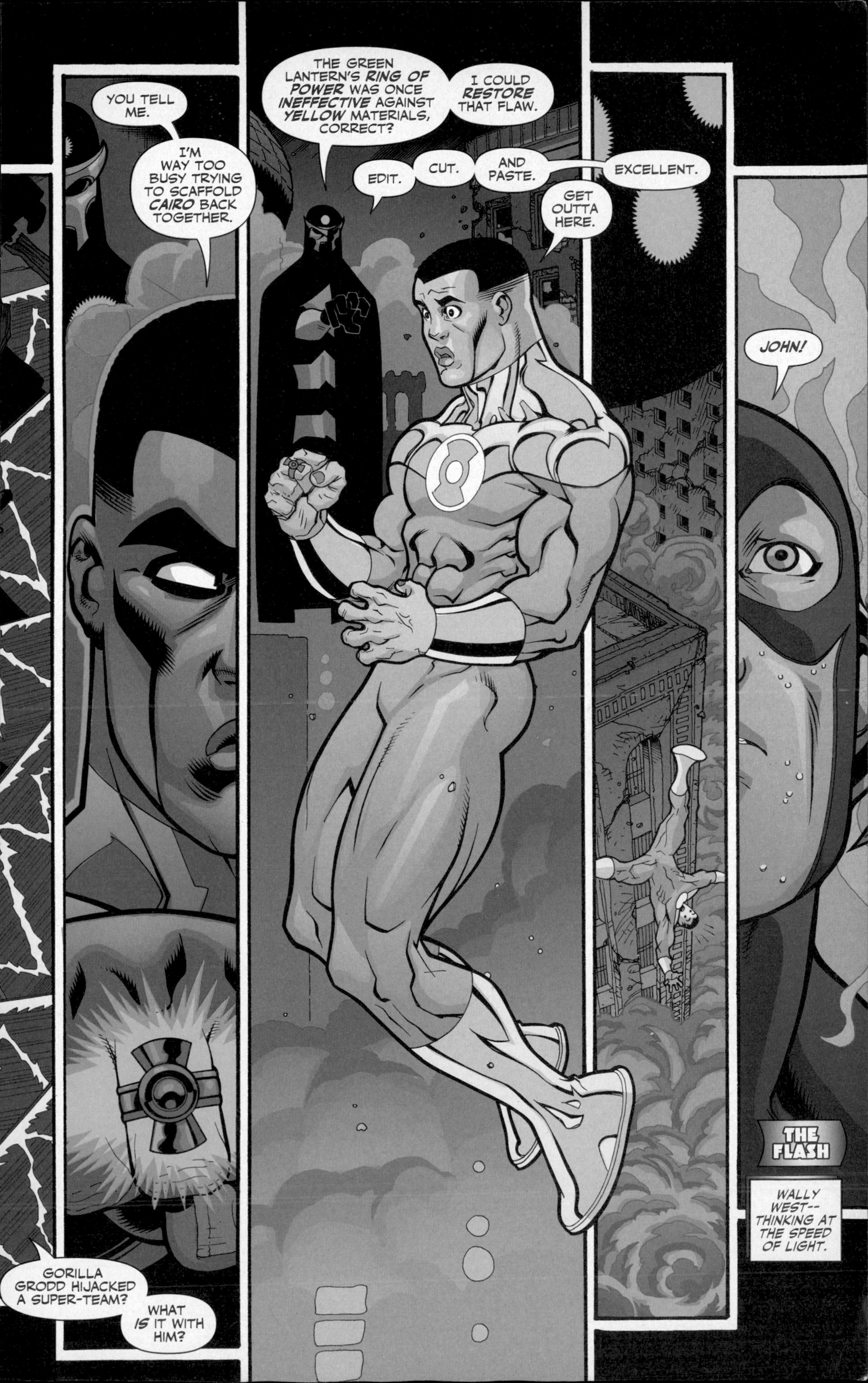

YOU TELL ME.
I'M WAY TOO BUSY TRYING TO SCAFFOLD CAIRO BACK TOGETHER.
THE GREEN LANTERN'S RING OF POWER WAS ONCE INEFFECTIVE AGAINST YELLOW MATERIALS, CORRECT?
I COULD RESTORE THAT FLAW.
EDIT.
CUT.
AND PASTE.
EXCELLENT.
GET OUTTA HERE.
JOHN!
THE FLASH
WALLY WEST-- THINKING AT THE SPEED OF LIGHT.
GORILLA GRODD HIJACKED A SUPER-TEAM?
WHAT IS IT WITH HIM?

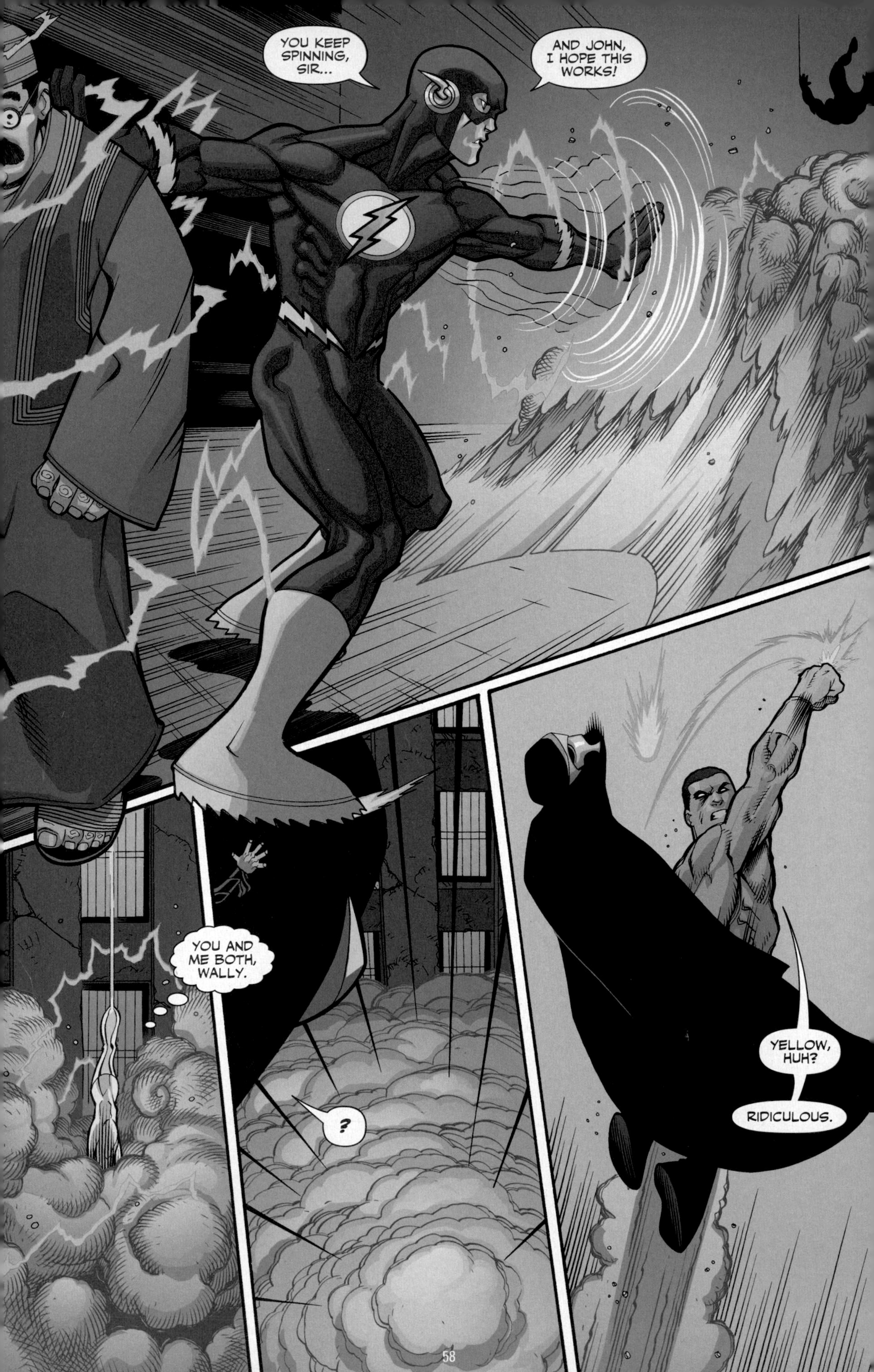
YOU KEEP SPINNING, SIR...
AND JOHN, I HOPE THIS WORKS!
YOU AND ME BOTH, WALLY.
?
YELLOW, HUH?
RIDICULOUS.

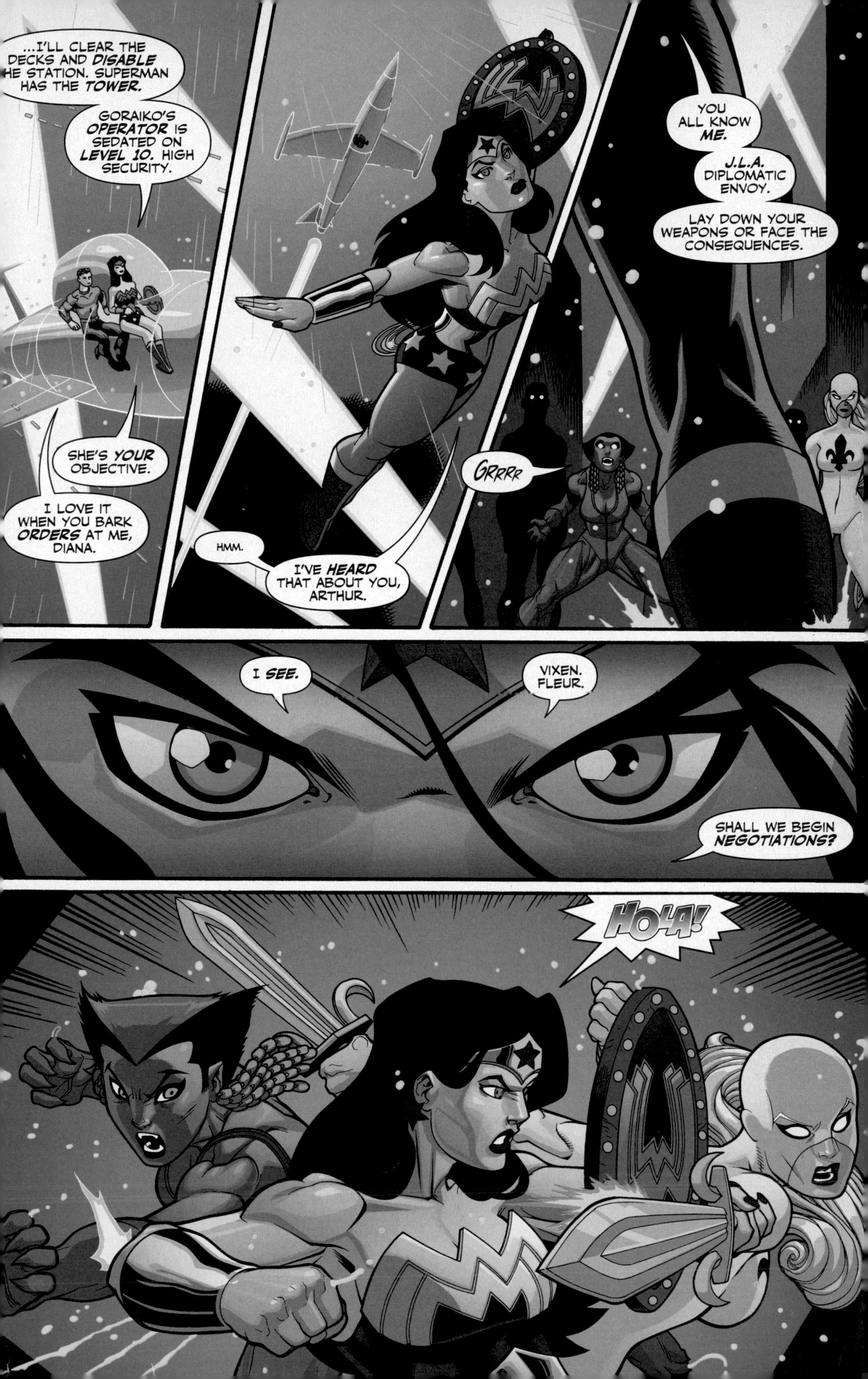
...I'LL CLEAR THE DECKS AND DISABLE HE STATION. SUPERMAN HAS THE TOWER.
GORAIKO'S OPERATOR IS SEDATED ON LEVEL 10. HIGH SECURITY.
SHE'S YOUR OBJECTIVE.
I LOVE IT WHEN YOU BARK ORDERS AT ME, DIANA.
HMM.
I'VE HEARD THAT ABOUT YOU, ARTHUR.
YOU ALL KNOW ME.
J.L.A. DIPLOMATIC ENVOY.
LAY DOWN YOUR WEAPONS OR FACE THE CONSEQUENCES.
GRRRR
I SEE.
VIXEN. FLEUR.
SHALL WE BEGIN NEGOTIATIONS?
HOLA!

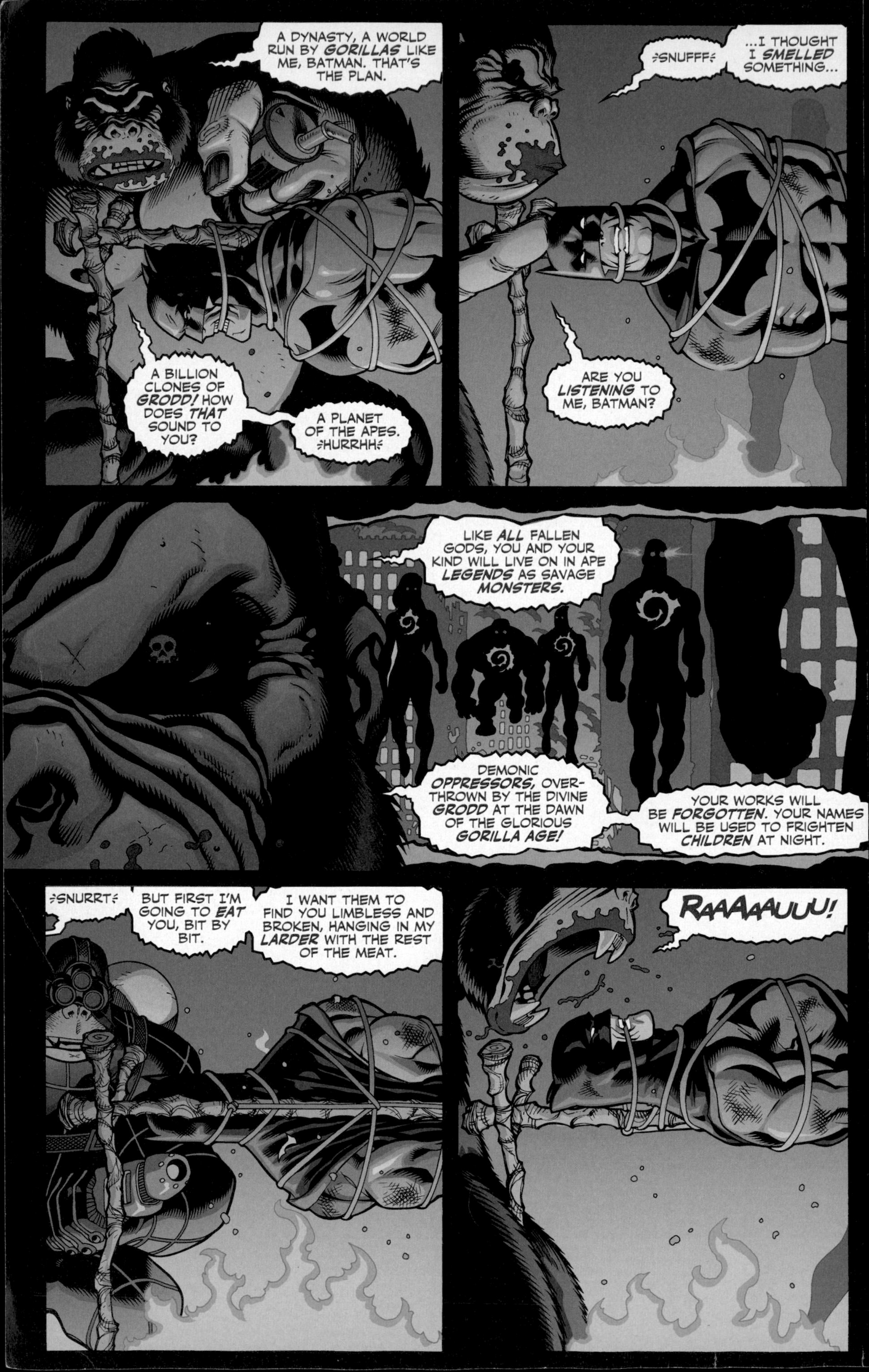
A DYNASTY, A WORLD RUN BY GORILLAS LIKE ME, BATMAN. THAT'S THE PLAN.
A BILLION CLONES OF GRODD! HOW DOES THAT SOUND TO YOU?
A PLANET OF THE APES. HURRHH
SNUFFF
...I THOUGHT I SMELLED SOMETHING...
ARE YOU LISTENING TO ME, BATMAN?
LIKE ALL FALLEN GODS, YOU AND YOUR KIND WILL LIVE ON IN APE LEGENDS AS SAVAGE MONSTERS.
DEMONIC OPPRESSORS, OVERTHROWN BY THE DIVINE GRODD AT THE DAWN OF THE GLORIOUS GORILLA AGE!
YOUR WORKS WILL BE FORGOTTEN. YOUR NAMES WILL BE USED TO FRIGHTEN CHILDREN AT NIGHT.
SNURRT
BUT FIRST I'M GOING TO EAT YOU, BIT BY BIT.
I WANT THEM TO FIND YOU LIMBLESS AND BROKEN, HANGING IN MY LARDER WITH THE REST OF THE MEAT.
RAAAAAUUU!

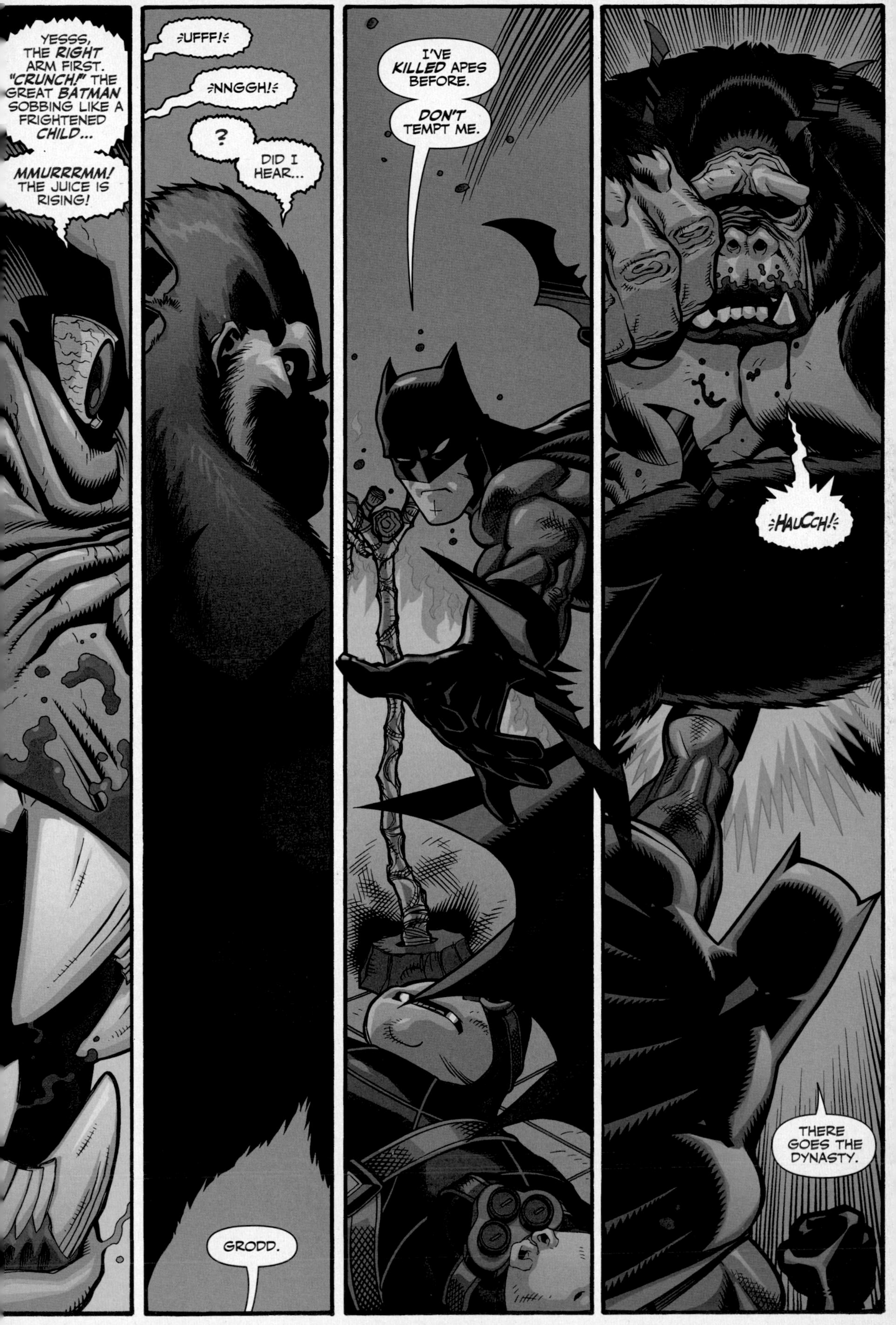
YESSS, THE RIGHT ARM FIRST. "CRUNCH!" THE GREAT BATMAN SOBBING LIKE A FRIGHTENED CHILD...
MMURRRMM! THE JUICE IS RISING!
UFFF!
NNGGH!
?
DID I HEAR...
GRODD.
I'VE KILLED APES BEFORE.
DON'T TEMPT ME.
HAUCCH!
THERE GOES THE DYNASTY.

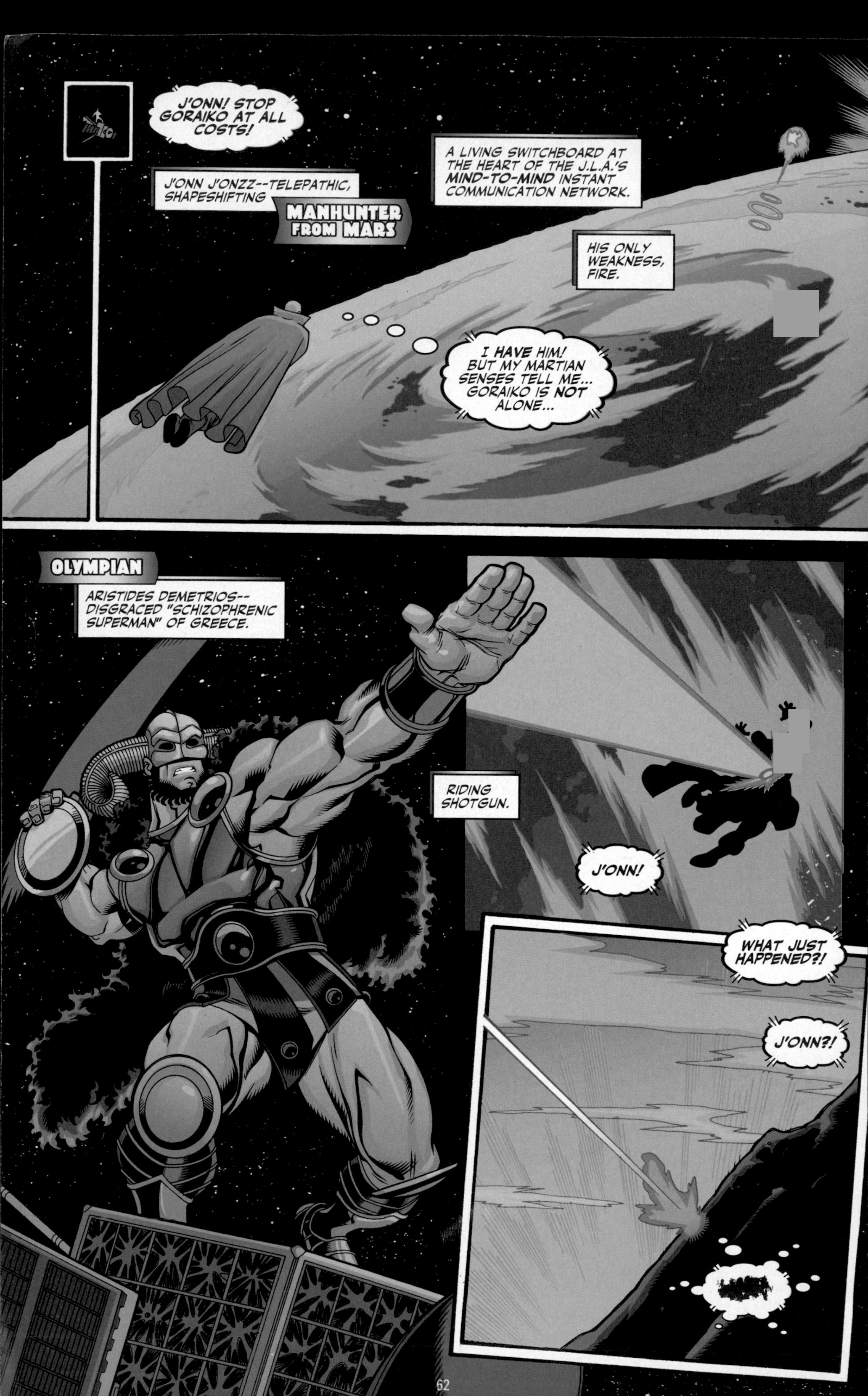
J'ONN! STOP GORAIKO AT ALL COSTS!
J'ONN J'ONZZ--TELEPATHIC, SHAPESHIFTING
MANHUNTER FROM MARS
A LIVING SWITCHBOARD AT THE HEART OF THE J.L.A.'S MIND-TO-MIND INSTANT COMMUNICATION NETWORK.
HIS ONLY WEAKNESS, FIRE.
I HAVE HIM! BUT MY MARTIAN SENSES TELL ME... GORAIKO IS NOT ALONE...
OLYMPIAN
ARISTIDES DEMETRIOS--DISGRACED "SCHIZOPHRENIC SUPERMAN" OF GREECE.
RIDING SHOTGUN.
J'ONN!
WHAT JUST HAPPENED?!
J'ONN?!

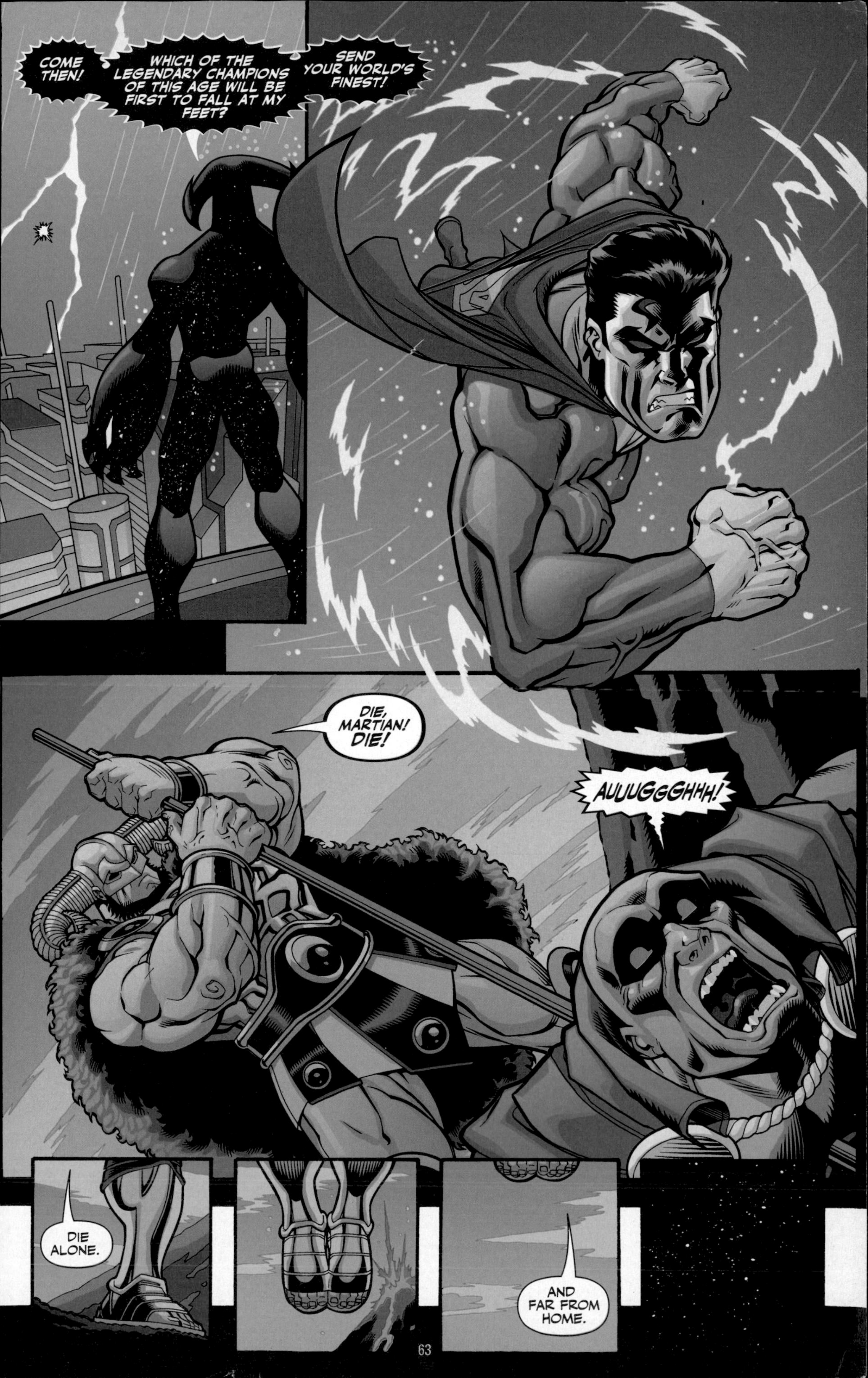
COME THEN!
WHICH OF THE LEGENDARY CHAMPIONS OF THIS AGE WILL BE FIRST TO FALL AT MY FEET?
SEND YOUR WORLD'S FINEST!
DIE, MARTIAN! DIE!
AUUUGGGHHH!
DIE ALONE.
AND FAR FROM HOME.

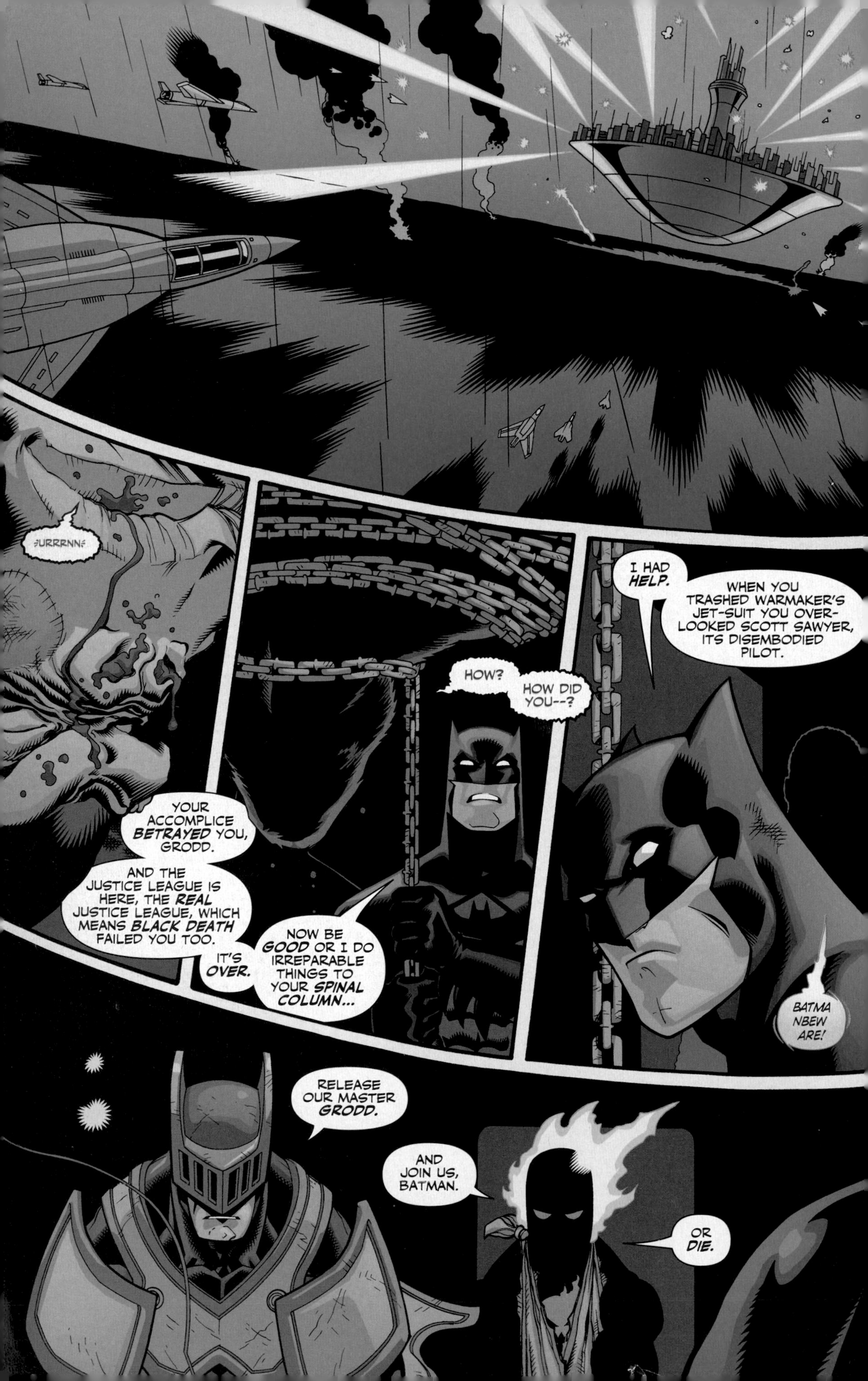

URRRNN
YOUR ACCOMPLICE BETRAYED YOU, GRODD.
AND THE JUSTICE LEAGUE IS HERE, THE REAL JUSTICE LEAGUE, WHICH MEANS BLACK DEATH FAILED YOU TOO.
IT'S OVER.
NOW BE GOOD OR I DO IRREPARABLE THINGS TO YOUR SPINAL COLUMN...
HOW?
HOW DID YOU--?
I HAD HELP.
WHEN YOU TRASHED WARMAKER'S JET-SUIT YOU OVER-LOOKED SCOTT SAWYER, ITS DISEMBODIED PILOT.
BATMA NBEW ARE!
RELEASE OUR MASTER GRODD.
AND JOIN US, BATMAN.
OR DIE.

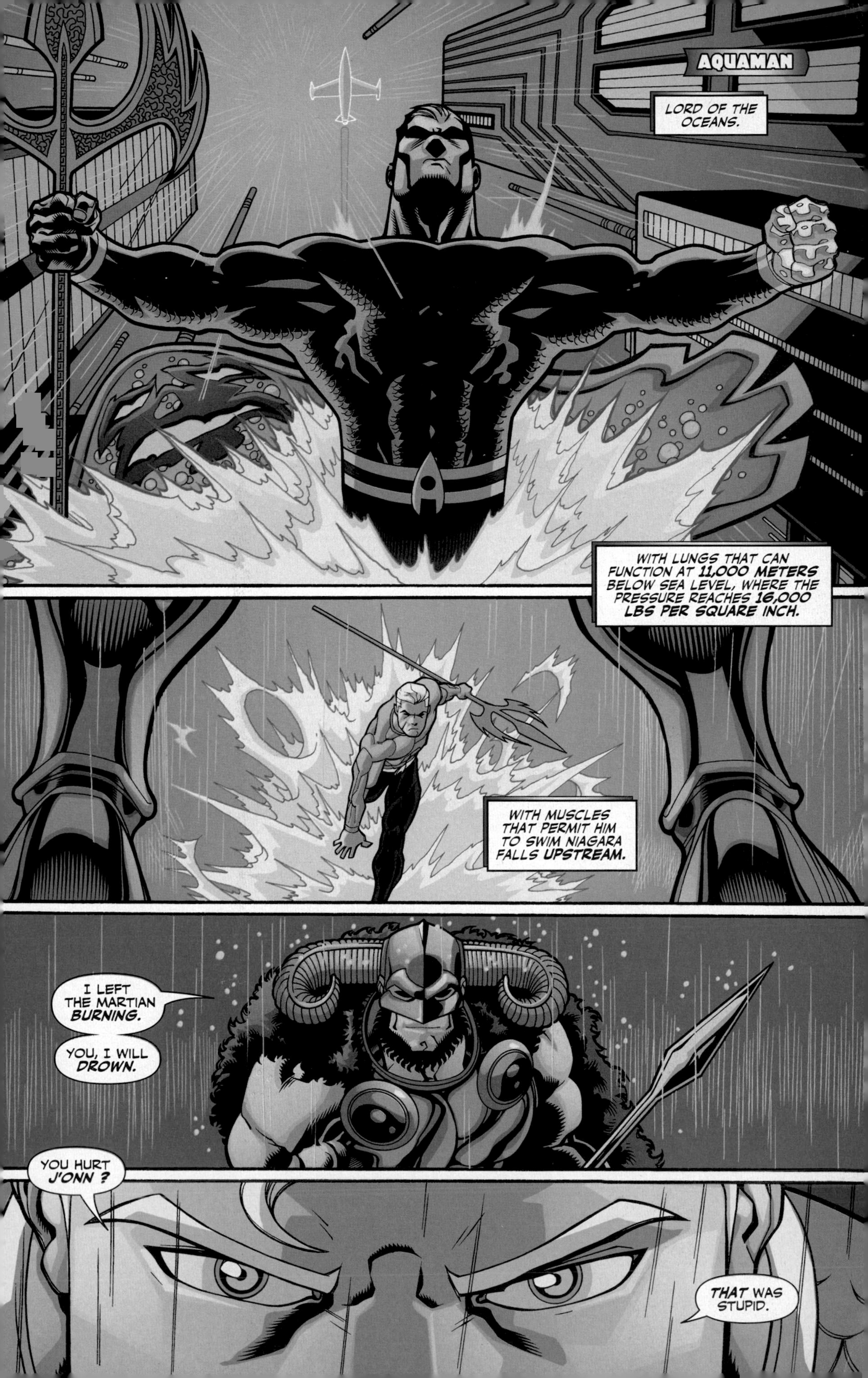
AQUAMAN
LORD OF THE OCEANS.
WITH LUNGS THAT CAN FUNCTION AT 11,000 METERS BELOW SEA LEVEL, WHERE THE PRESSURE REACHES 16,000 LBS PER SQUARE INCH.
WITH MUSCLES THAT PERMIT HIM TO SWIM NIAGARA FALLS UPSTREAM.
I LEFT THE MARTIAN BURNING.
YOU, I WILL DROWN.
YOU HURT J'ONN ?
THAT WAS STUPID.

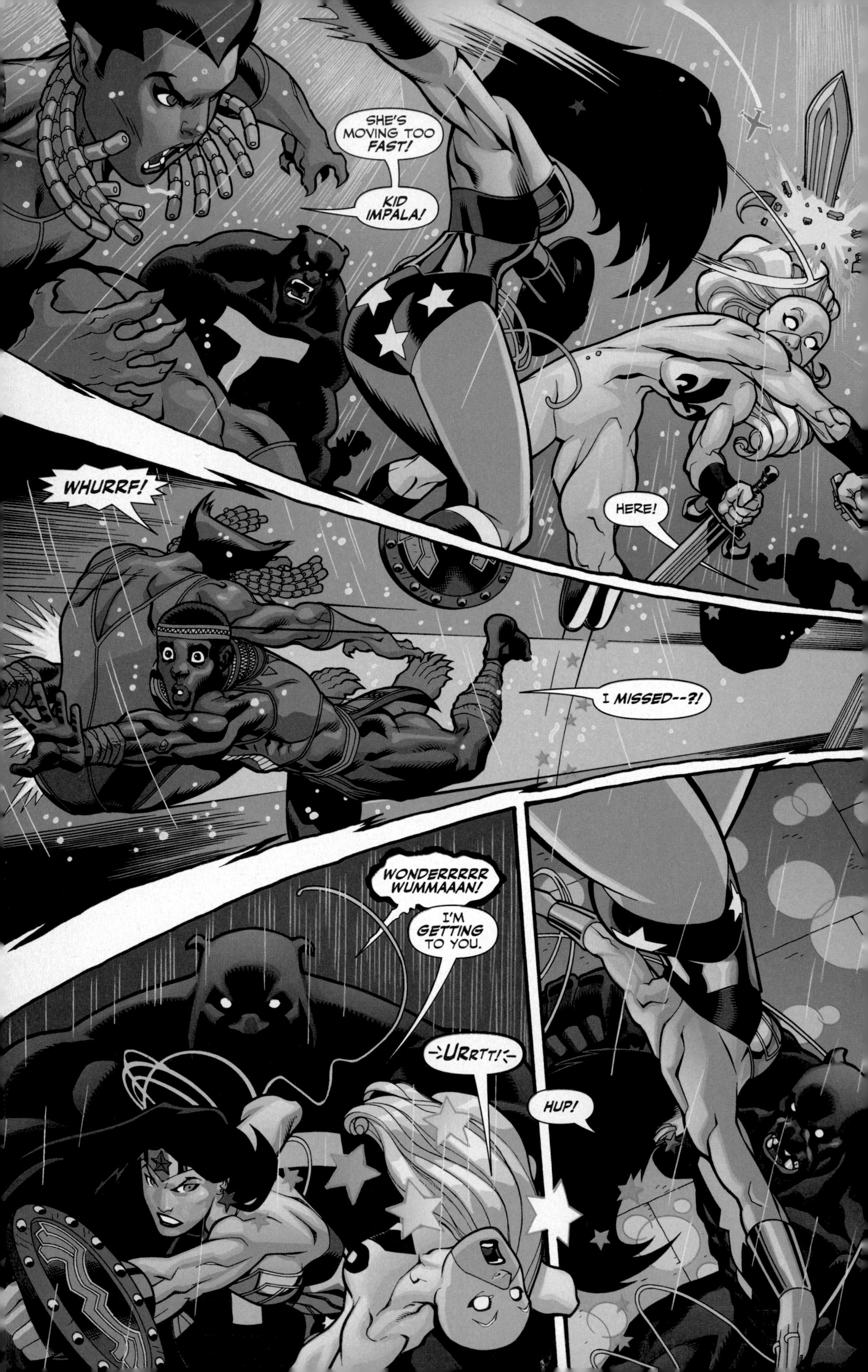
SHE'S MOVING TOO FAST!
KID IMPALA!
WHURRF!
HERE!
I MISSED--?!
WONDERRRRR WUMMAAAN!
I'M GETTING TO YOU.
URRTT!
HUP!

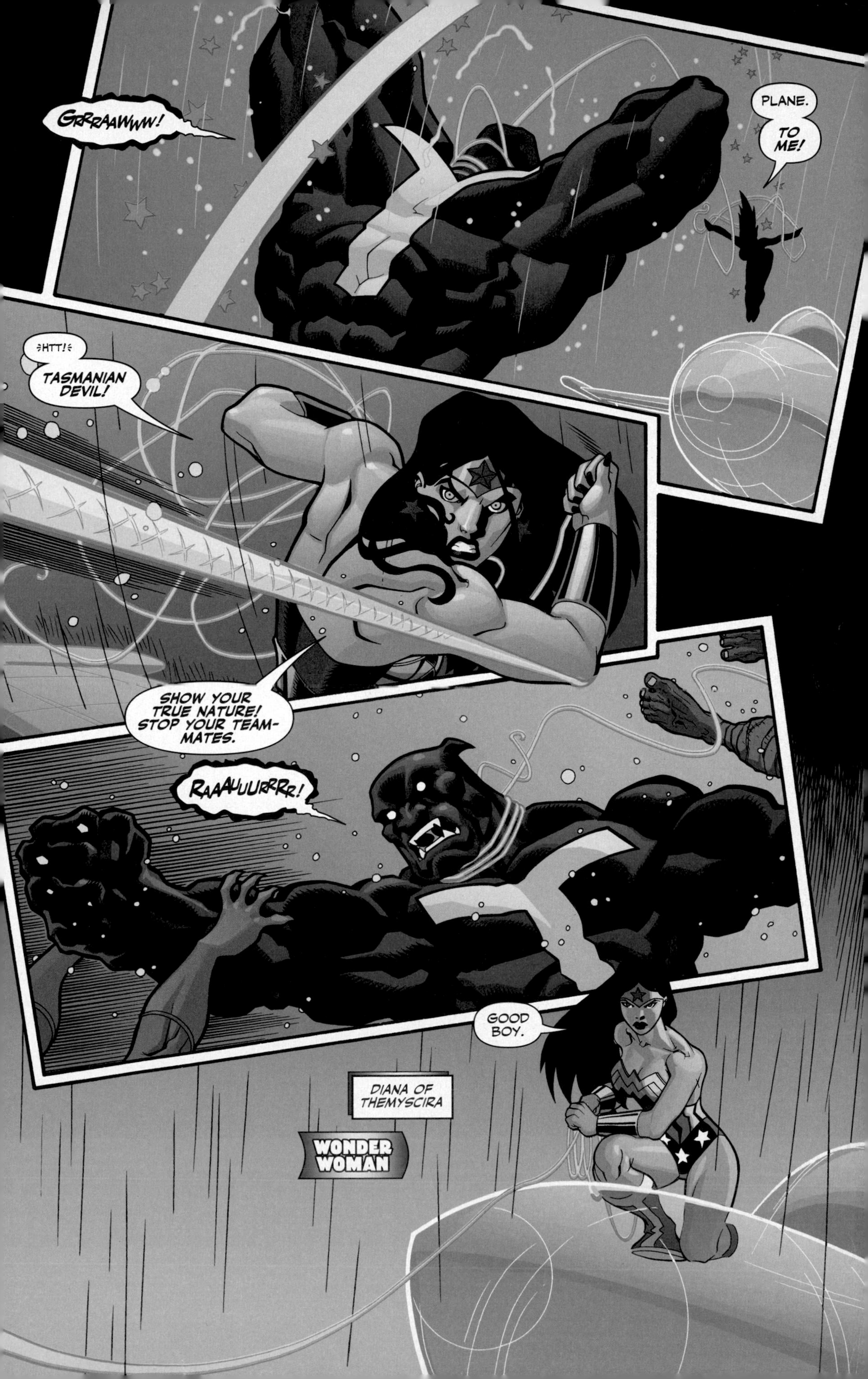
GRRRAAWWW!
PLANE.
TO ME!
HTT!
TASMANIAN DEVIL!
SHOW YOUR TRUE NATURE! STOP YOUR TEAM-MATES.
RAAAUUURRRR!
GOOD BOY.
DIANA OF THEMYSCIRA
WONDER WOMAN

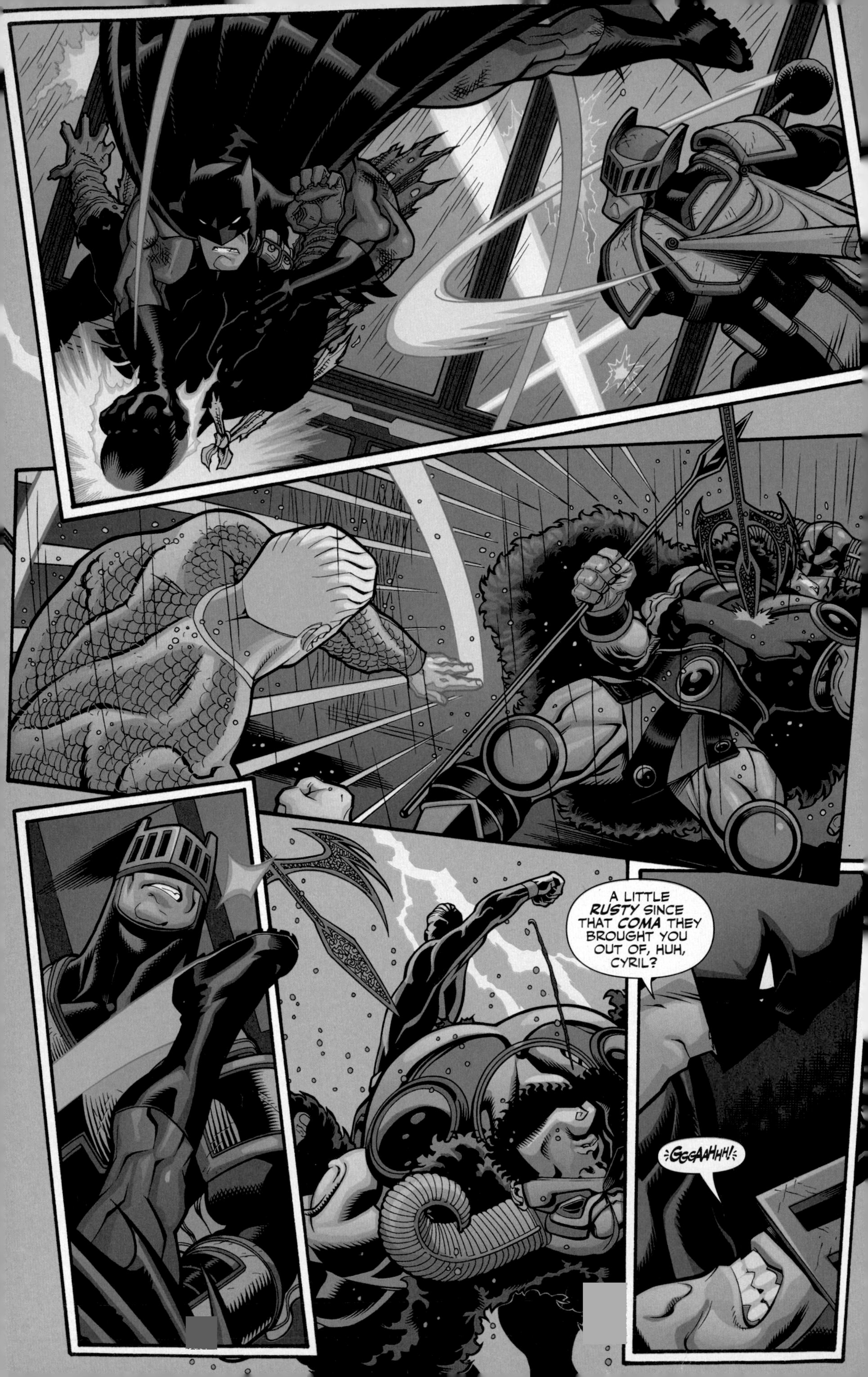
A LITTLE RUSTY SINCE THAT COMA THEY BROUGHT YOU OUT OF, HUH, CYRIL?
GGGAAHHH!

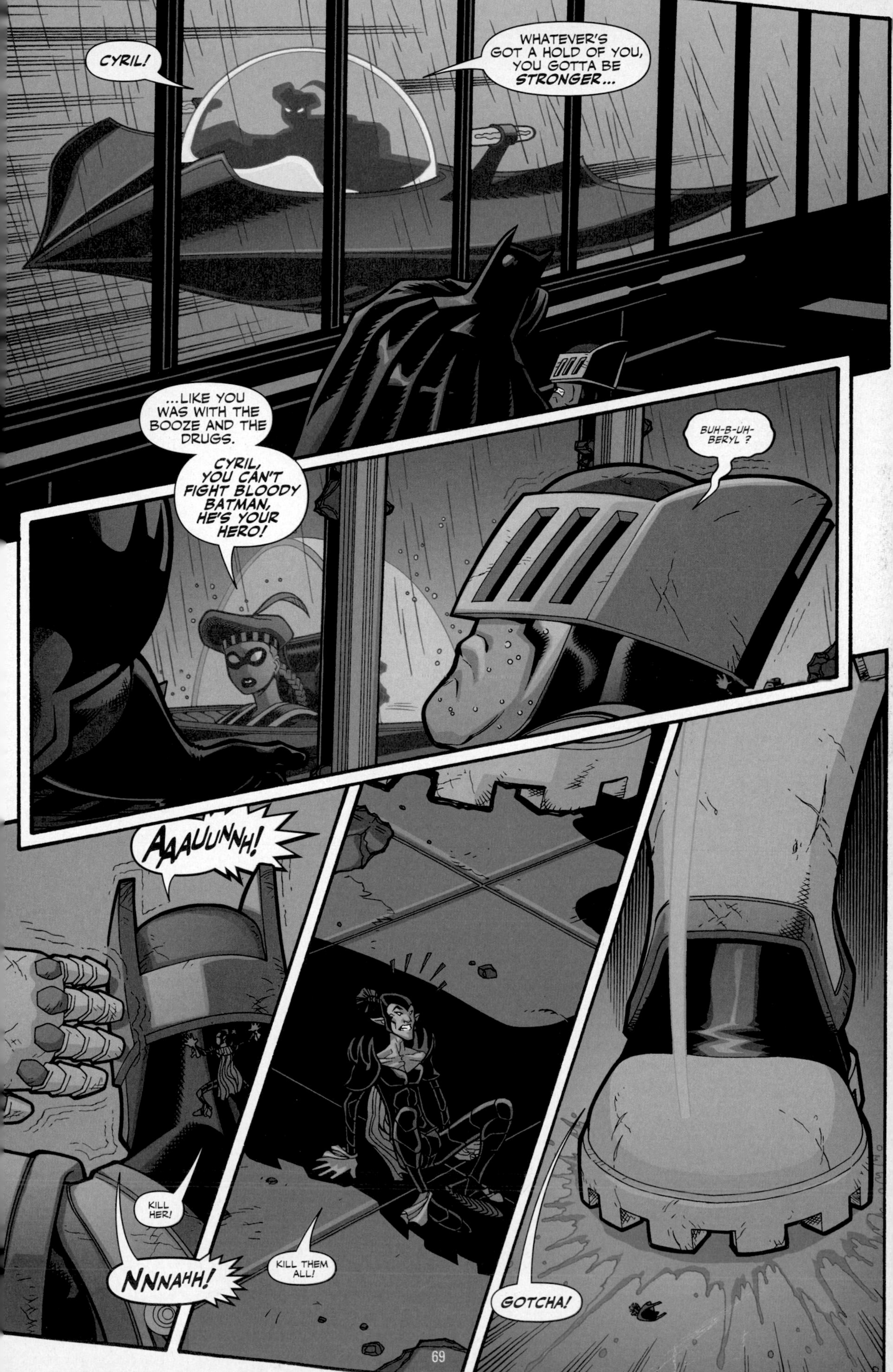
CYRIL!
WHATEVER'S GOT A HOLD OF YOU, YOU GOTTA BE STRONGER...
...LIKE YOU WAS WITH THE BOOZE AND THE DRUGS.
CYRIL, YOU CAN'T FIGHT BLOODY BATMAN, HE'S YOUR HERO!
BUH-B-UH-BERYL ?
AAAUUNNH!
KILL HER!
NNNAHH!
KILL THEM ALL!
GOTCHA!

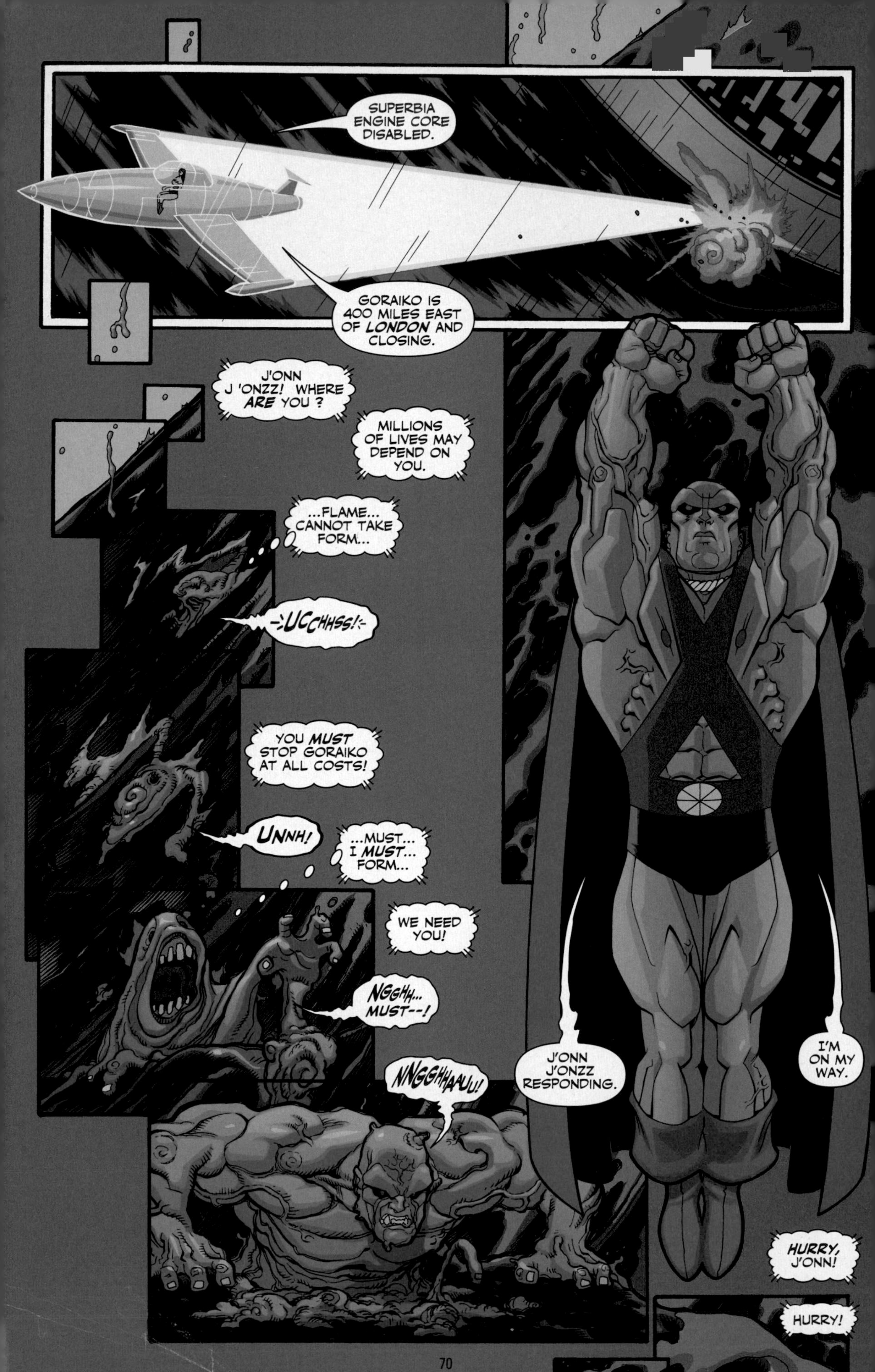
SUPERBIA ENGINE CORE DISABLED.
GORAIKO IS 400 MILES EAST OF LONDON AND CLOSING.
J'ONN J 'ONZZ! WHERE ARE YOU ?
MILLIONS OF LIVES MAY DEPEND ON YOU.
...FLAME... CANNOT TAKE FORM...
UCCHHSS!
YOU MUST STOP GORAIKO AT ALL COSTS!
UNNH!
...MUST... I MUST... FORM...
WE NEED YOU!
NGGHH... MUST--!
NNGGHHAAUU!
J'ONN J'ONZZ RESPONDING.
I'M ON MY WAY.
HURRY, J'ONN!
HURRY!

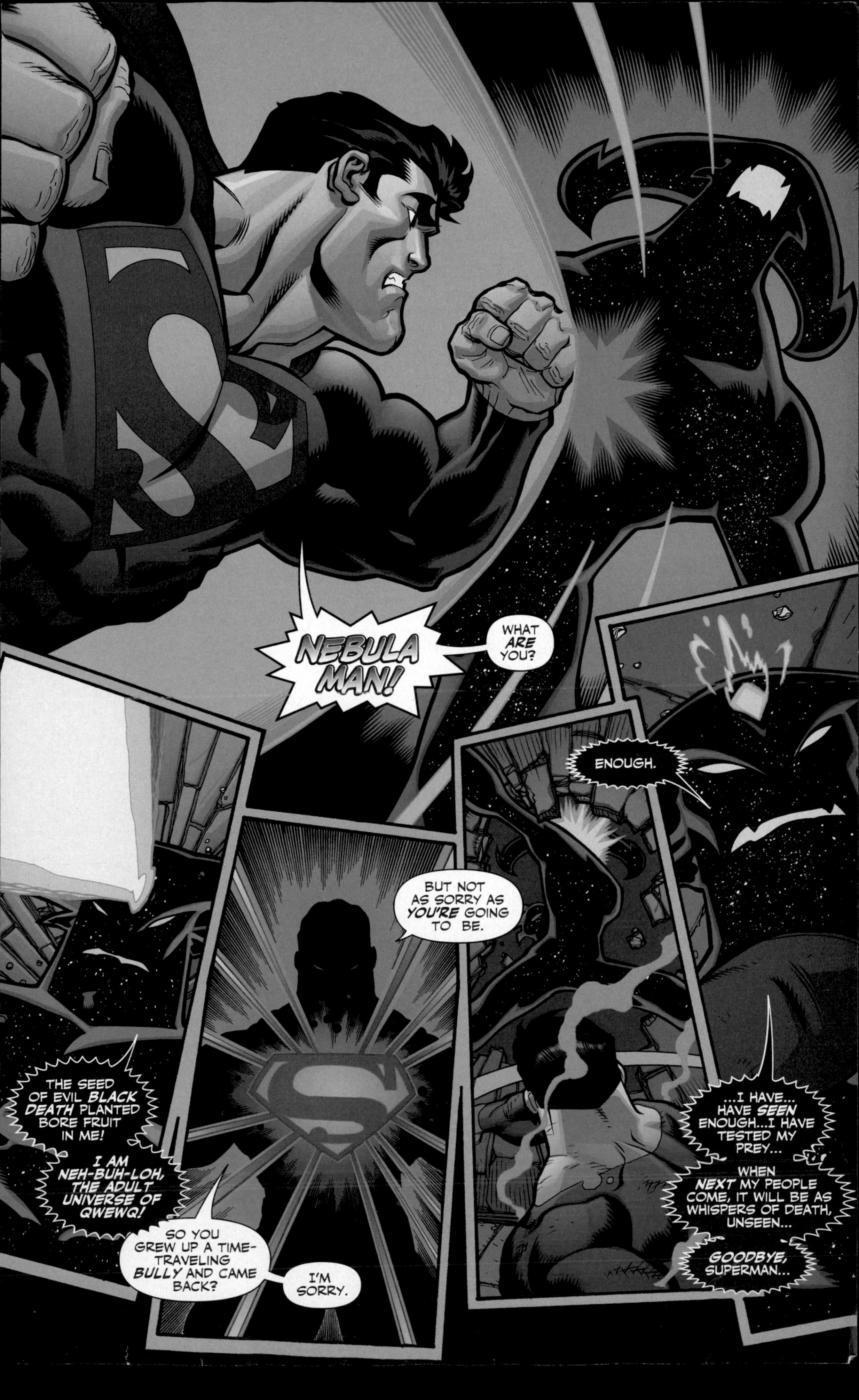
NEBULA MAN!
WHAT ARE YOU?
THE SEED OF EVIL BLACK DEATH PLANTED BORE FRUIT IN ME!
I AM NEH-BUH-LOH, THE ADULT UNIVERSE OF QWEWQ!
SO YOU GREW UP A TIME-TRAVELING BULLY AND CAME BACK?
I'M SORRY.
BUT NOT AS SORRY AS YOU'RE GOING TO BE.
ENOUGH.
...I HAVE... HAVE SEEN ENOUGH...I HAVE TESTED MY PREY...
WHEN NEXT MY PEOPLE COME, IT WILL BE AS WHISPERS OF DEATH, UNSEEN...
GOODBYE, SUPERMAN...

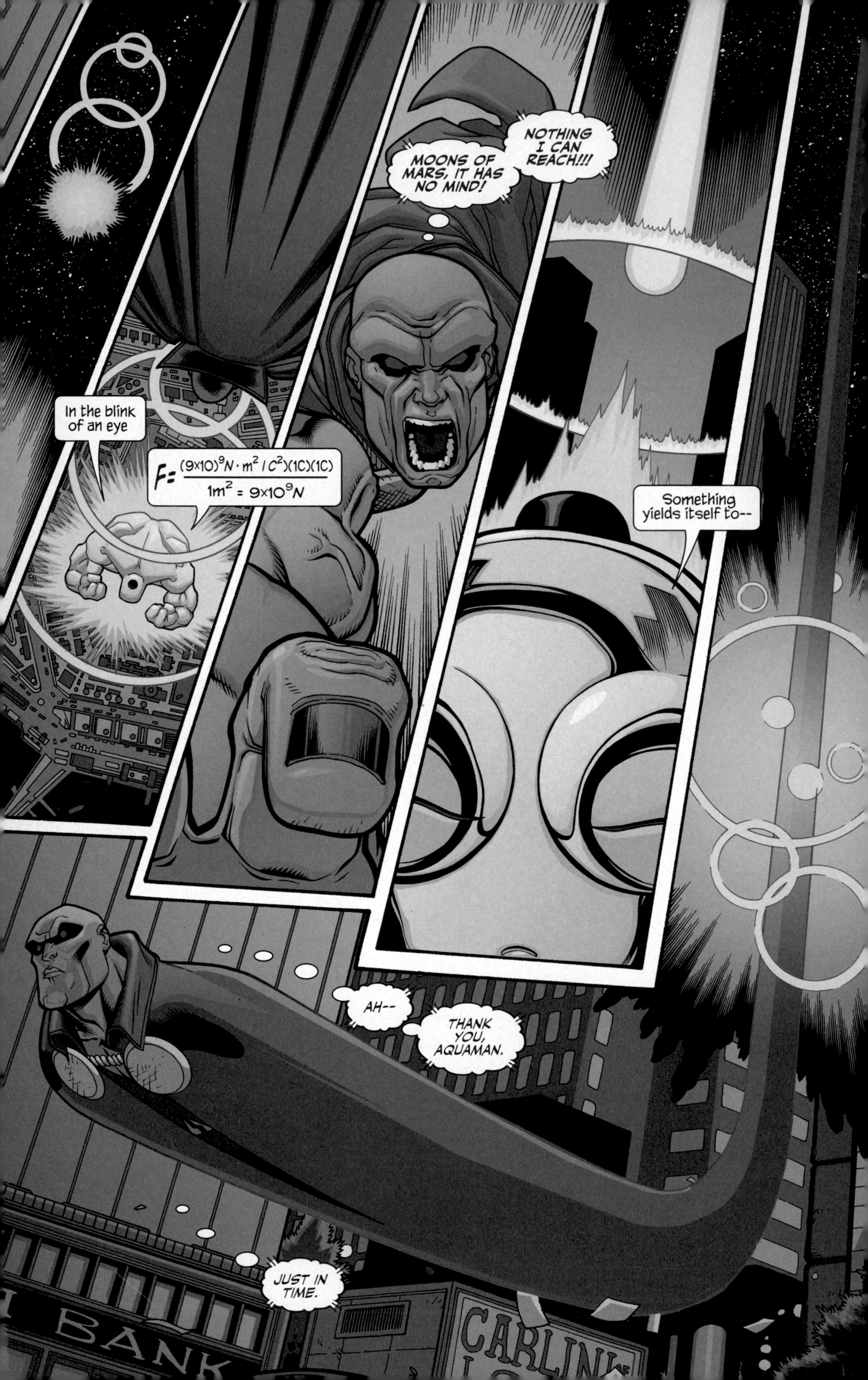
In the blink of an eye
$F = \frac{(9\times10)^9 N \cdot m^2 / C^2)(1C)(1C)}{1m^2} = 9\times10^9 N$
MOONS OF MARS, IT HAS NO MIND!
NOTHING I CAN REACH!!!
Something yields itself to--
AH--
THANK YOU, AQUAMAN.
JUST IN TIME.
BANK
CARLINI

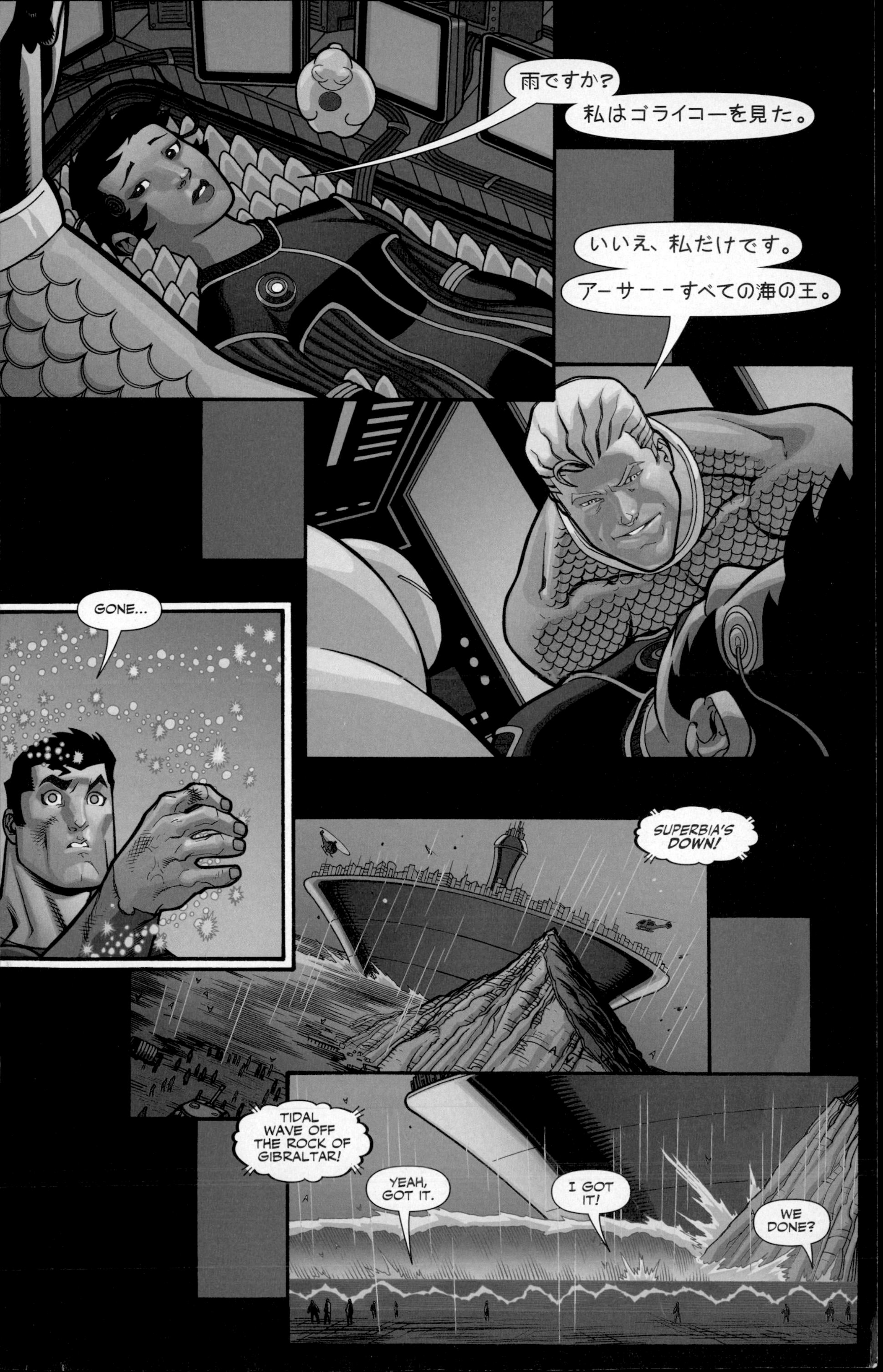
雨ですか?
私はゴライコーを見た。
いいえ、私だけです。
アーサー－すべての海の王。
GONE...
SUPERBIA'S DOWN!
TIDAL WAVE OFF THE ROCK OF GIBRALTAR!
YEAH, GOT IT.
I GOT IT!
WE DONE?

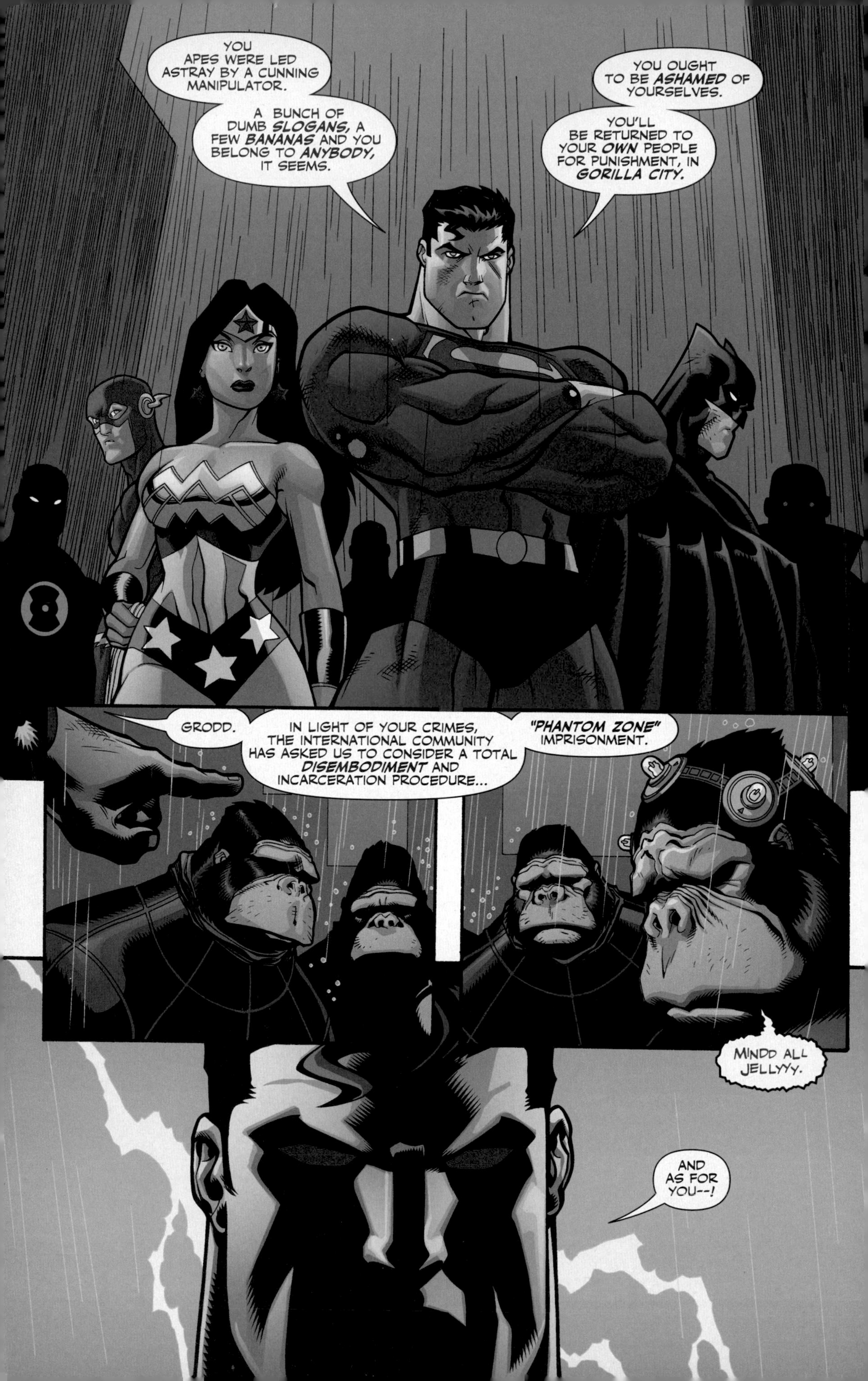
YOU APES WERE LED ASTRAY BY A CUNNING MANIPULATOR.
A BUNCH OF DUMB *SLOGANS*, A FEW *BANANAS* AND YOU BELONG TO *ANYBODY*, IT SEEMS.
YOU OUGHT TO BE *ASHAMED* OF YOURSELVES.
YOU'LL BE RETURNED TO YOUR *OWN* PEOPLE FOR PUNISHMENT, IN *GORILLA CITY*.
GRODD.
IN LIGHT OF YOUR CRIMES, THE INTERNATIONAL COMMUNITY HAS ASKED US TO CONSIDER A TOTAL *DISEMBODIMENT* AND INCARCERATION PROCEDURE...
"PHANTOM ZONE" IMPRISONMENT.
MINDD ALL JELLYYY.
AND AS FOR YOU--!

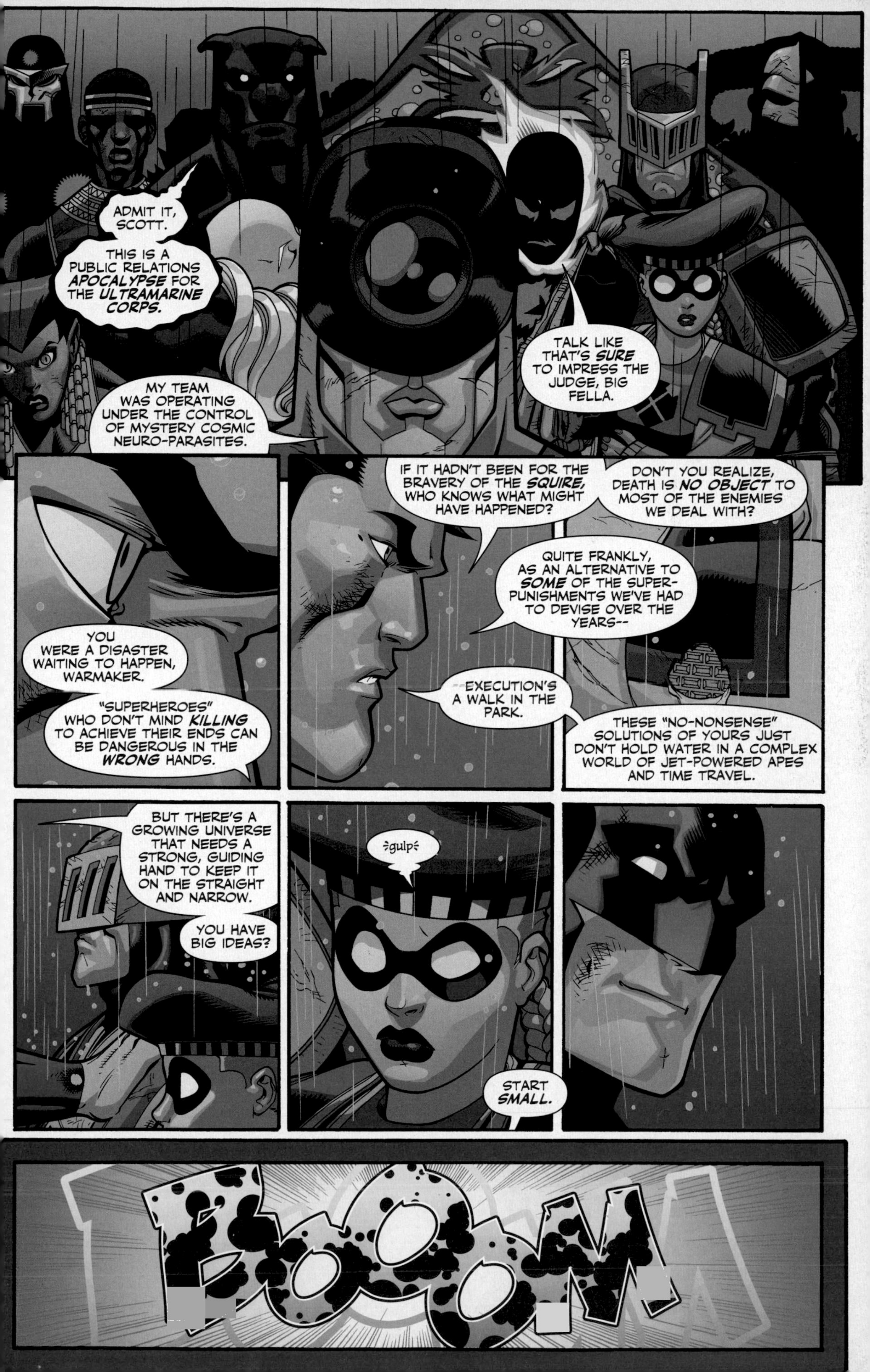
ADMIT IT, SCOTT.
THIS IS A PUBLIC RELATIONS APOCALYPSE FOR THE ULTRAMARINE CORPS.
MY TEAM WAS OPERATING UNDER THE CONTROL OF MYSTERY COSMIC NEURO-PARASITES.
TALK LIKE THAT'S SURE TO IMPRESS THE JUDGE, BIG FELLA.
YOU WERE A DISASTER WAITING TO HAPPEN, WARMAKER.
"SUPERHEROES" WHO DON'T MIND KILLING TO ACHIEVE THEIR ENDS CAN BE DANGEROUS IN THE WRONG HANDS.
IF IT HADN'T BEEN FOR THE BRAVERY OF THE SQUIRE, WHO KNOWS WHAT MIGHT HAVE HAPPENED?
DON'T YOU REALIZE, DEATH IS NO OBJECT TO MOST OF THE ENEMIES WE DEAL WITH?
QUITE FRANKLY, AS AN ALTERNATIVE TO SOME OF THE SUPER-PUNISHMENTS WE'VE HAD TO DEVISE OVER THE YEARS--
--EXECUTION'S A WALK IN THE PARK.
THESE "NO-NONSENSE" SOLUTIONS OF YOURS JUST DON'T HOLD WATER IN A COMPLEX WORLD OF JET-POWERED APES AND TIME TRAVEL.
BUT THERE'S A GROWING UNIVERSE THAT NEEDS A STRONG, GUIDING HAND TO KEEP IT ON THE STRAIGHT AND NARROW.
YOU HAVE BIG IDEAS?
gulp
START SMALL.
BOOOM

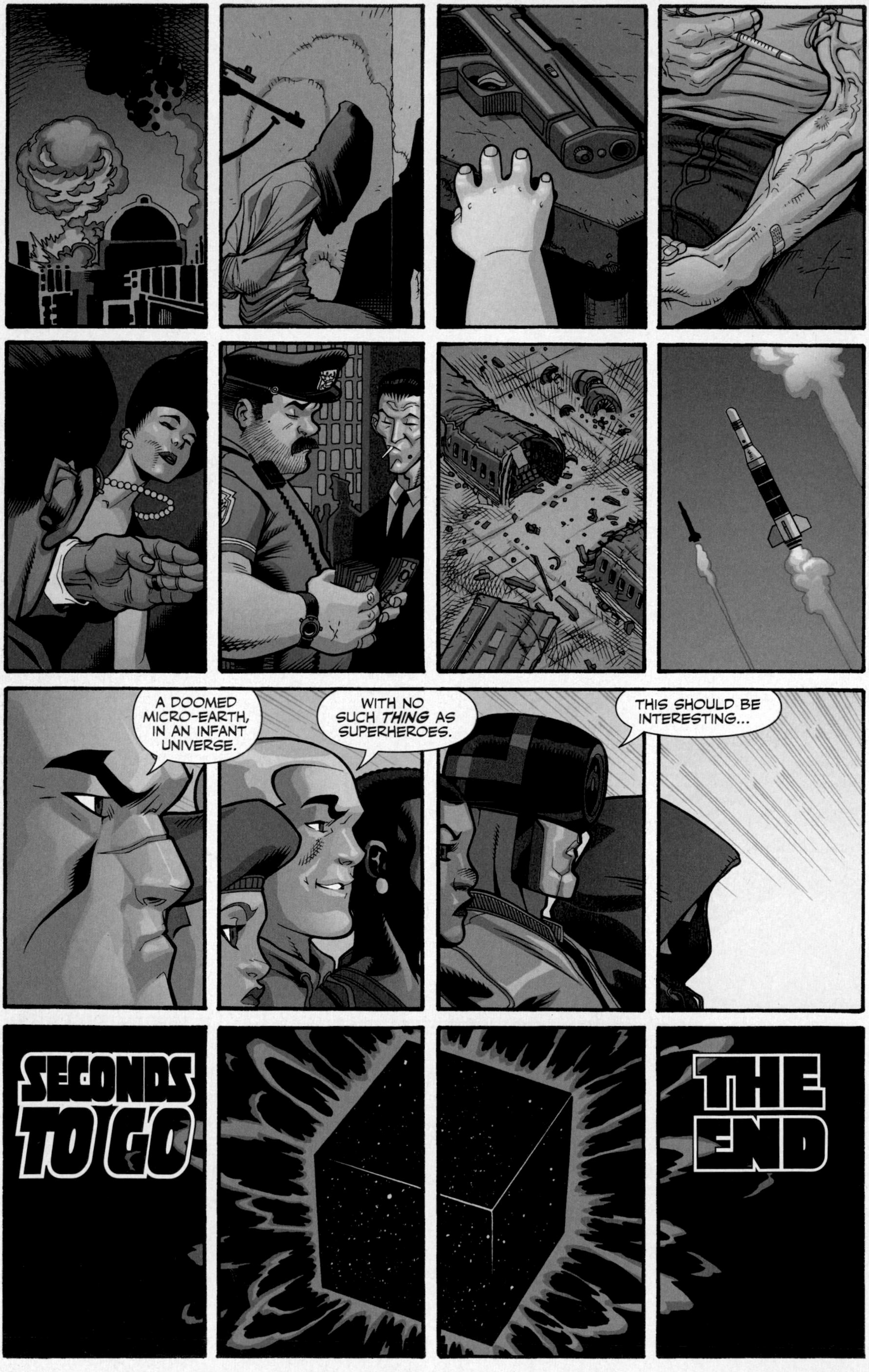
A DOOMED MICRO-EARTH, IN AN INFANT UNIVERSE.
WITH NO SUCH *THING* AS SUPERHEROES.
THIS SHOULD BE INTERESTING...
SECONDS TO GO
THE END

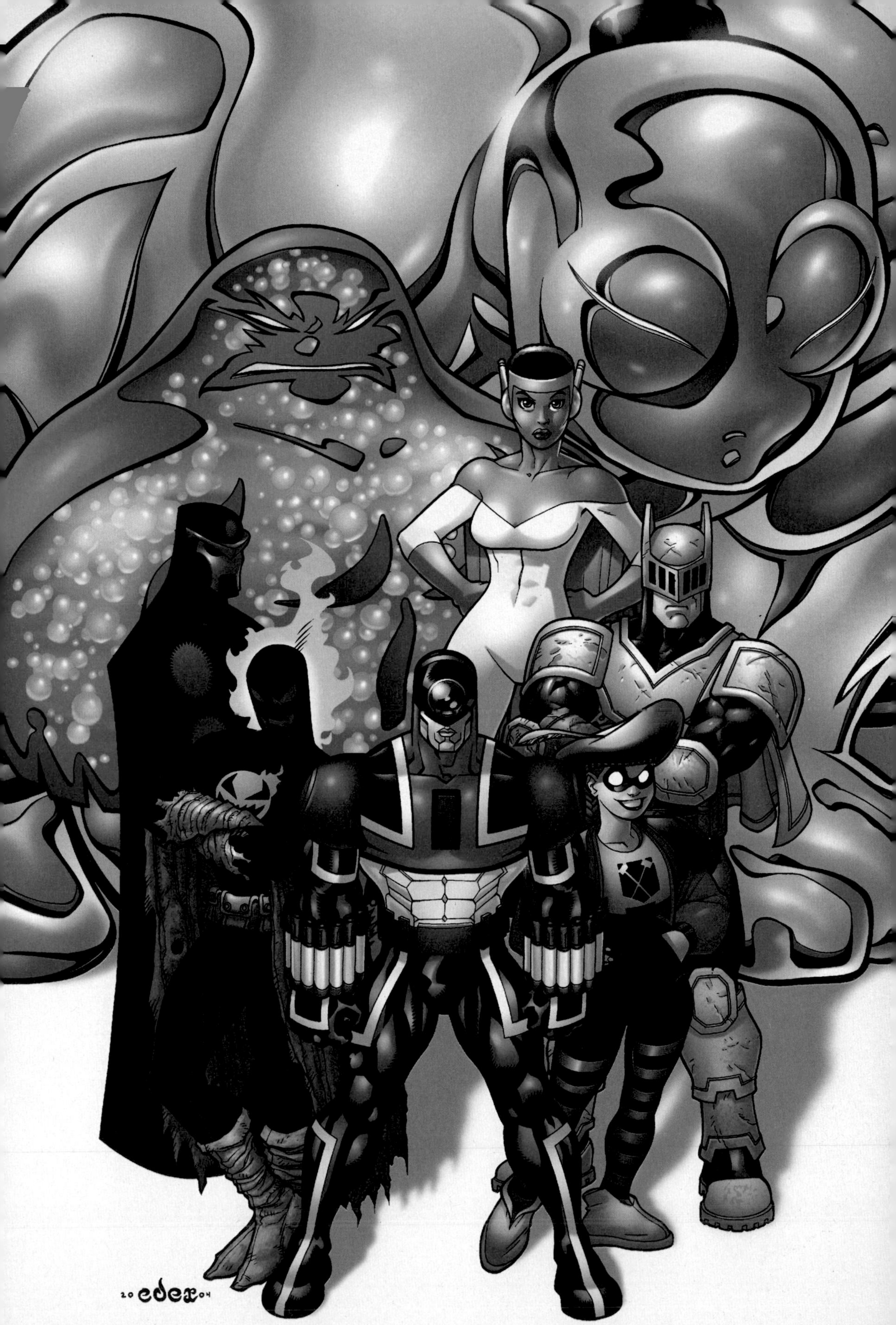
20 edex 04

JLA CLASSIFIED #1 ALTERNATE COVER

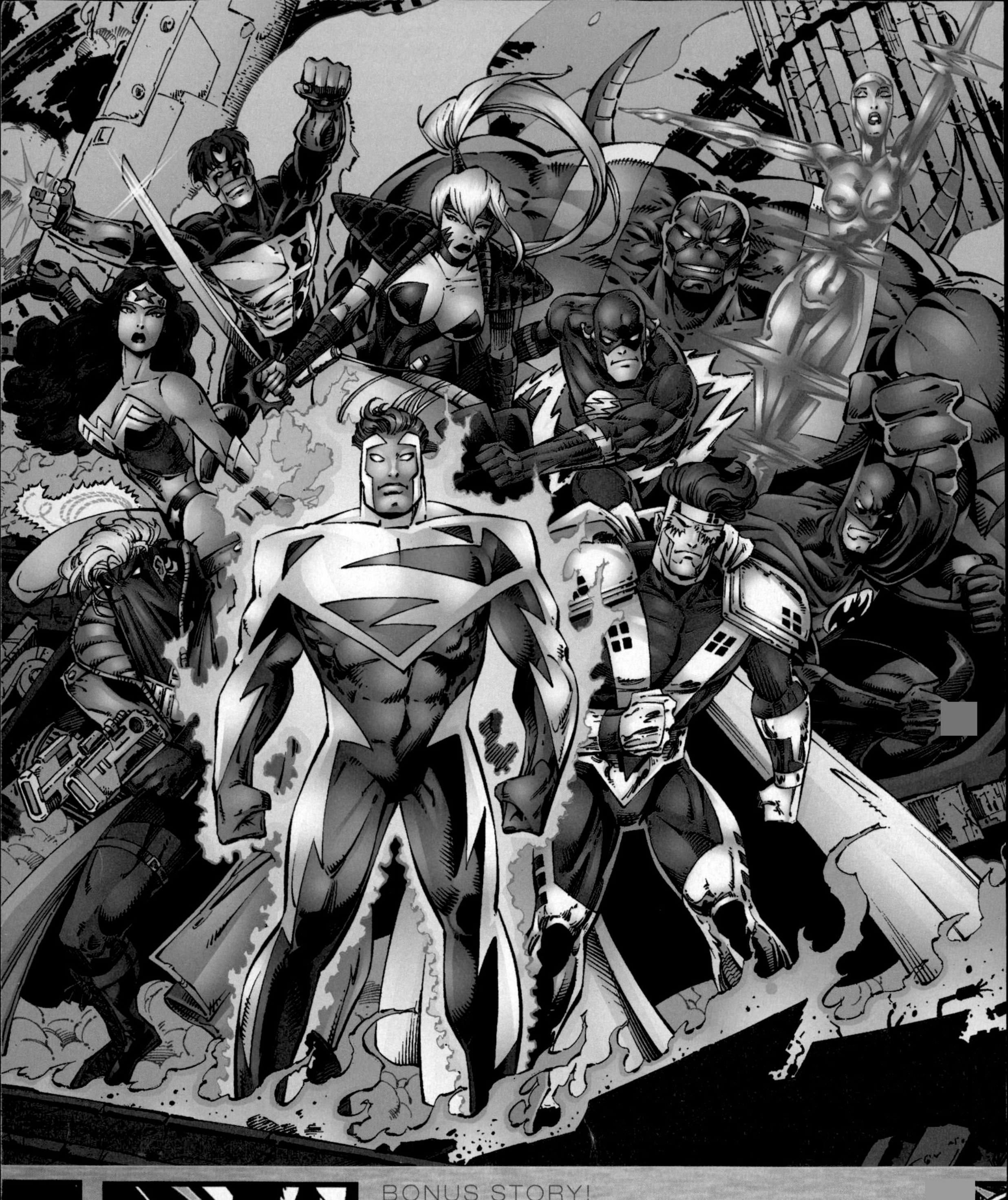

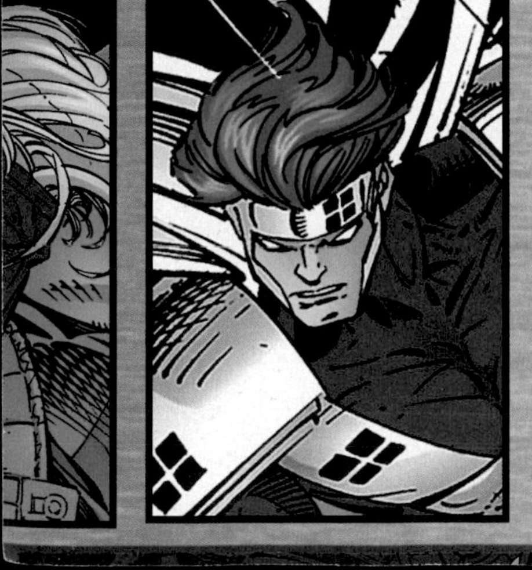

BONUS STORY!

JLA/WILDCATS

GRANT MORRISON WRITER

VAL SEMEIKS PENCILS

KEVIN CONRAD AND RAY KRYSSING INKERS

PAT GARRAHY COLORIST

KEN LOPEZ LETTERER

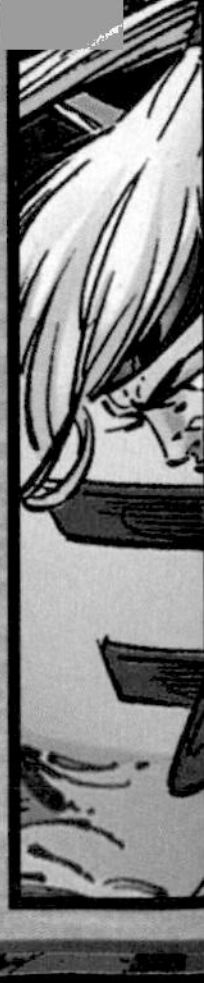

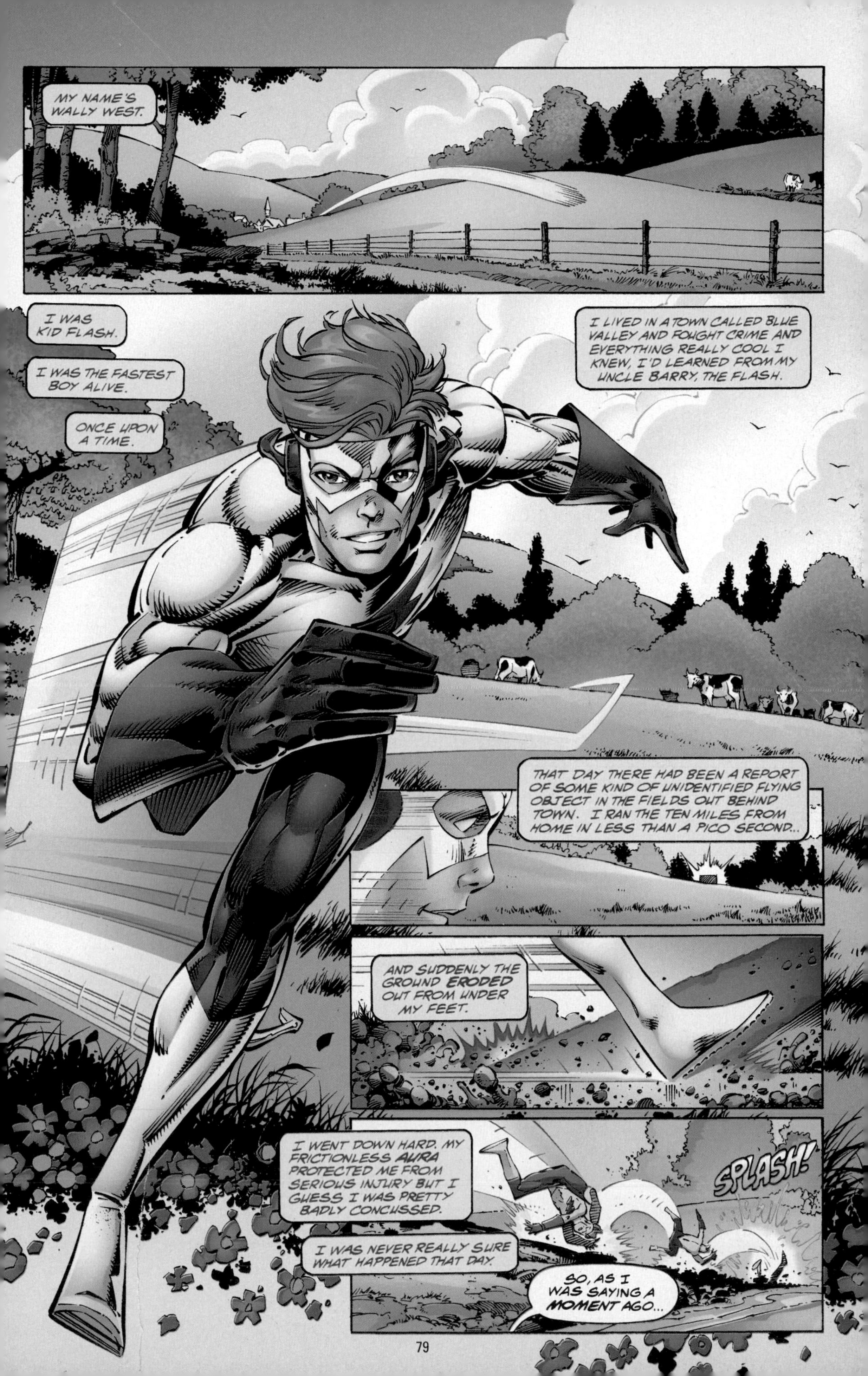
MY NAME'S WALLY WEST.
I WAS KID FLASH.
I WAS THE FASTEST BOY ALIVE.
ONCE UPON A TIME.
I LIVED IN A TOWN CALLED BLUE VALLEY AND FOUGHT CRIME AND EVERYTHING REALLY COOL I KNEW, I'D LEARNED FROM MY UNCLE BARRY, THE FLASH.
THAT DAY THERE HAD BEEN A REPORT OF SOME KIND OF UNIDENTIFIED FLYING OBJECT IN THE FIELDS OUT BEHIND TOWN. I RAN THE TEN MILES FROM HOME IN LESS THAN A PICO SECOND...
AND SUDDENLY THE GROUND ERODED OUT FROM UNDER MY FEET.
I WENT DOWN HARD. MY FRICTIONLESS AURA PROTECTED ME FROM SERIOUS INJURY BUT I GUESS I WAS PRETTY BADLY CONCUSSED.
I WAS NEVER REALLY SURE WHAT HAPPENED THAT DAY.
SPLASH!
SO, AS I WAS SAYING A MOMENT AGO...

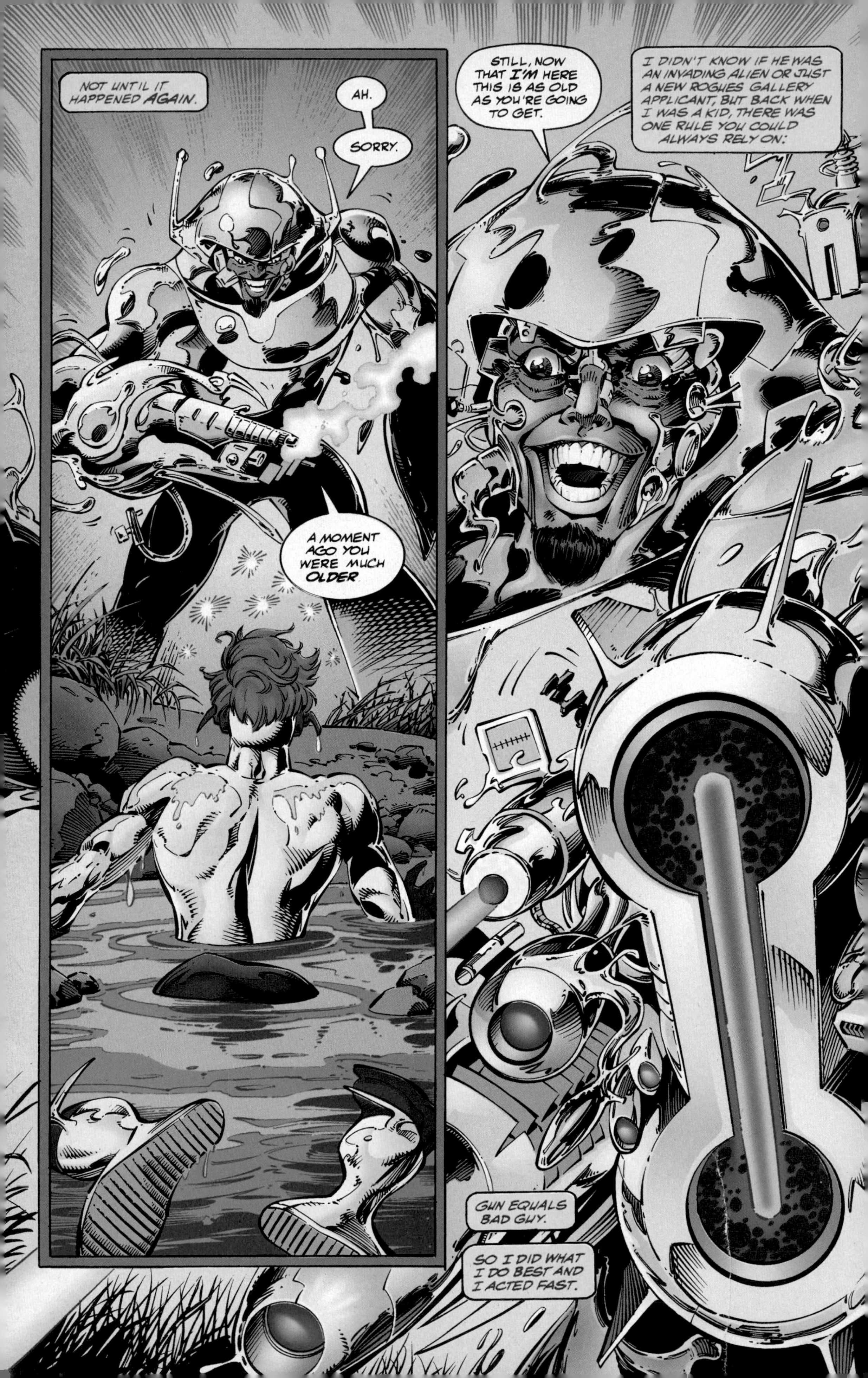
NOT UNTIL IT HAPPENED AGAIN.
AH.
SORRY.
A MOMENT AGO YOU WERE MUCH OLDER.
STILL, NOW THAT I'M HERE THIS IS AS OLD AS YOU'RE GOING TO GET.
I DIDN'T KNOW IF HE WAS AN INVADING ALIEN OR JUST A NEW ROGUES GALLERY APPLICANT, BUT BACK WHEN I WAS A KID, THERE WAS ONE RULE YOU COULD ALWAYS RELY ON:
GUN EQUALS BAD GUY.
SO I DID WHAT I DO BEST AND I ACTED FAST.

I STARTED VIBRATING MY FINGERS, SUPER-ACCELERATING A STREAM OF AIR MOLECULES UNTIL THE OXYGEN ITSELF BEGAN TO COMBUST AROUND HIS FEET.

AS I WAS SAYING, THE *BATTLESUIT* IS STATE OF THE ART *41ST CENTURY* TECHNOLOGY: TELEKINETICALLY-CONTROLLED SUPER-CONDUCTING LIQUID POLYALLOY...

...EXPIALIDOCIOUS...

AH...YOU'RE ALL SUCH... *COMEDIANS*, YOU SUPER PEOPLE.

THE ARMOR CAN BE PROGRAMMED WITH *DAXAMITE* STRENGTH OR *MARTIAN* AND *DURLAN* GENETIC CHARACTERISTICS, GIVING ME A FULL RANGE OF STEALTH AND CAMOUFLAGE OPTIONS...

;SNFF;

WHAT A CLEVER LITTLE BOY YOU ARE.

BUT AGAINST MY TECHNOLOGY, I'M AFRAID...

I'M GOING TO *KILL* YOU NOW. OR SHOULD THAT BE "*THEN*"?

OH, AND I FORGOT TO INTRODUCE MYSELF PROPERLY: I'M *EPOCH*. I'M THE *LORD OF TIME.*

AND *YOURS* JUST RAN OUT.

SSWWRRRP

I GUESS IT WAS ROUND ABOUT *THEN* THINGS REALLY STARTED TO GET WEIRD...

AS THE GUNS WENT OFF IN MY FACE I REMEMBER PRAYING FOR HELP AND THEN THERE WAS A BIG NOISE LIKE A HURRICANE COMING TO A STOP...

KKKKKRRR TWUKKACHAKA

AND SOMEBODY ANSWERED.

NO. IT DIDN'T HAPPEN THAT WAY.

ALL OF YOUR PROJECTILES WERE SNATCHED OUT OF THE AIR AT *SUPERSPEED.*

I *KNOW.*

UNCLE BARRY?

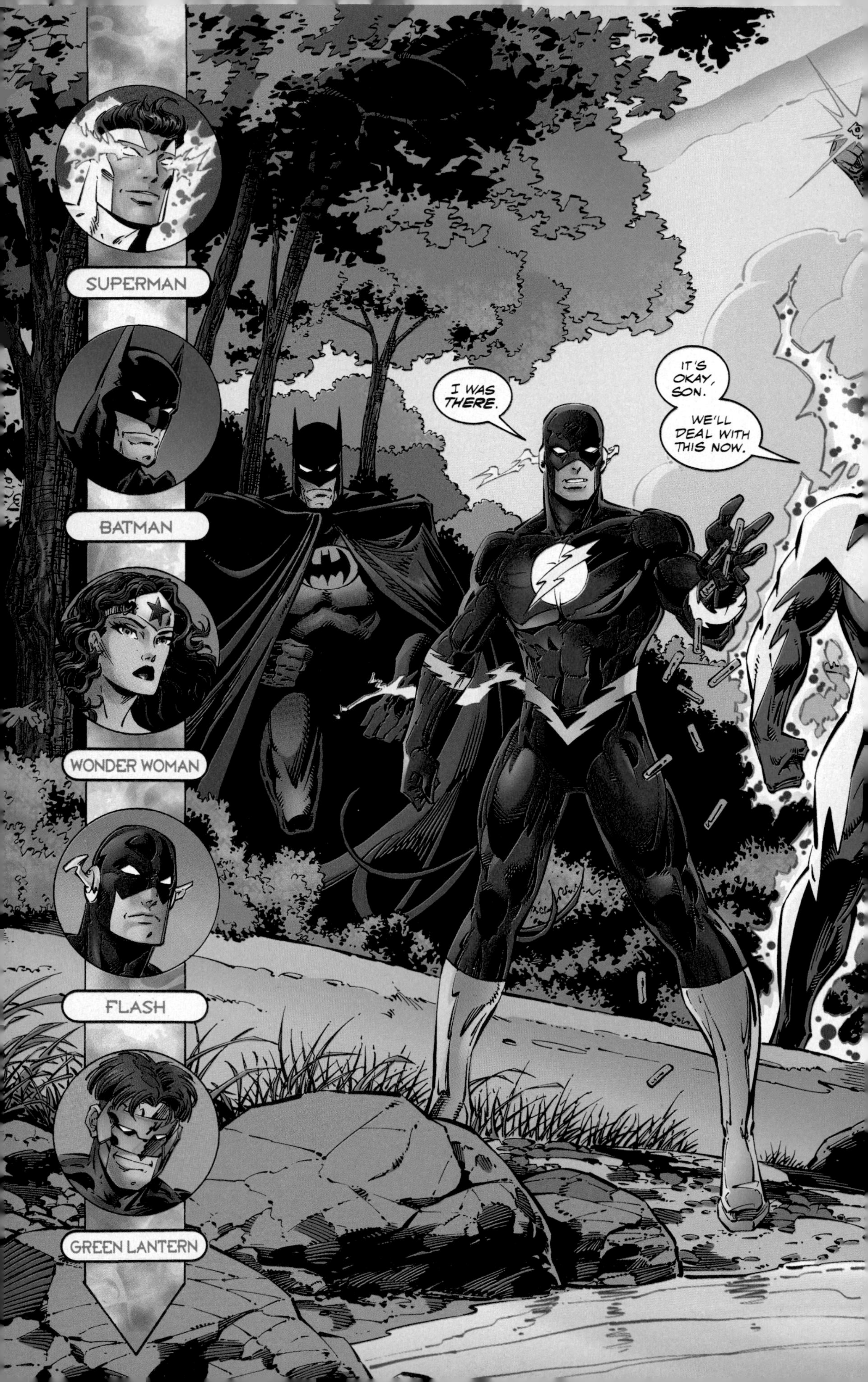
SUPERMAN
BATMAN
WONDER WOMAN
FLASH
GREEN LANTERN
I WAS THERE.
IT'S OKAY, SON.
WE'LL DEAL WITH THIS NOW.

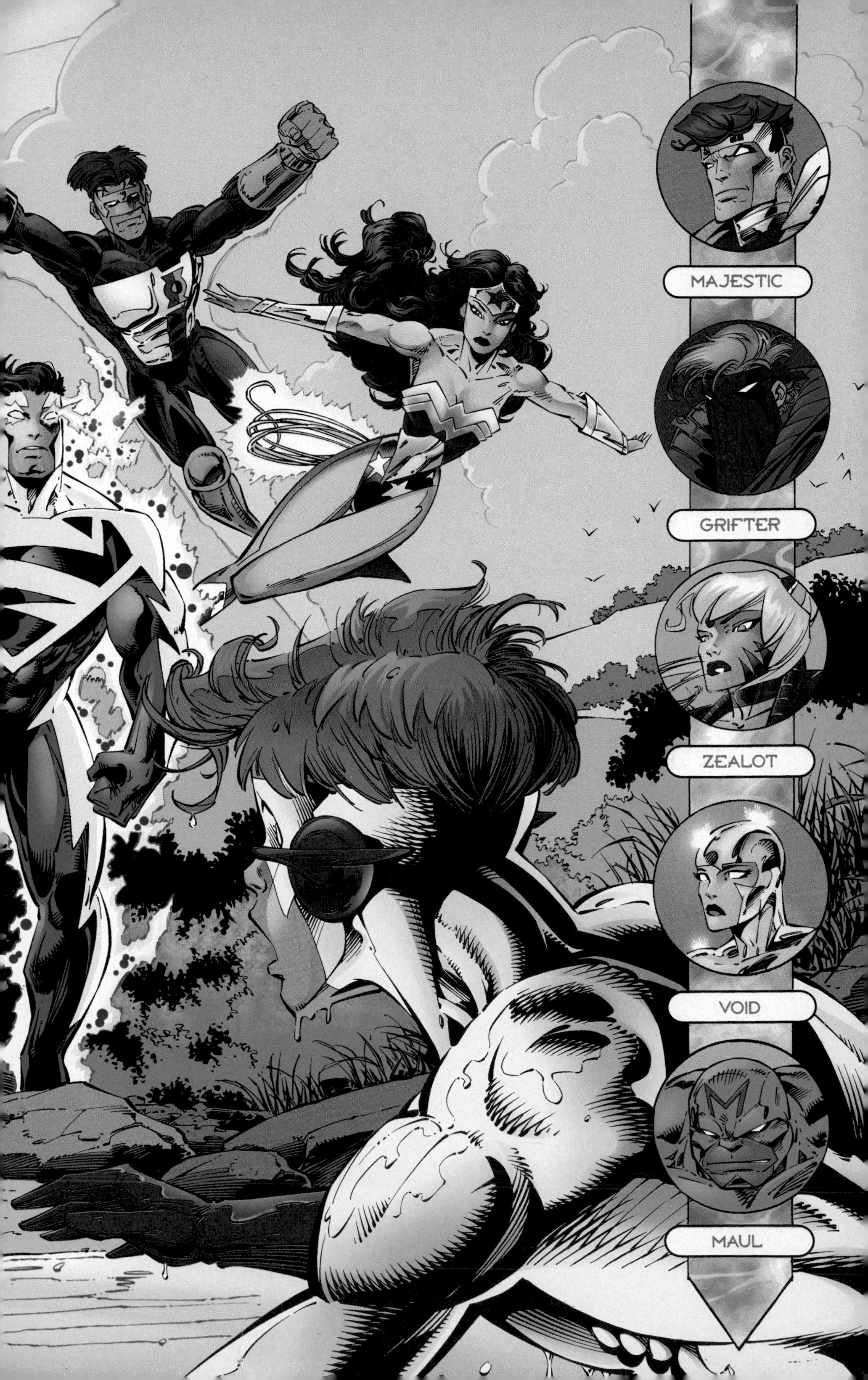
MAJESTIC
GRIFTER
ZEALOT
VOID
MAUL

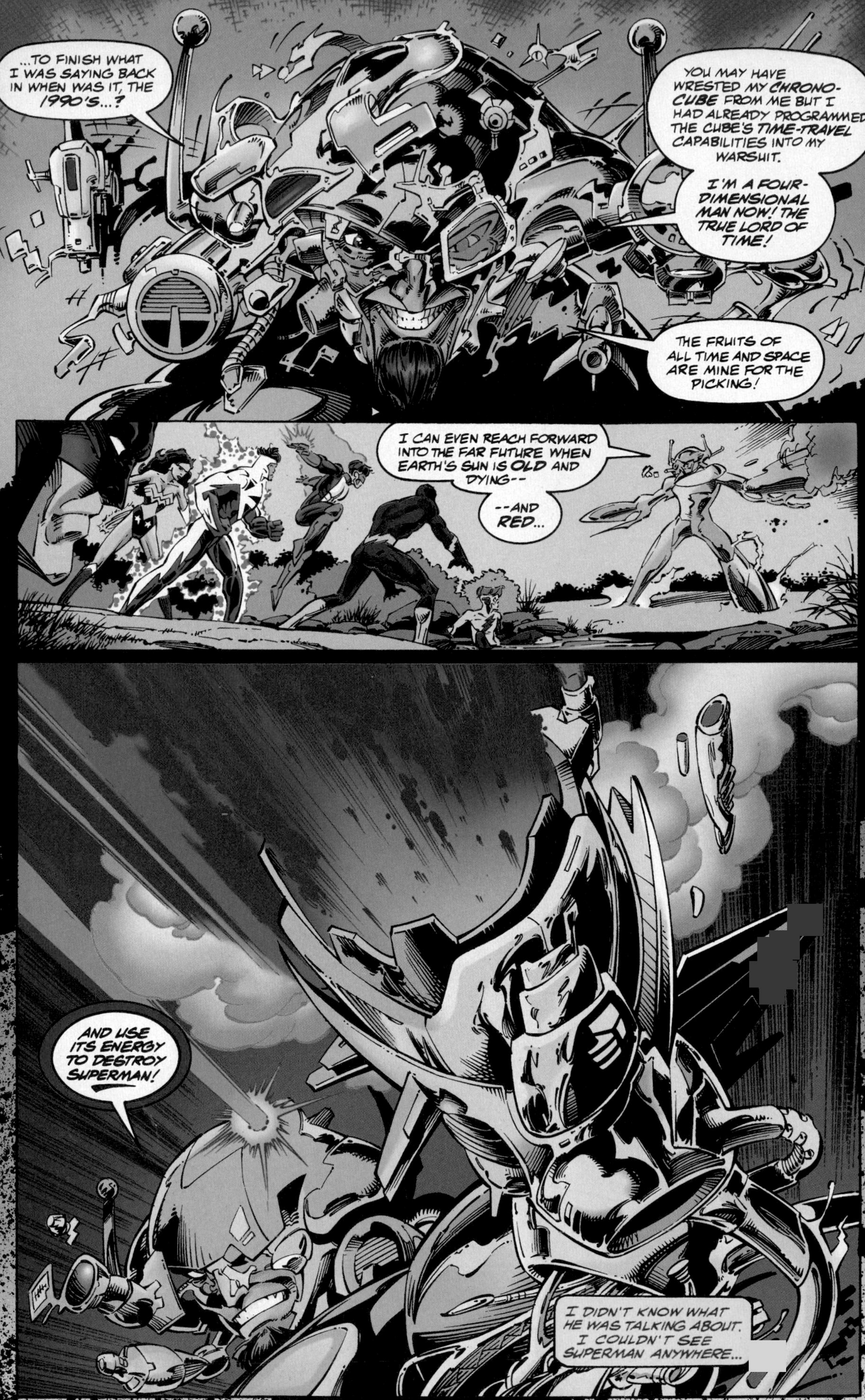
...TO FINISH WHAT I WAS SAYING BACK IN WHEN WAS IT, THE 1990'S...?
YOU MAY HAVE WRESTED MY CHRONO-CUBE FROM ME BUT I HAD ALREADY PROGRAMMED THE CUBE'S TIME-TRAVEL CAPABILITIES INTO MY WARSUIT.
I'M A FOUR-DIMENSIONAL MAN NOW! THE TRUE LORD OF TIME!
THE FRUITS OF ALL TIME AND SPACE ARE MINE FOR THE PICKING!
I CAN EVEN REACH FORWARD INTO THE FAR FUTURE WHEN EARTH'S SUN IS OLD AND DYING--
--AND RED...
AND USE ITS ENERGY TO DESTROY SUPERMAN!
I DIDN'T KNOW WHAT HE WAS TALKING ABOUT. I COULDN'T SEE SUPERMAN ANYWHERE...

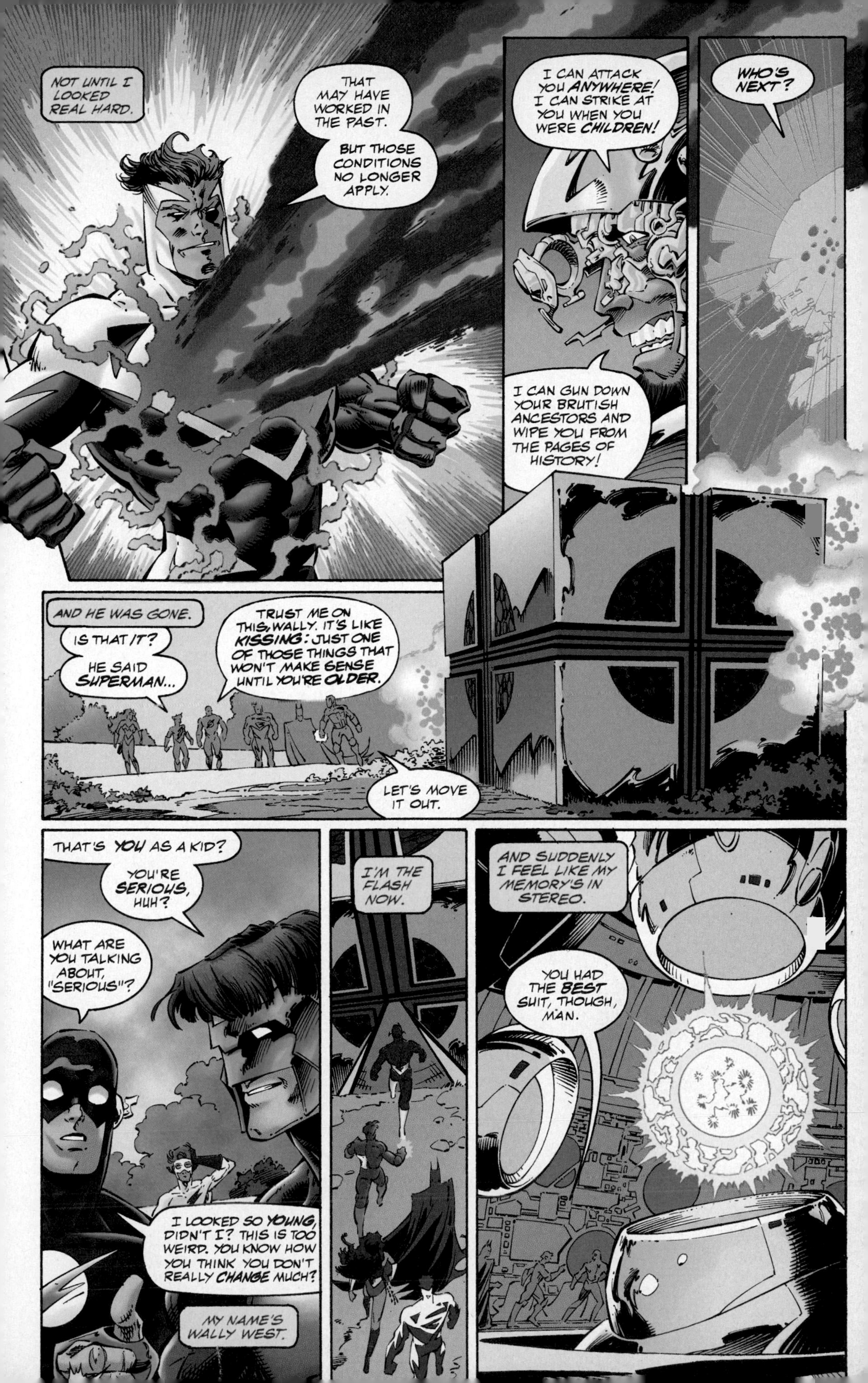
NOT UNTIL I LOOKED REAL HARD.
THAT MAY HAVE WORKED IN THE PAST.
BUT THOSE CONDITIONS NO LONGER APPLY.
I CAN ATTACK YOU ANYWHERE! I CAN STRIKE AT YOU WHEN YOU WERE CHILDREN!
I CAN GUN DOWN YOUR BRUTISH ANCESTORS AND WIPE YOU FROM THE PAGES OF HISTORY!
WHO'S NEXT?
AND HE WAS GONE.
IS THAT IT?
HE SAID SUPERMAN...
TRUST ME ON THIS, WALLY. IT'S LIKE KISSING: JUST ONE OF THOSE THINGS THAT WON'T MAKE SENSE UNTIL YOU'RE OLDER.
LET'S MOVE IT OUT.
THAT'S YOU AS A KID?
YOU'RE SERIOUS, HUH?
WHAT ARE YOU TALKING ABOUT, "SERIOUS"?
I LOOKED SO YOUNG, DIDN'T I? THIS IS TOO WEIRD. YOU KNOW HOW YOU THINK YOU DON'T REALLY CHANGE MUCH?
MY NAME'S WALLY WEST.
I'M THE FLASH NOW.
AND SUDDENLY I FEEL LIKE MY MEMORY'S IN STEREO.
YOU HAD THE BEST SUIT, THOUGH, MAN.

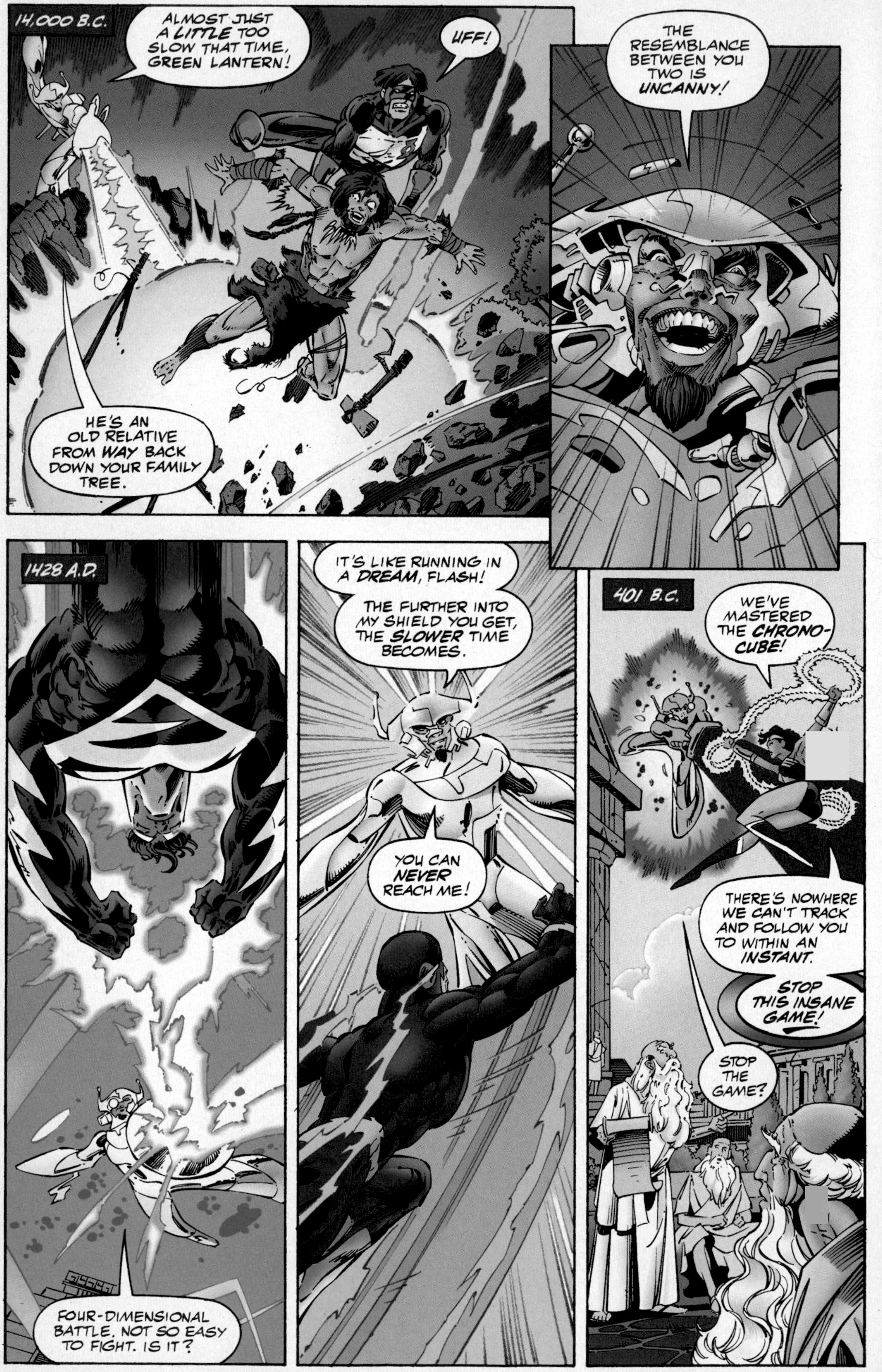
14,000 B.C.
ALMOST JUST A LITTLE TOO SLOW THAT TIME, GREEN LANTERN!
UFF!
HE'S AN OLD RELATIVE FROM WAY BACK DOWN YOUR FAMILY TREE.
THE RESEMBLANCE BETWEEN YOU TWO IS UNCANNY!
1428 A.D.
FOUR-DIMENSIONAL BATTLE. NOT SO EASY TO FIGHT. IS IT?
IT'S LIKE RUNNING IN A DREAM, FLASH!
THE FURTHER INTO MY SHIELD YOU GET, THE SLOWER TIME BECOMES.
YOU CAN NEVER REACH ME!
401 B.C.
WE'VE MASTERED THE CHRONO-CUBE!
THERE'S NOWHERE WE CAN'T TRACK AND FOLLOW YOU TO WITHIN AN INSTANT.
STOP THIS INSANE GAME!
STOP THE GAME?

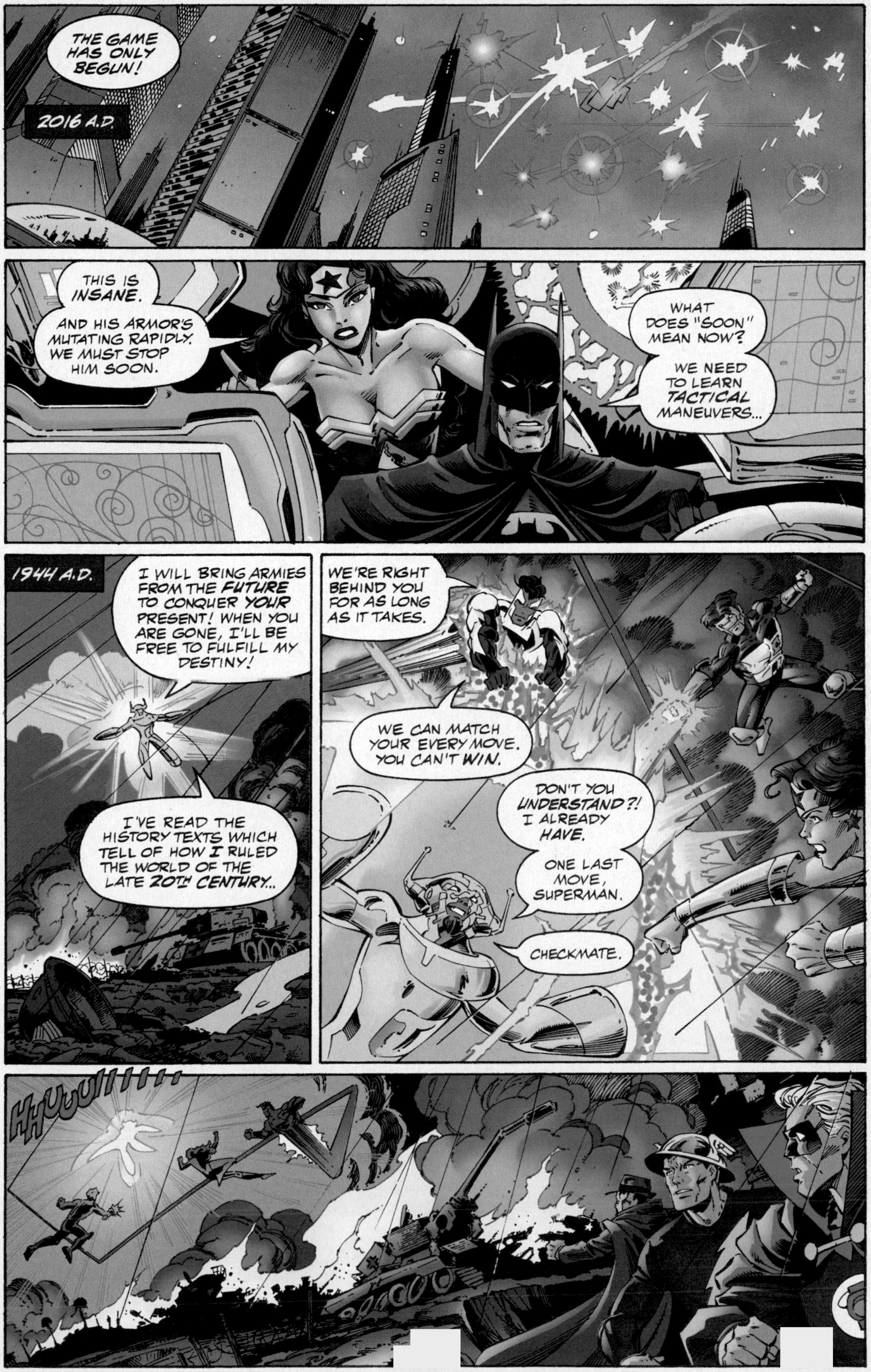
THE GAME HAS ONLY BEGUN!
2016 A.D.
THIS IS INSANE.
AND HIS ARMOR'S MUTATING RAPIDLY. WE MUST STOP HIM SOON.
WHAT DOES "SOON" MEAN NOW?
WE NEED TO LEARN TACTICAL MANEUVERS...
1944 A.D.
I WILL BRING ARMIES FROM THE FUTURE TO CONQUER YOUR PRESENT! WHEN YOU ARE GONE, I'LL BE FREE TO FULFILL MY DESTINY!
I'VE READ THE HISTORY TEXTS WHICH TELL OF HOW I RULED THE WORLD OF THE LATE 20TH CENTURY...
WE'RE RIGHT BEHIND YOU FOR AS LONG AS IT TAKES.
WE CAN MATCH YOUR EVERY MOVE. YOU CAN'T WIN.
DON'T YOU UNDERSTAND?! I ALREADY HAVE.
ONE LAST MOVE, SUPERMAN.
CHECKMATE.
HHUUUIIIIII

65,000,000 B.C.

UUUUNNNNNNNN

WOHH!

LOOK AT THE SKY! DID *HE* DO THAT?

WE DIDN'T DO THAT, DID WE?

NO. SOMETHING'S OCCURRING IN *SPACE*. SOME KIND OF... *DARK NOVA* EVENT. IT'S LIKE A SMALL BLACK *SUN* BLOTTING OUT THE SKY. WHATEVER IT IS, IT MAY BE ABSORBING *LIGHT* AS IT COLLAPSES...

"*I THINK HE'S FEEDING ON IT.*

...ENERGY STREAMING BACKWARDS THROUGH TIME... ANTI-TACHYONS STRIPMINED BY THE... GRAVITY OF THE DARK NOVA...ABSORBED THROUGH THE WARSUIT'S SMARTSKIN CASING... FEEDING THE ARMOR'S COMPUTER COLONIES... I MUST RECORD THIS MOMENT...

MY GOD!

THIS IS THE GREATEST MOMENT OF MY LIFE!

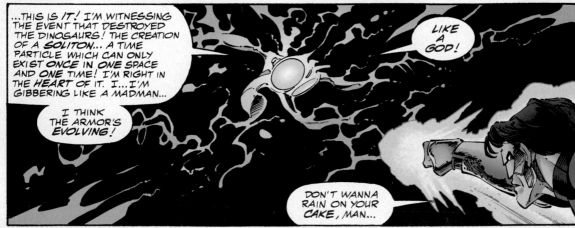

...THIS IS *IT!* I'M WITNESSING THE EVENT THAT DESTROYED THE DINOSAURS! THE CREATION OF A *SOLITON*... A TIME PARTICLE WHICH CAN ONLY *EXIST ONCE* IN *ONE SPACE* AND *ONE TIME!* I'M RIGHT IN THE *HEART* OF IT. I...I'M GIBBERING LIKE A MADMAN...

I THINK THE ARMOR'S *EVOLVING!*

LIKE A GOD!

DON'T WANNA RAIN ON YOUR *CAKE,* MAN...

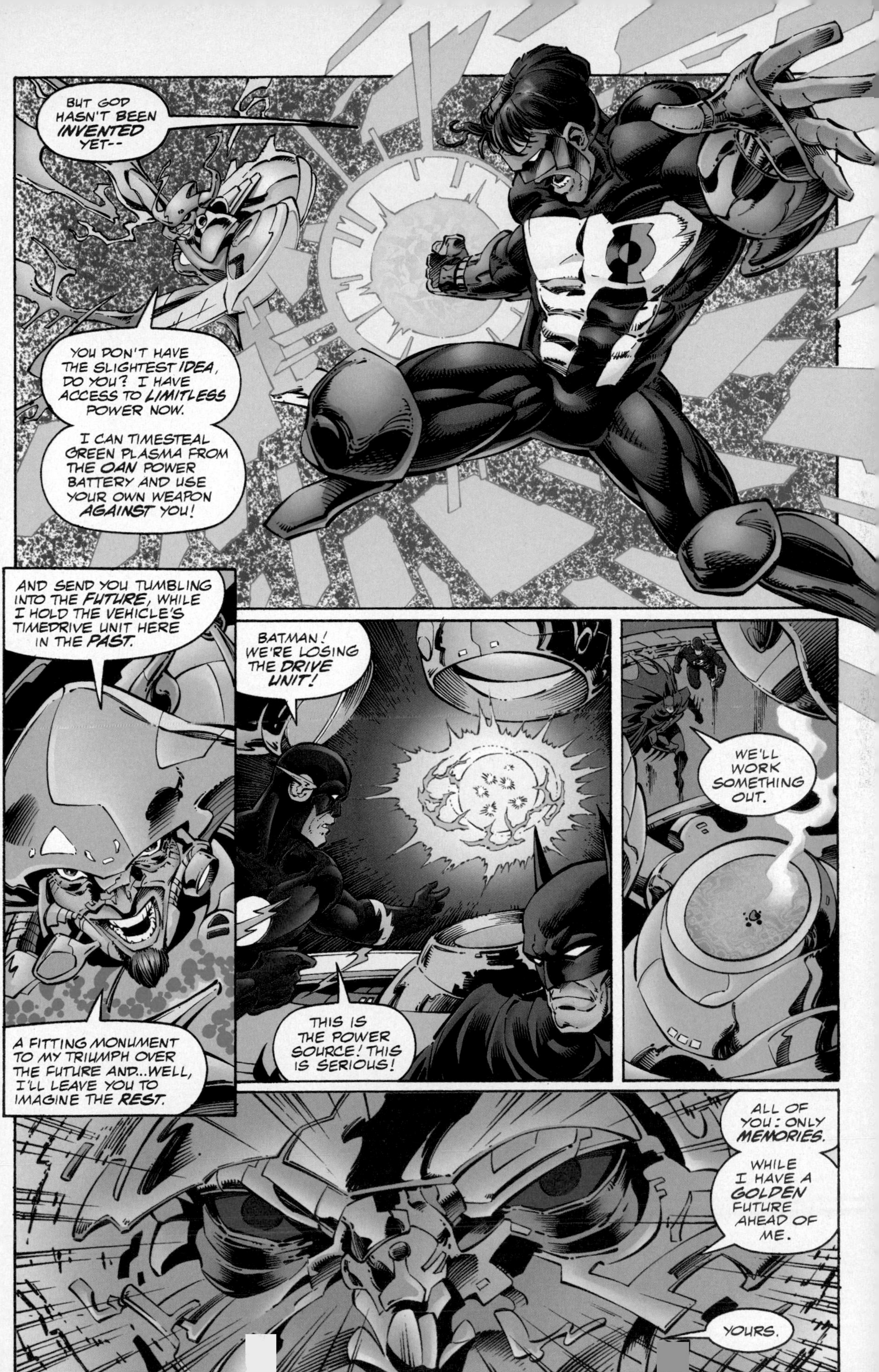
BUT GOD HASN'T BEEN INVENTED YET--
YOU DON'T HAVE THE SLIGHTEST IDEA, DO YOU? I HAVE ACCESS TO LIMITLESS POWER NOW.
I CAN TIMESTEAL GREEN PLASMA FROM THE OAN POWER BATTERY AND USE YOUR OWN WEAPON AGAINST YOU!
AND SEND YOU TUMBLING INTO THE FUTURE, WHILE I HOLD THE VEHICLE'S TIMEDRIVE UNIT HERE IN THE PAST.
A FITTING MONUMENT TO MY TRIUMPH OVER THE FUTURE AND...WELL, I'LL LEAVE YOU TO IMAGINE THE REST.
BATMAN! WE'RE LOSING THE DRIVE UNIT!
THIS IS THE POWER SOURCE! THIS IS SERIOUS!
WE'LL WORK SOMETHING OUT.
ALL OF YOU: ONLY MEMORIES.
WHILE I HAVE A GOLDEN FUTURE AHEAD OF ME.
YOURS.

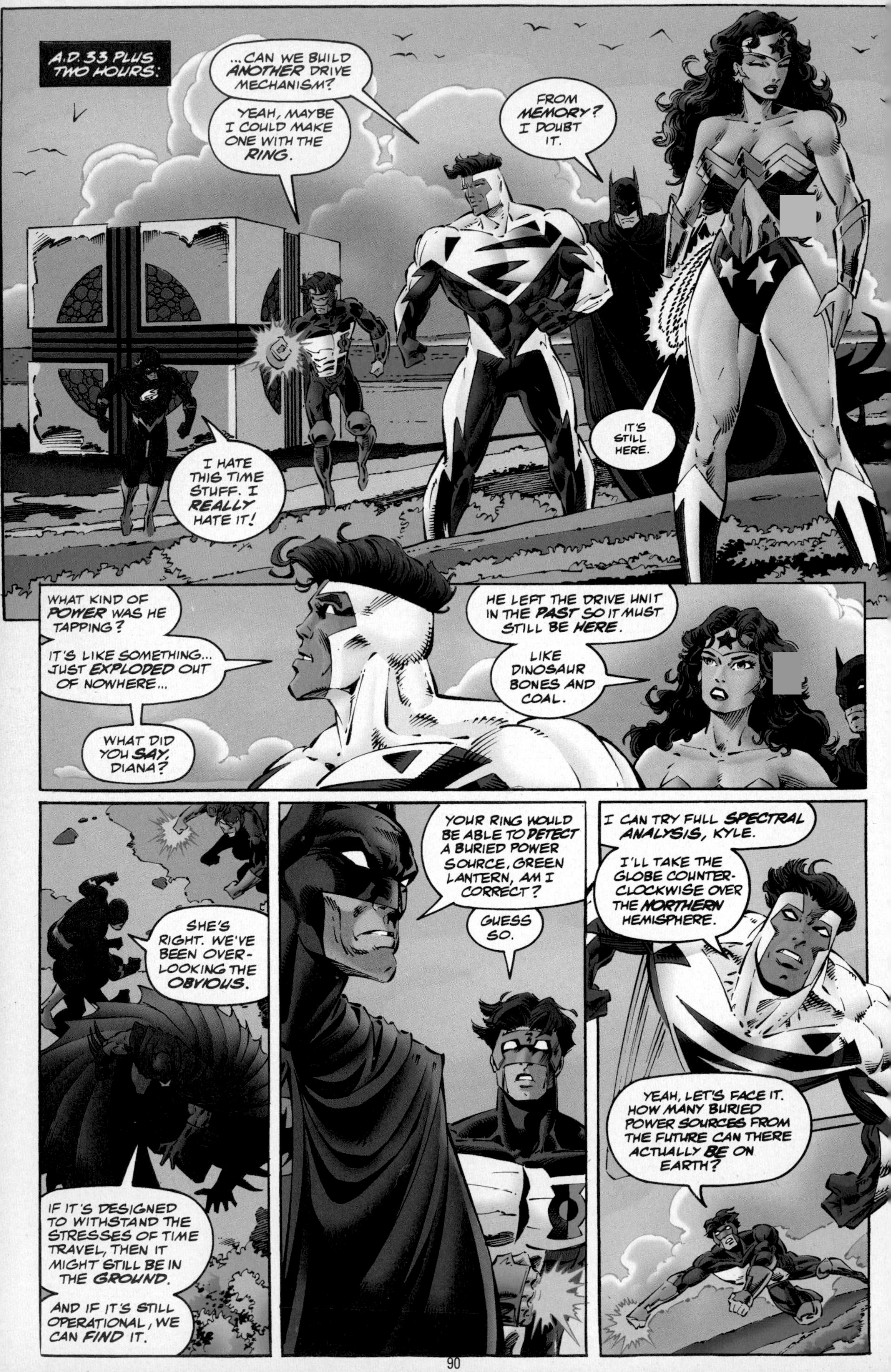
A.D. 33 PLUS TWO HOURS:
...CAN WE BUILD ANOTHER DRIVE MECHANISM?
YEAH, MAYBE I COULD MAKE ONE WITH THE RING.
FROM MEMORY? I DOUBT IT.
IT'S STILL HERE.
I HATE THIS TIME STUFF. I REALLY HATE IT!
WHAT KIND OF POWER WAS HE TAPPING?
IT'S LIKE SOMETHING... JUST EXPLODED OUT OF NOWHERE...
WHAT DID YOU SAY, DIANA?
HE LEFT THE DRIVE UNIT IN THE PAST SO IT MUST STILL BE HERE.
LIKE DINOSAUR BONES AND COAL.
SHE'S RIGHT. WE'VE BEEN OVER-LOOKING THE OBVIOUS.
IF IT'S DESIGNED TO WITHSTAND THE STRESSES OF TIME TRAVEL, THEN IT MIGHT STILL BE IN THE GROUND.
AND IF IT'S STILL OPERATIONAL, WE CAN FIND IT.
YOUR RING WOULD BE ABLE TO DETECT A BURIED POWER SOURCE, GREEN LANTERN, AM I CORRECT?
GUESS SO.
I CAN TRY FULL SPECTRAL ANALYSIS, KYLE.
I'LL TAKE THE GLOBE COUNTER-CLOCKWISE OVER THE NORTHERN HEMISPHERE.
YEAH, LET'S FACE IT. HOW MANY BURIED POWER SOURCES FROM THE FUTURE CAN THERE ACTUALLY BE ON EARTH?

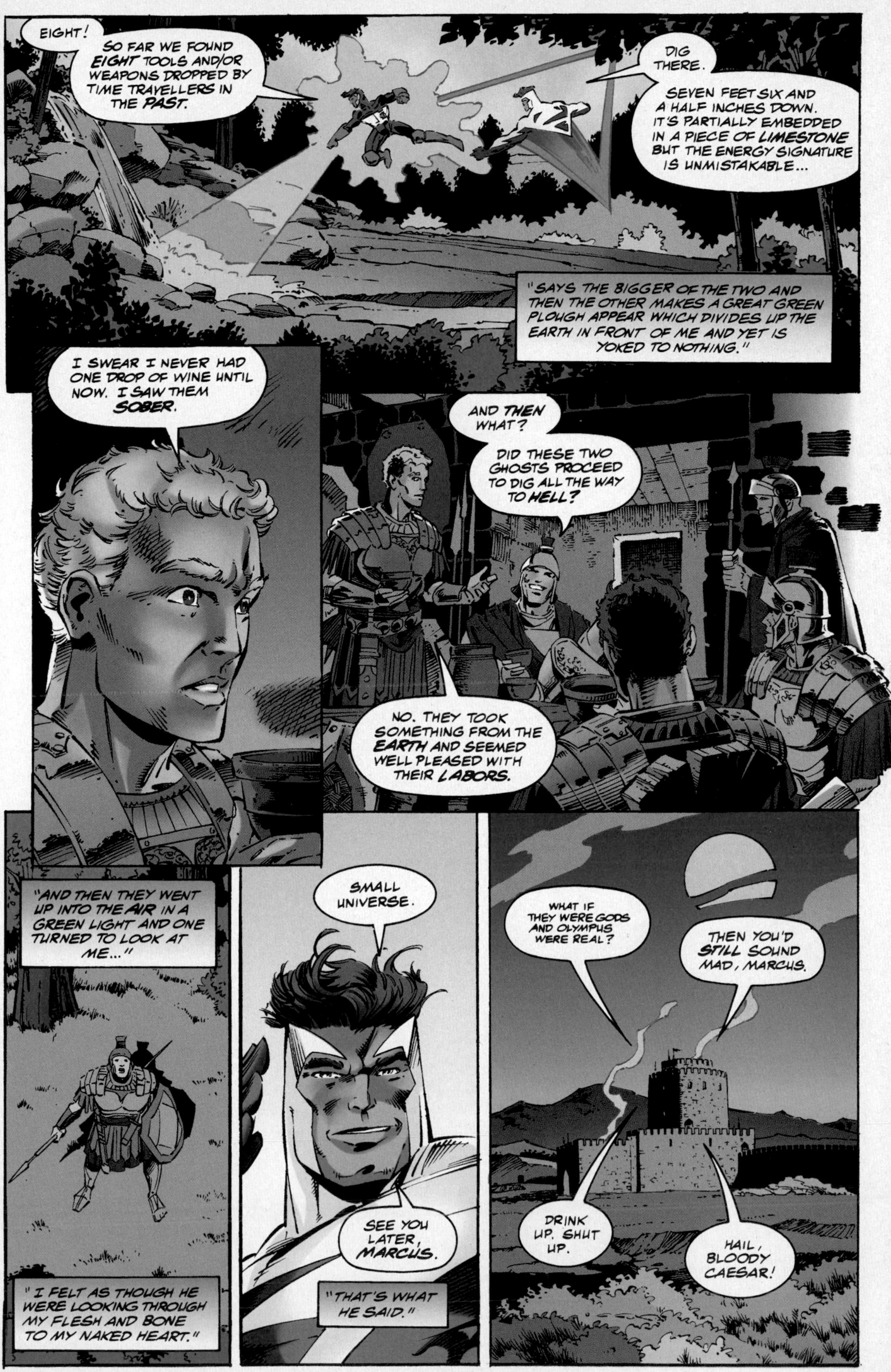
EIGHT!
SO FAR WE FOUND EIGHT TOOLS AND/OR WEAPONS DROPPED BY TIME TRAVELLERS IN THE PAST.
DIG THERE.
SEVEN FEET SIX AND A HALF INCHES DOWN. IT'S PARTIALLY EMBEDDED IN A PIECE OF LIMESTONE BUT THE ENERGY SIGNATURE IS UNMISTAKABLE...
"SAYS THE BIGGER OF THE TWO AND THEN THE OTHER MAKES A GREAT GREEN PLOUGH APPEAR WHICH DIVIDES UP THE EARTH IN FRONT OF ME AND YET IS YOKED TO NOTHING."
I SWEAR I NEVER HAD ONE DROP OF WINE UNTIL NOW. I SAW THEM SOBER.
AND THEN WHAT?
DID THESE TWO GHOSTS PROCEED TO DIG ALL THE WAY TO HELL?
NO. THEY TOOK SOMETHING FROM THE EARTH AND SEEMED WELL PLEASED WITH THEIR LABORS.
"AND THEN THEY WENT UP INTO THE AIR IN A GREEN LIGHT AND ONE TURNED TO LOOK AT ME..."
"I FELT AS THOUGH HE WERE LOOKING THROUGH MY FLESH AND BONE TO MY NAKED HEART."
SMALL UNIVERSE.
SEE YOU LATER, MARCUS.
"THAT'S WHAT HE SAID."
WHAT IF THEY WERE GODS AND OLYMPUS WERE REAL?
THEN YOU'D STILL SOUND MAD, MARCUS.
DRINK UP. SHUT UP.
HAIL, BLOODY CAESAR!

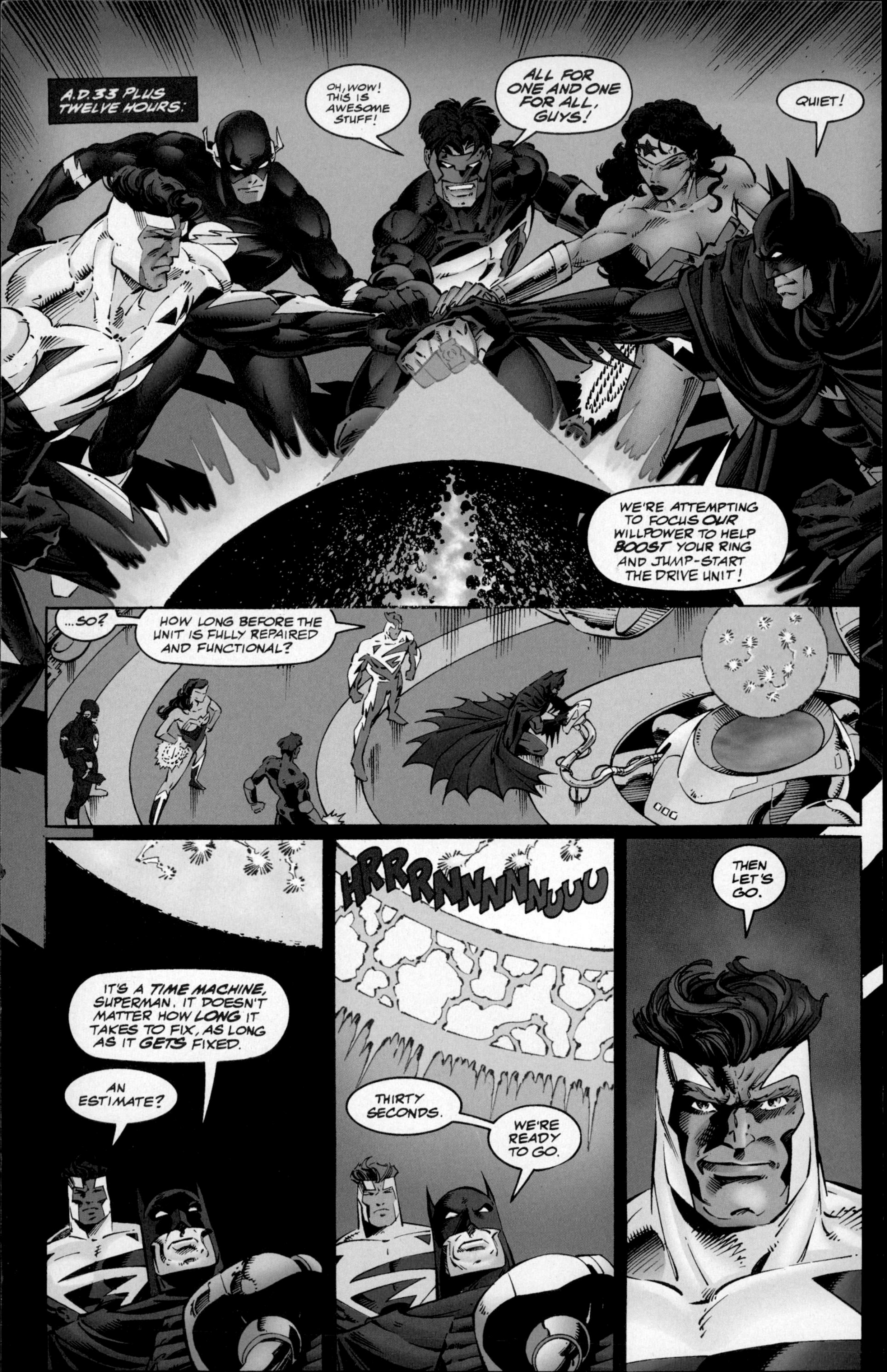

A.D. 33 PLUS TWELVE HOURS:
OH, WOW! THIS IS AWESOME STUFF!
ALL FOR ONE AND ONE FOR ALL, GUYS!
QUIET!
WE'RE ATTEMPTING TO FOCUS OUR WILLPOWER TO HELP BOOST YOUR RING AND JUMP-START THE DRIVE UNIT!
...SO?
HOW LONG BEFORE THE UNIT IS FULLY REPAIRED AND FUNCTIONAL?
IT'S A TIME MACHINE, SUPERMAN. IT DOESN'T MATTER HOW LONG IT TAKES TO FIX, AS LONG AS IT GETS FIXED.
AN ESTIMATE?
HRRRNNNNNNUUU
THIRTY SECONDS.
WE'RE READY TO GO.
THEN LET'S GO.

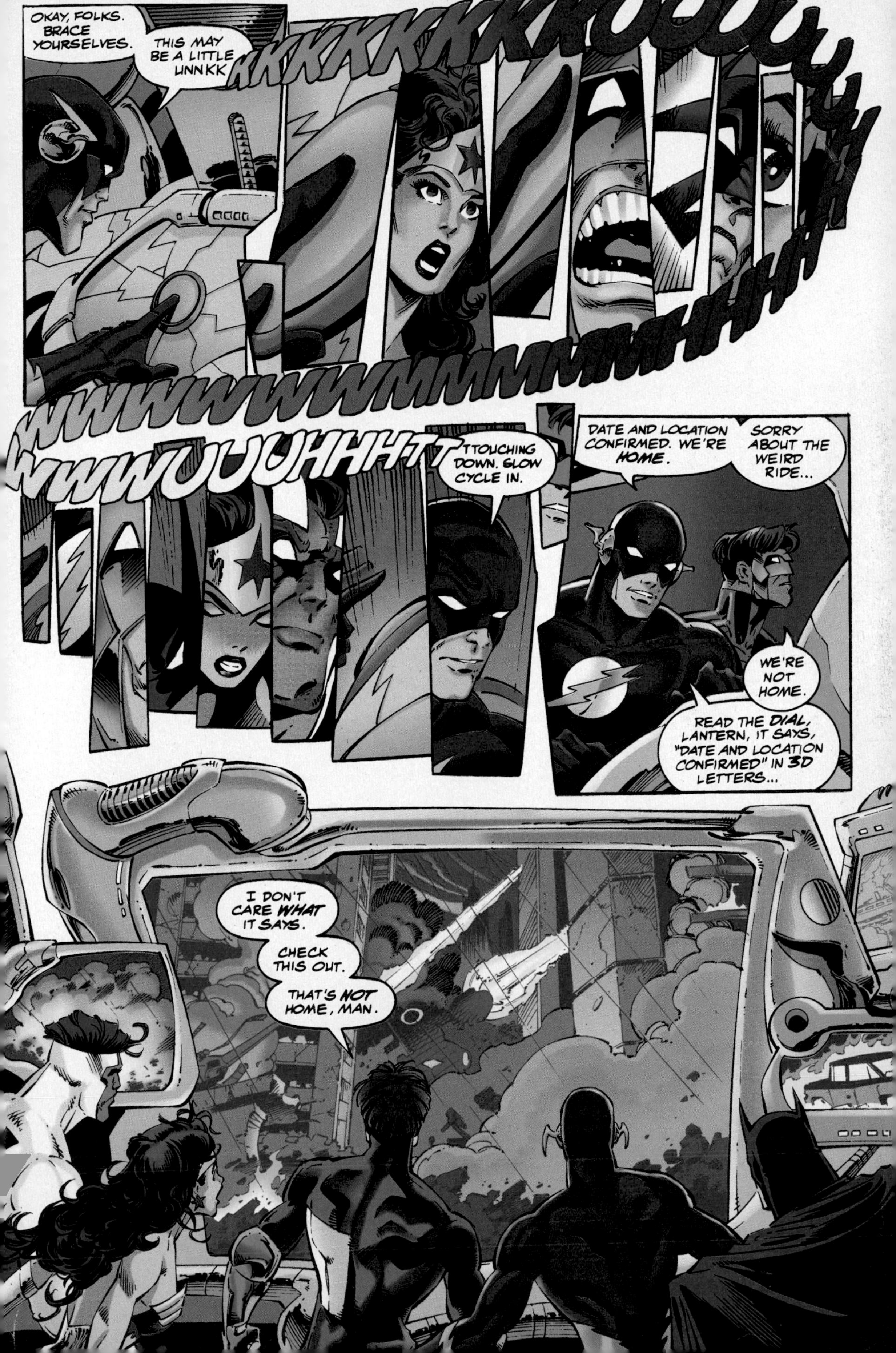
OKAY, FOLKS. BRACE YOURSELVES.
THIS MAY BE A LITTLE UNNKK
KKKKKKKKKKKKVVUUUUUUUHHHHHHHHMMMMMMMWWWWWWWWWWWWWW
WWWWWUUUUHHHTT
TTOUCHING DOWN. SLOW CYCLE IN.
DATE AND LOCATION CONFIRMED. WE'RE HOME.
SORRY ABOUT THE WEIRD RIDE...
WE'RE NOT HOME.
READ THE DIAL, LANTERN, IT SAYS, "DATE AND LOCATION CONFIRMED" IN 3D LETTERS...
I DON'T CARE WHAT IT SAYS.
CHECK THIS OUT.
THAT'S NOT HOME, MAN.

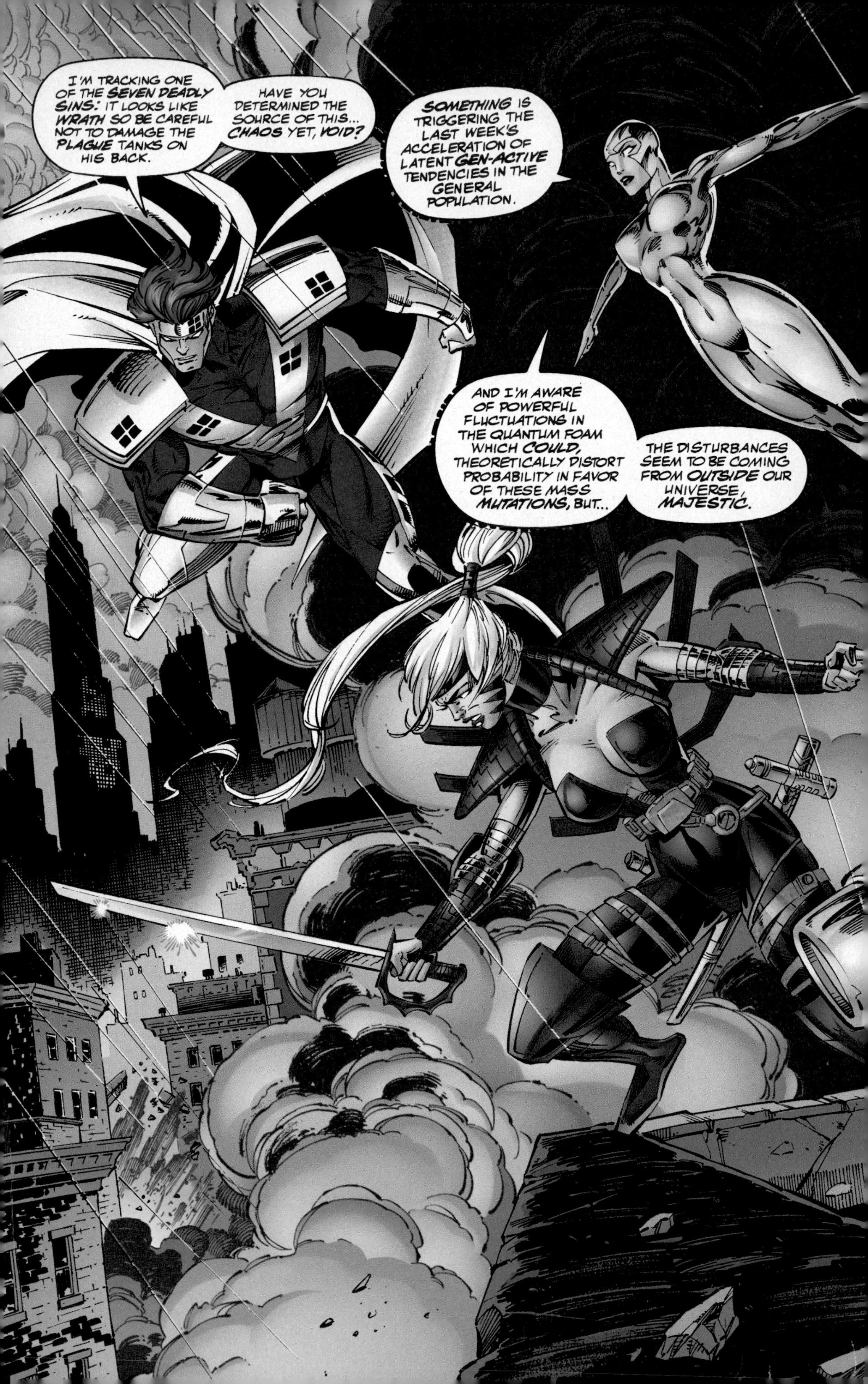
I'M TRACKING ONE OF THE SEVEN DEADLY SINS: IT LOOKS LIKE WRATH SO BE CAREFUL NOT TO DAMAGE THE PLAGUE TANKS ON HIS BACK.
HAVE YOU DETERMINED THE SOURCE OF THIS... CHAOS YET, VOID?
SOMETHING IS TRIGGERING THE LAST WEEK'S ACCELERATION OF LATENT GEN-ACTIVE TENDENCIES IN THE GENERAL POPULATION.
AND I'M AWARE OF POWERFUL FLUCTUATIONS IN THE QUANTUM FOAM WHICH COULD, THEORETICALLY DISTORT PROBABILITY IN FAVOR OF THESE MASS MUTATIONS, BUT...
THE DISTURBANCES SEEM TO BE COMING FROM OUTSIDE OUR UNIVERSE, MAJESTIC.

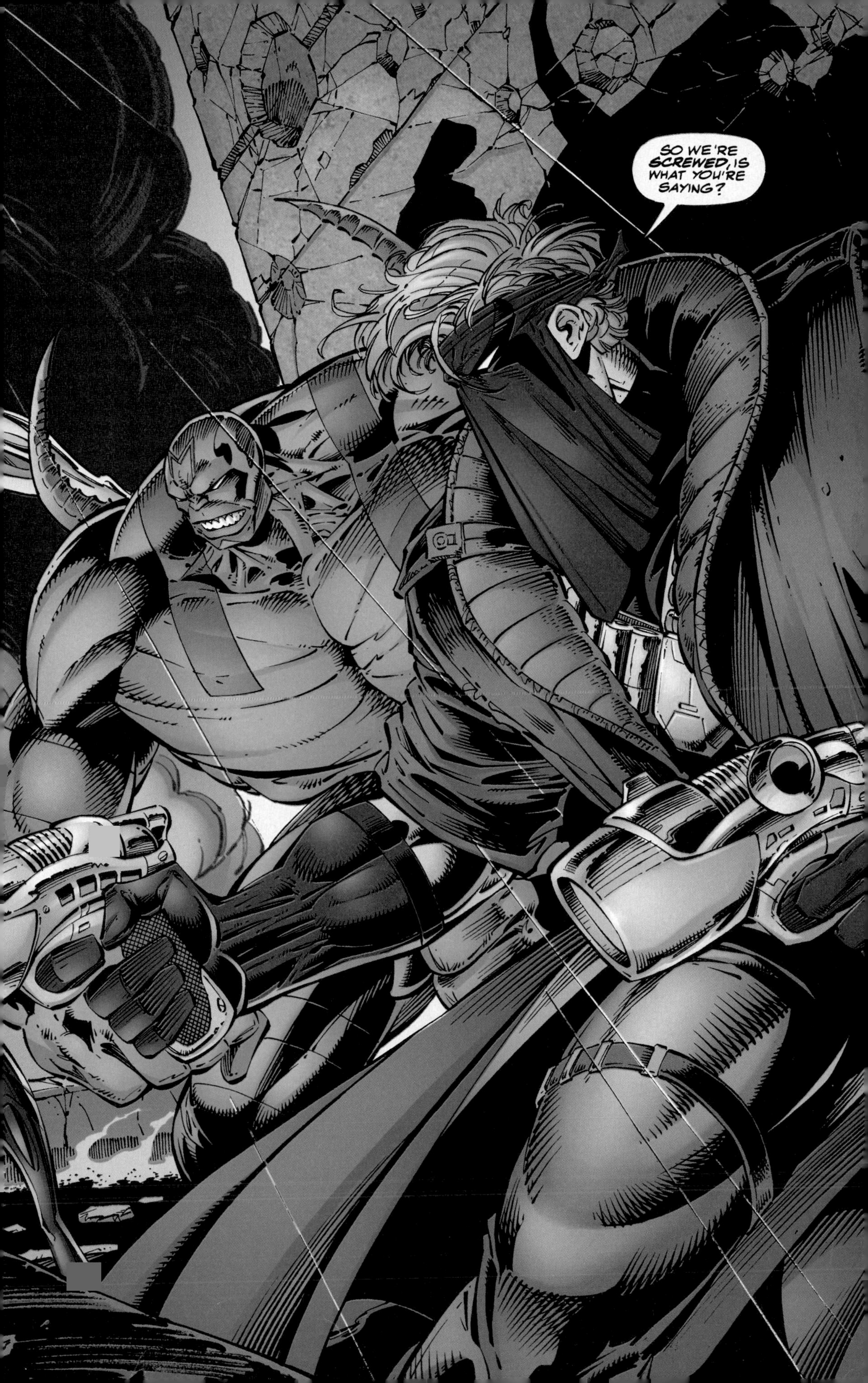
SO WE'RE SCREWED, IS WHAT YOU'RE SAYING?

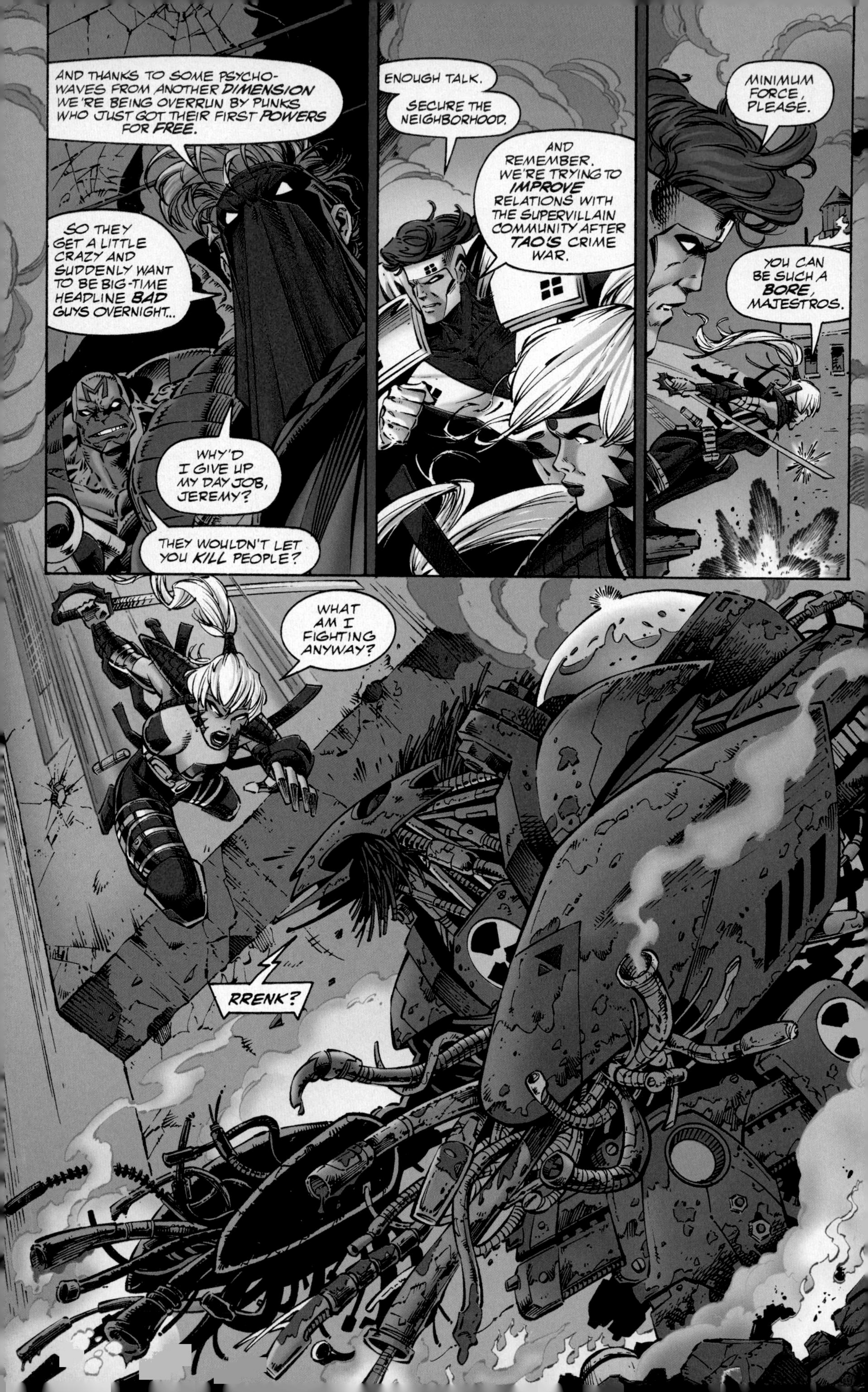
AND THANKS TO SOME PSYCHO-WAVES FROM ANOTHER DIMENSION WE'RE BEING OVERRUN BY PUNKS WHO JUST GOT THEIR FIRST POWERS FOR FREE.
SO THEY GET A LITTLE CRAZY AND SUDDENLY WANT TO BE BIG-TIME HEADLINE BAD GUYS OVERNIGHT...
WHY'D I GIVE UP MY DAY JOB, JEREMY?
THEY WOULDN'T LET YOU KILL PEOPLE?
ENOUGH TALK.
SECURE THE NEIGHBORHOOD.
AND REMEMBER. WE'RE TRYING TO IMPROVE RELATIONS WITH THE SUPERVILLAIN COMMUNITY AFTER TAO'S CRIME WAR.
MINIMUM FORCE, PLEASE.
YOU CAN BE SUCH A BORE, MAJESTROS.
WHAT AM I FIGHTING ANYWAY?
RRENK?

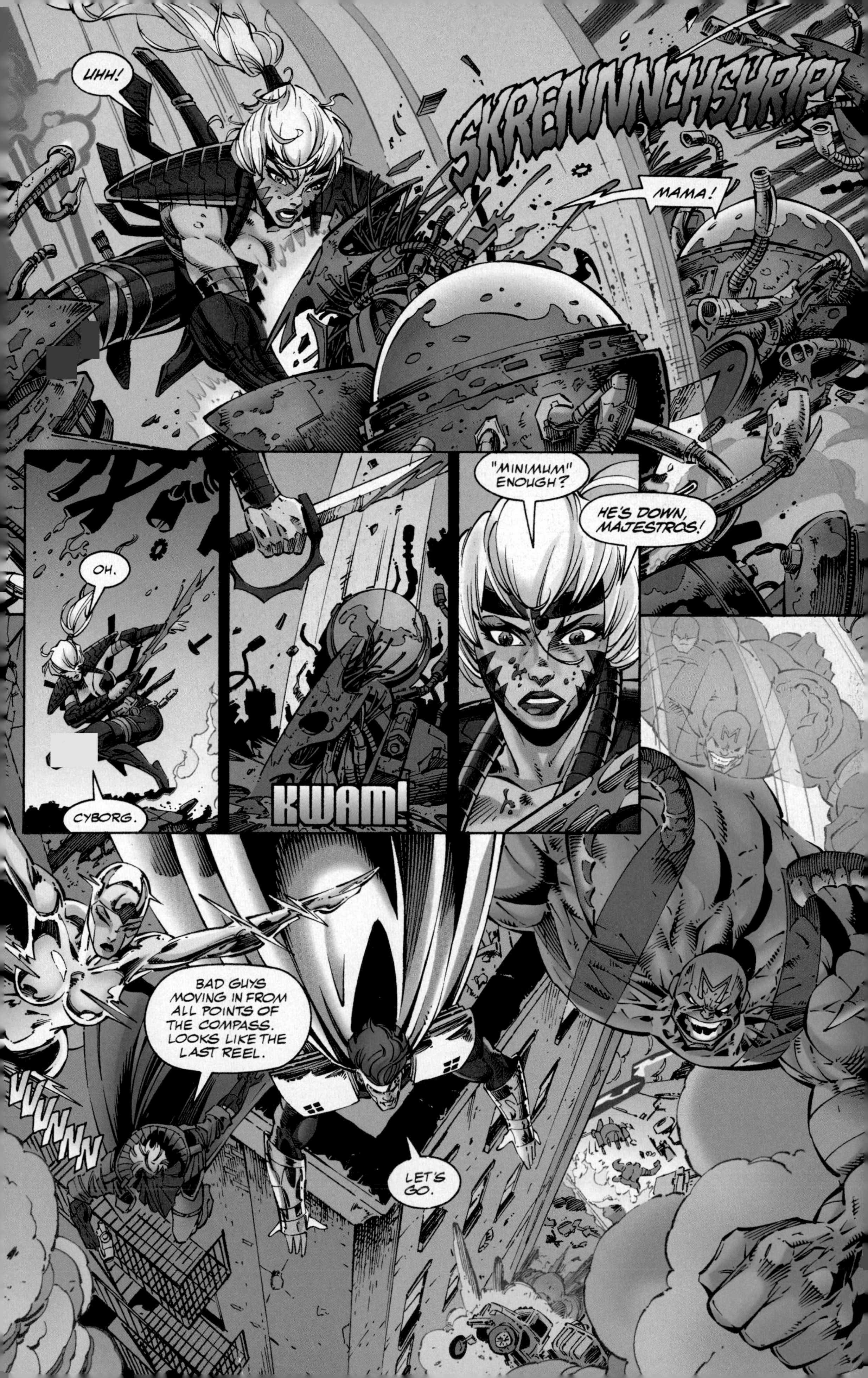
UHH!
SKRENNNNCHSHRIP!
MAMA!
OH.
CYBORG.
KWAM!
"MINIMUM" ENOUGH?
HE'S DOWN, MAJESTROS!
BAD GUYS MOVING IN FROM ALL POINTS OF THE COMPASS. LOOKS LIKE THE LAST REEL.
VVVNNNN
LET'S GO.

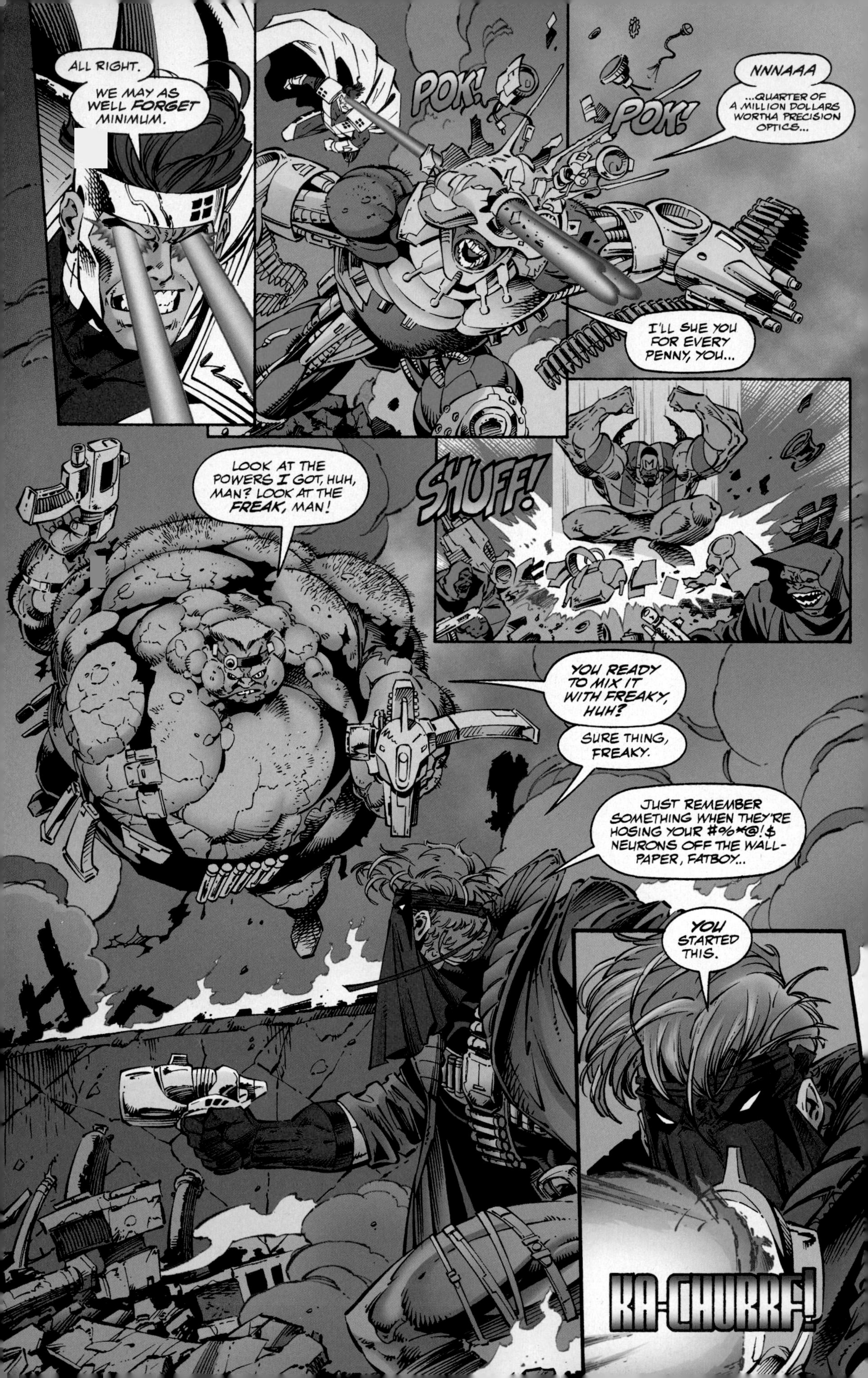
ALL RIGHT.
WE MAY AS WELL FORGET MINIMUM.
POK!
POK!
NNNAAA
...QUARTER OF A MILLION DOLLARS WORTHA PRECISION OPTICS...
I'LL SUE YOU FOR EVERY PENNY, YOU...
SHUFF!
LOOK AT THE POWERS I GOT, HUH, MAN? LOOK AT THE FREAK, MAN!
YOU READY TO MIX IT WITH FREAKY, HUH?
SURE THING, FREAKY.
JUST REMEMBER SOMETHING WHEN THEY'RE HOSING YOUR #%*@!$ NEURONS OFF THE WALL-PAPER, FATBOY...
YOU STARTED THIS.
KA-CHURRF!

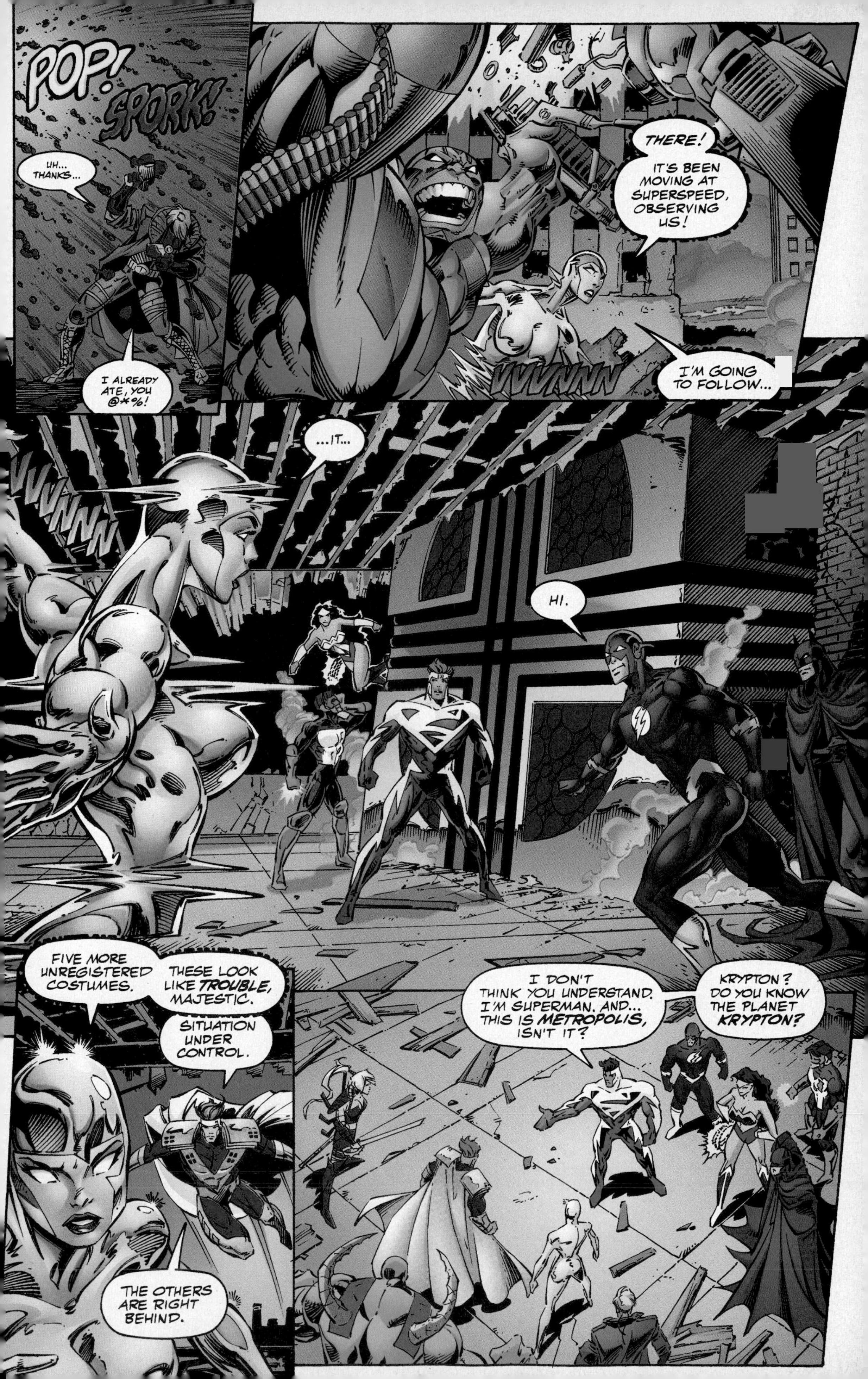
POP!
SPORK!
UH... THANKS...
I ALREADY ATE, YOU @*%!
THERE!
IT'S BEEN MOVING AT SUPERSPEED, OBSERVING US!
VVVNNNN
I'M GOING TO FOLLOW...
VVVNNNN
...IT...
HI.
FIVE MORE UNREGISTERED COSTUMES.
THESE LOOK LIKE TROUBLE, MAJESTIC.
SITUATION UNDER CONTROL.
THE OTHERS ARE RIGHT BEHIND.
I DON'T THINK YOU UNDERSTAND. I'M SUPERMAN. AND... THIS IS METROPOLIS, ISN'T IT?
KRYPTON? DO YOU KNOW THE PLANET KRYPTON?

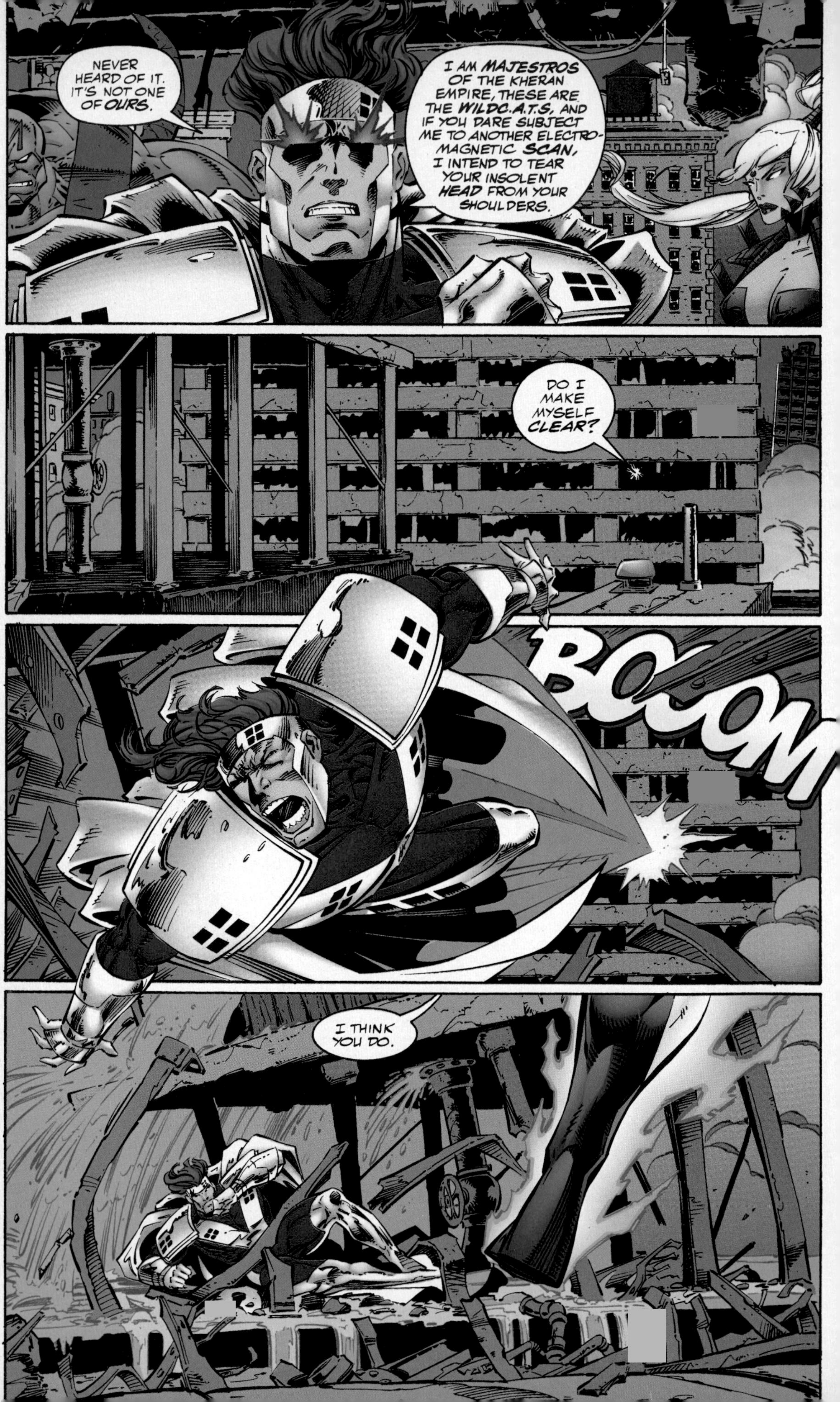
NEVER HEARD OF IT. IT'S NOT ONE OF OURS.
I AM MAJESTROS OF THE KHERAN EMPIRE, THESE ARE THE WILDC.A.T.S, AND IF YOU DARE SUBJECT ME TO ANOTHER ELECTRO-MAGNETIC SCAN, I INTEND TO TEAR YOUR INSOLENT HEAD FROM YOUR SHOULDERS.
DO I MAKE MYSELF CLEAR?
BOOOM
I THINK YOU DO.

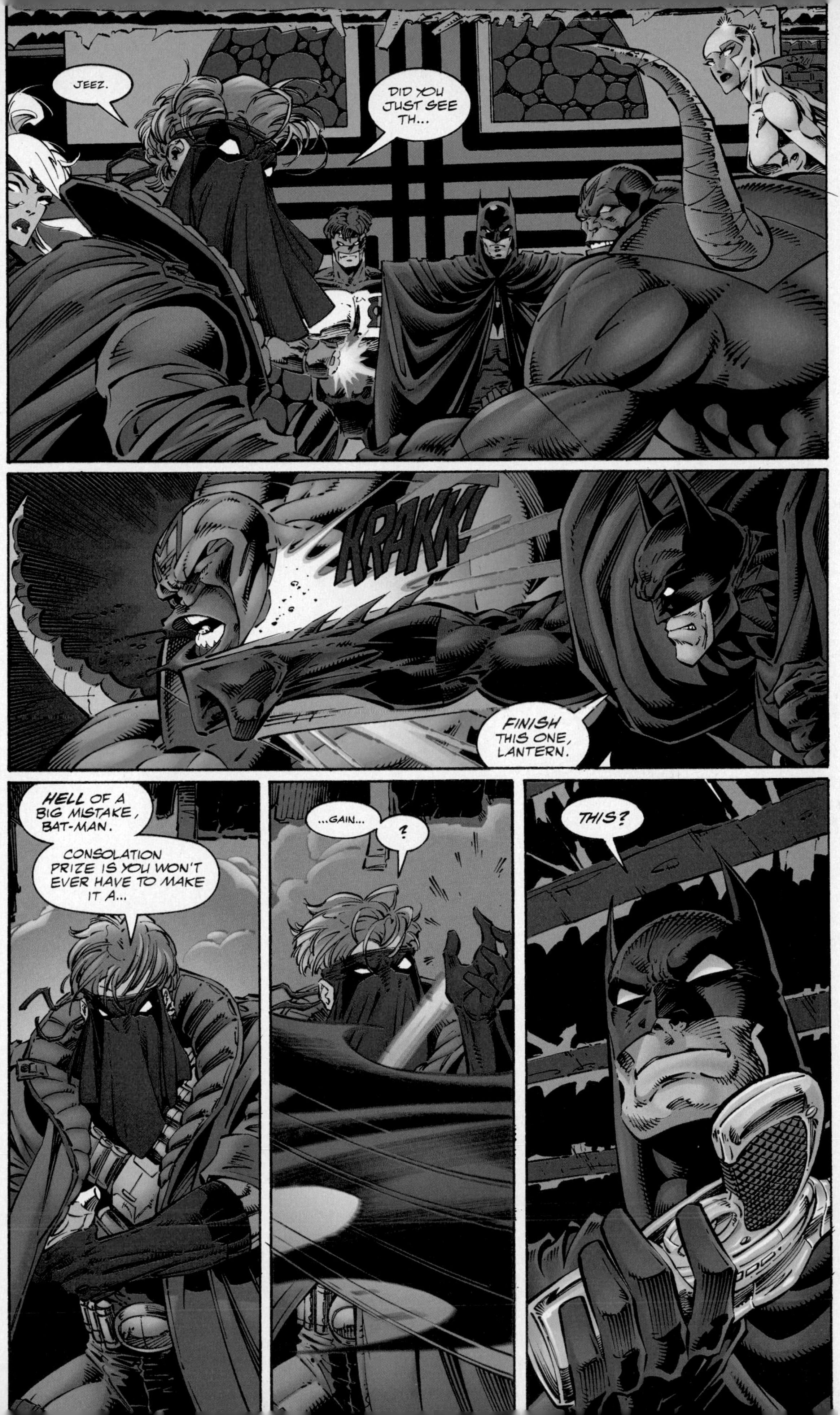
JEEZ.
DID YOU JUST SEE TH...
KRAKK!
FINISH THIS ONE, LANTERN.
HELL OF A BIG MISTAKE, BAT-MAN.
CONSOLATION PRIZE IS YOU WON'T EVER HAVE TO MAKE IT A...
...GAIN...
?
THIS?

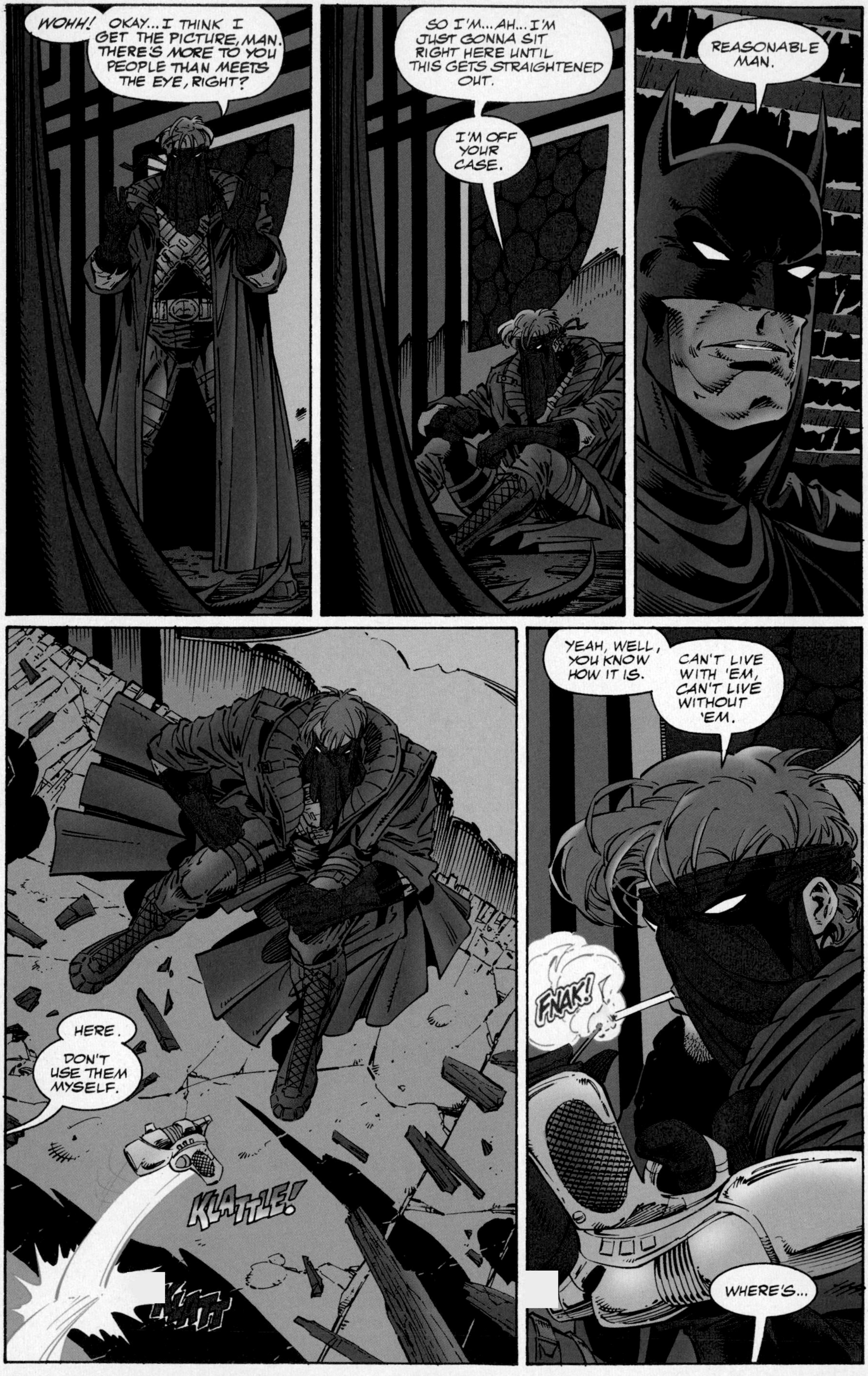
WOHH!
OKAY...I THINK I GET THE PICTURE, MAN. THERE'S MORE TO YOU PEOPLE THAN MEETS THE EYE, RIGHT?
SO I'M...AH...I'M JUST GONNA SIT RIGHT HERE UNTIL THIS GETS STRAIGHTENED OUT.
I'M OFF YOUR CASE.
REASONABLE MAN.
HERE.
DON'T USE THEM MYSELF.
KLATTLE!
YEAH, WELL, YOU KNOW HOW IT IS.
CAN'T LIVE WITH 'EM, CAN'T LIVE WITHOUT 'EM.
FNAK!
WHERE'S...

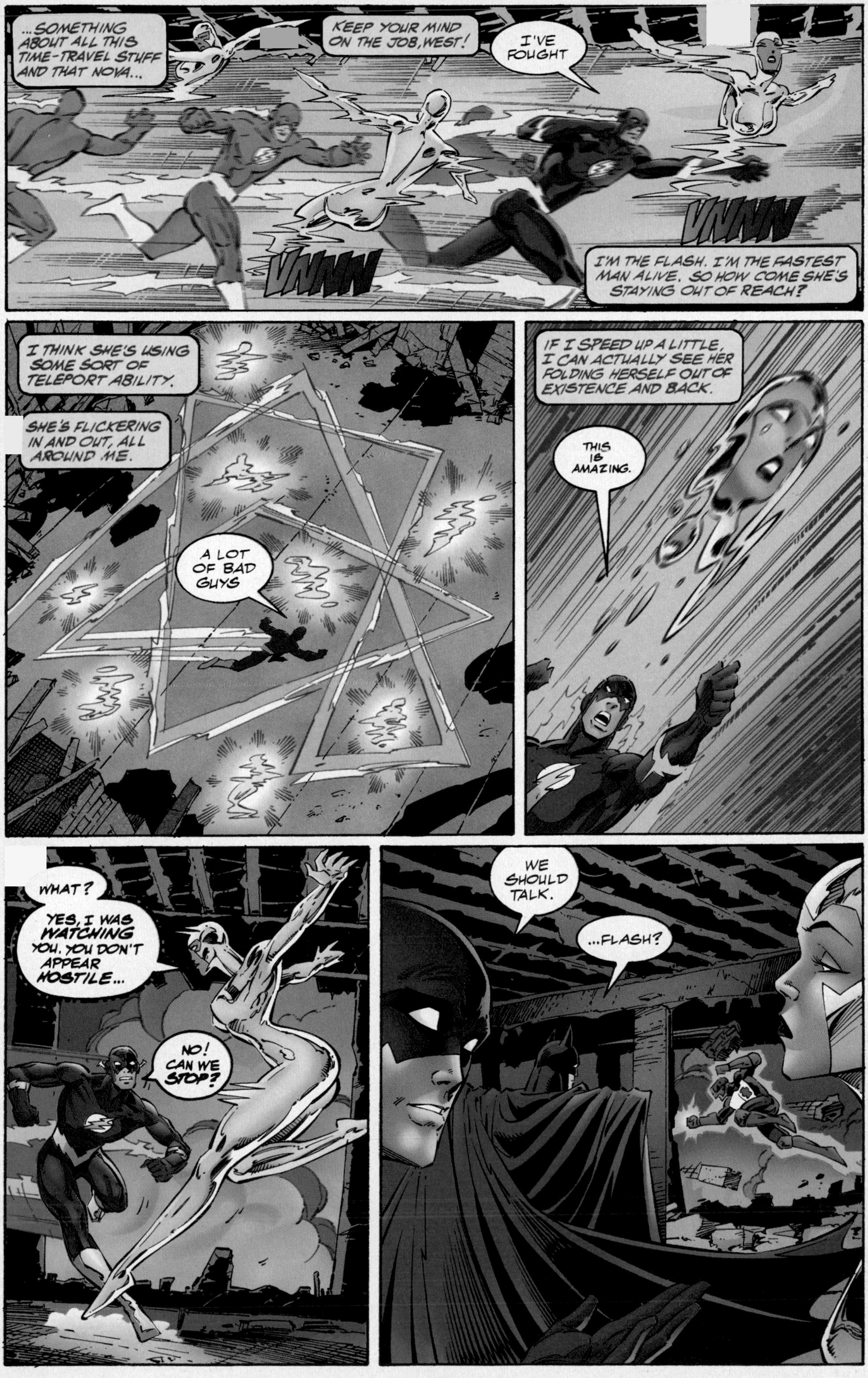
...SOMETHING ABOUT ALL THIS TIME-TRAVEL STUFF AND THAT NOVA...
KEEP YOUR MIND ON THE JOB, WEST!
I'VE FOUGHT
VNNN
VNNN
I'M THE FLASH. I'M THE FASTEST MAN ALIVE. SO HOW COME SHE'S STAYING OUT OF REACH?
I THINK SHE'S USING SOME SORT OF TELEPORT ABILITY.
SHE'S FLICKERING IN AND OUT, ALL AROUND ME.
A LOT OF BAD GUYS
IF I SPEED UP A LITTLE, I CAN ACTUALLY SEE HER FOLDING HERSELF OUT OF EXISTENCE AND BACK.
THIS IS AMAZING.
WHAT?
YES, I WAS WATCHING YOU. YOU DON'T APPEAR HOSTILE...
NO! CAN WE STOP?
WE SHOULD TALK.
...FLASH?

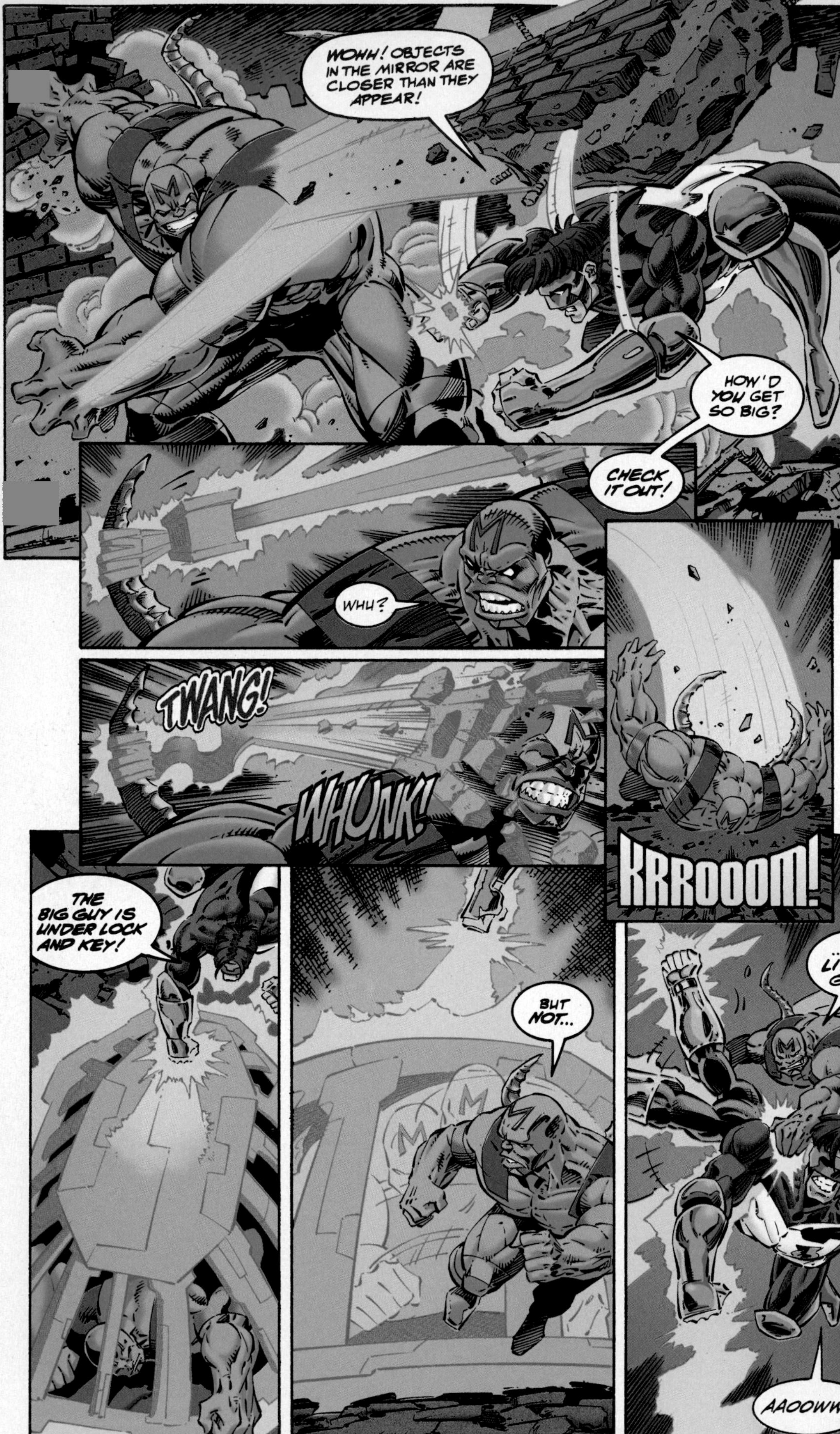
WOHH! OBJECTS IN THE MIRROR ARE CLOSER THAN THEY APPEAR!
HOW'D YOU GET SO BIG?
CHECK IT OUT!
WHU?
TWANG!
WHUNK!
KRROOOM!
THE BIG GUY IS UNDER LOCK AND KEY!
BUT NOT...
...THE LITTLE GUY!
AAOOWW!

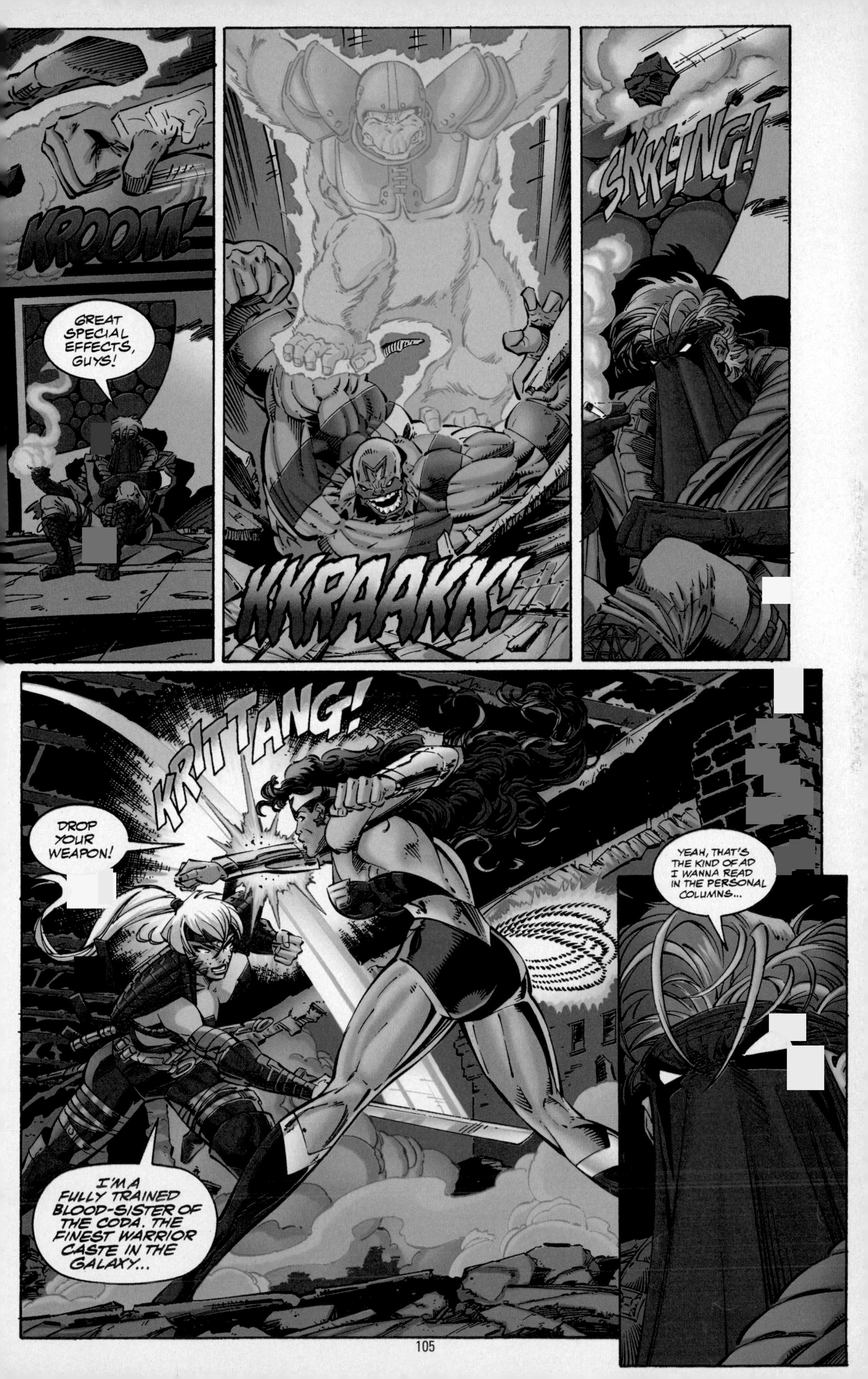
KROOM!
GREAT SPECIAL EFFECTS, GUYS!
KKRAAKK!
SKKLING!
KRITTANG!
DROP YOUR WEAPON!
I'M A FULLY TRAINED BLOOD-SISTER OF THE CODA. THE FINEST WARRIOR CASTE IN THE GALAXY...
YEAH, THAT'S THE KIND OF AD I WANNA READ IN THE PERSONAL COLUMNS...

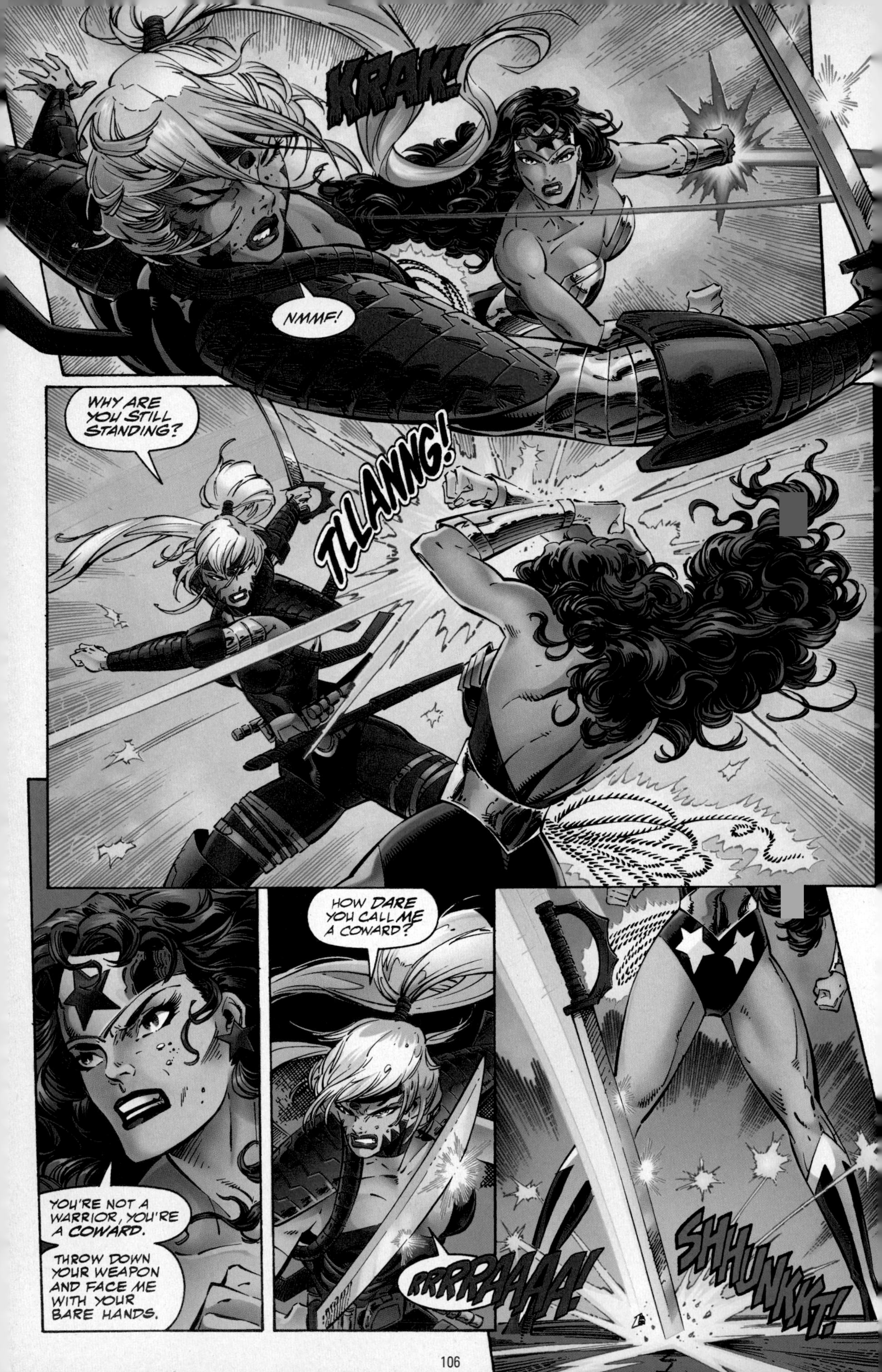
KRAK!
NMMF!
WHY ARE YOU STILL STANDING?
TLLANNG!
YOU'RE NOT A WARRIOR, YOU'RE A COWARD.
THROW DOWN YOUR WEAPON AND FACE ME WITH YOUR BARE HANDS.
HOW DARE YOU CALL ME A COWARD?
RRRRAAAA!
SHHUNKKT!

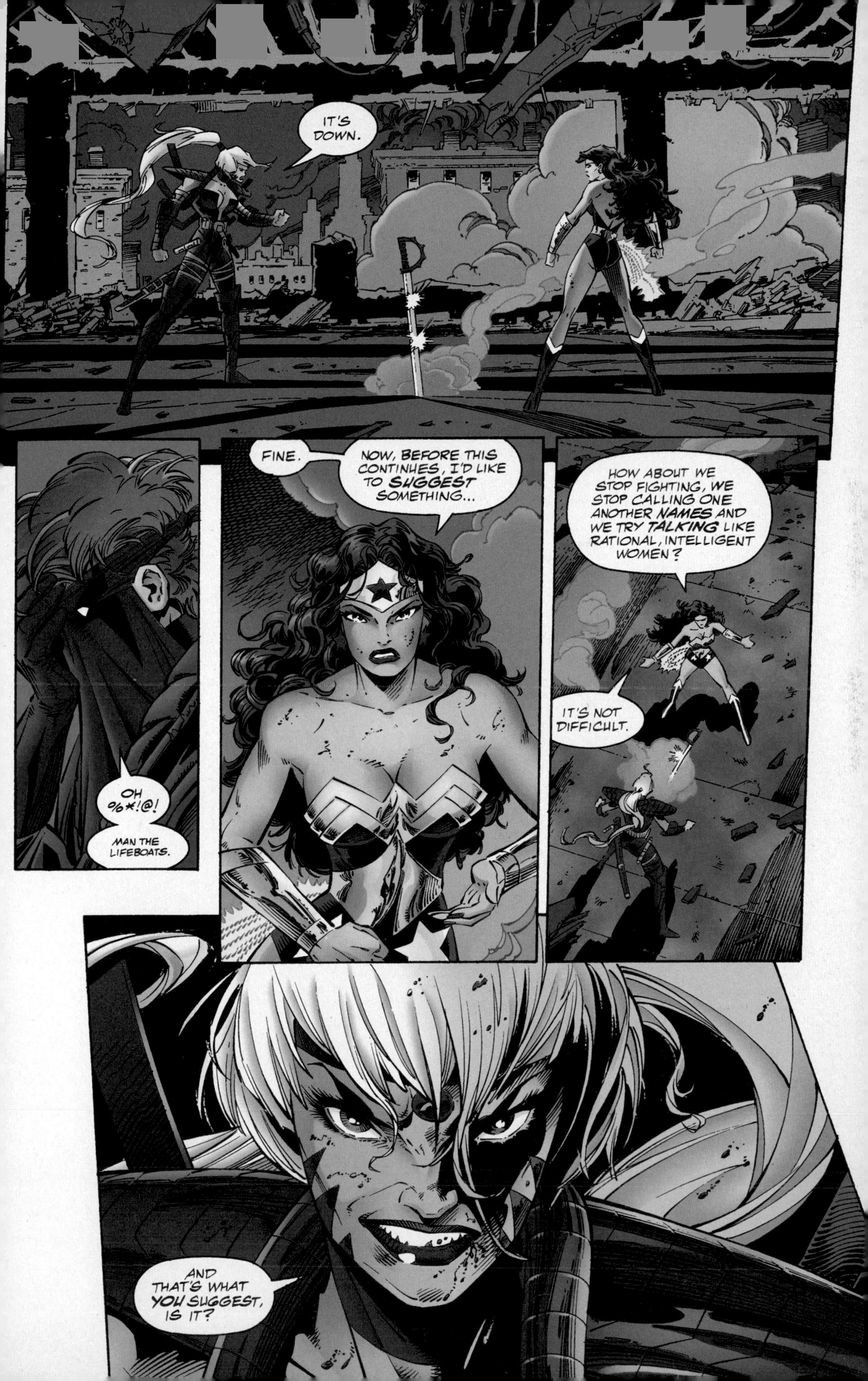
IT'S DOWN.
OH %*!@!
MAN THE LIFEBOATS.
FINE.
NOW, BEFORE THIS CONTINUES, I'D LIKE TO SUGGEST SOMETHING...
HOW ABOUT WE STOP FIGHTING, WE STOP CALLING ONE ANOTHER NAMES AND WE TRY TALKING LIKE RATIONAL, INTELLIGENT WOMEN?
IT'S NOT DIFFICULT.
AND THAT'S WHAT YOU SUGGEST, IS IT?

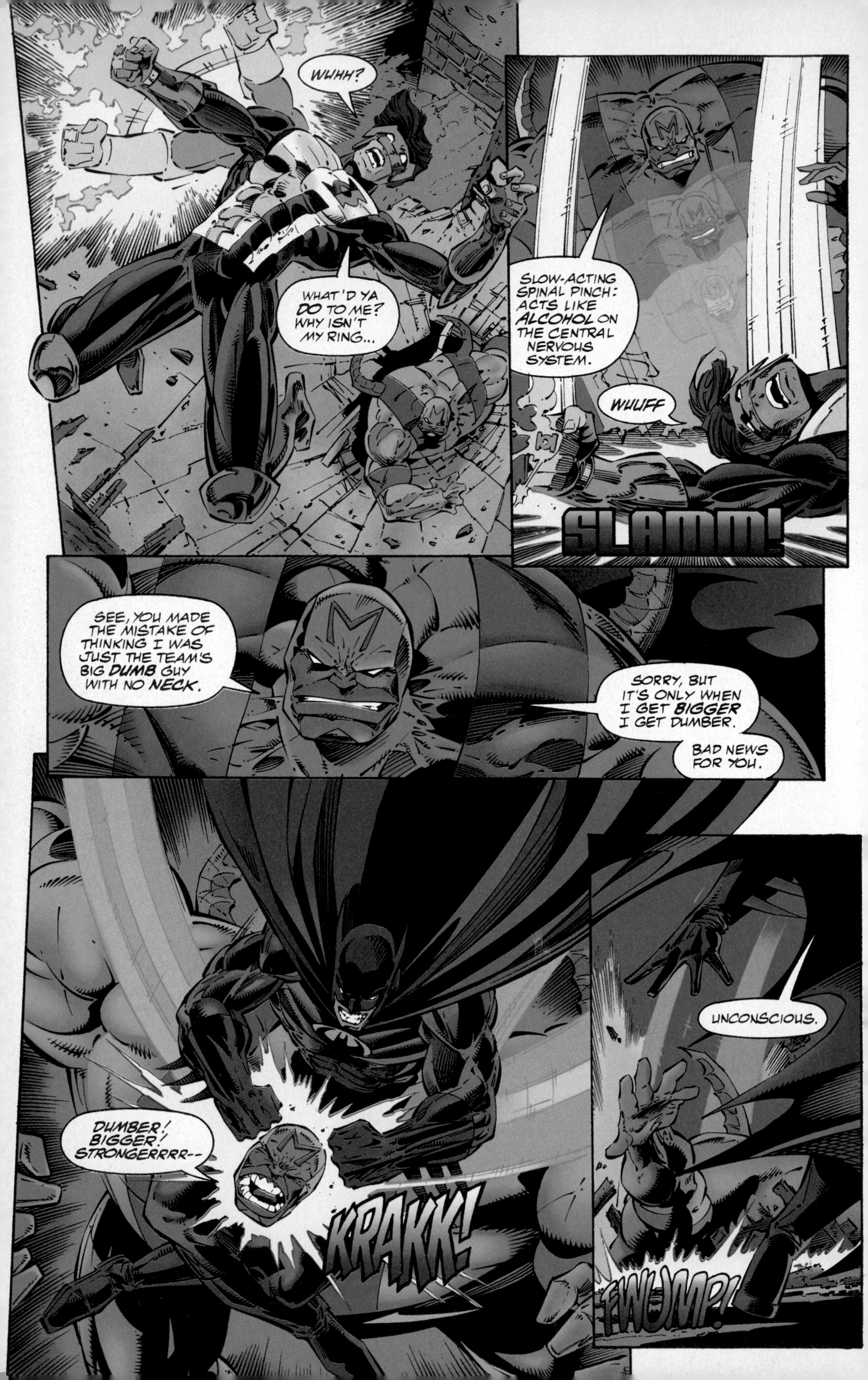
WUHH?
WHAT'D YA DO TO ME? WHY ISN'T MY RING...
SLOW-ACTING SPINAL PINCH: ACTS LIKE ALCOHOL ON THE CENTRAL NERVOUS SYSTEM.
WUUFF
SLAMM!
SEE, YOU MADE THE MISTAKE OF THINKING I WAS JUST THE TEAM'S BIG DUMB GUY WITH NO NECK.
SORRY, BUT IT'S ONLY WHEN I GET BIGGER I GET DUMBER.
BAD NEWS FOR YOU.
DUMBER! BIGGER! STRONGERRRR--
KRAKK!
UNCONSCIOUS.
FWUMP!

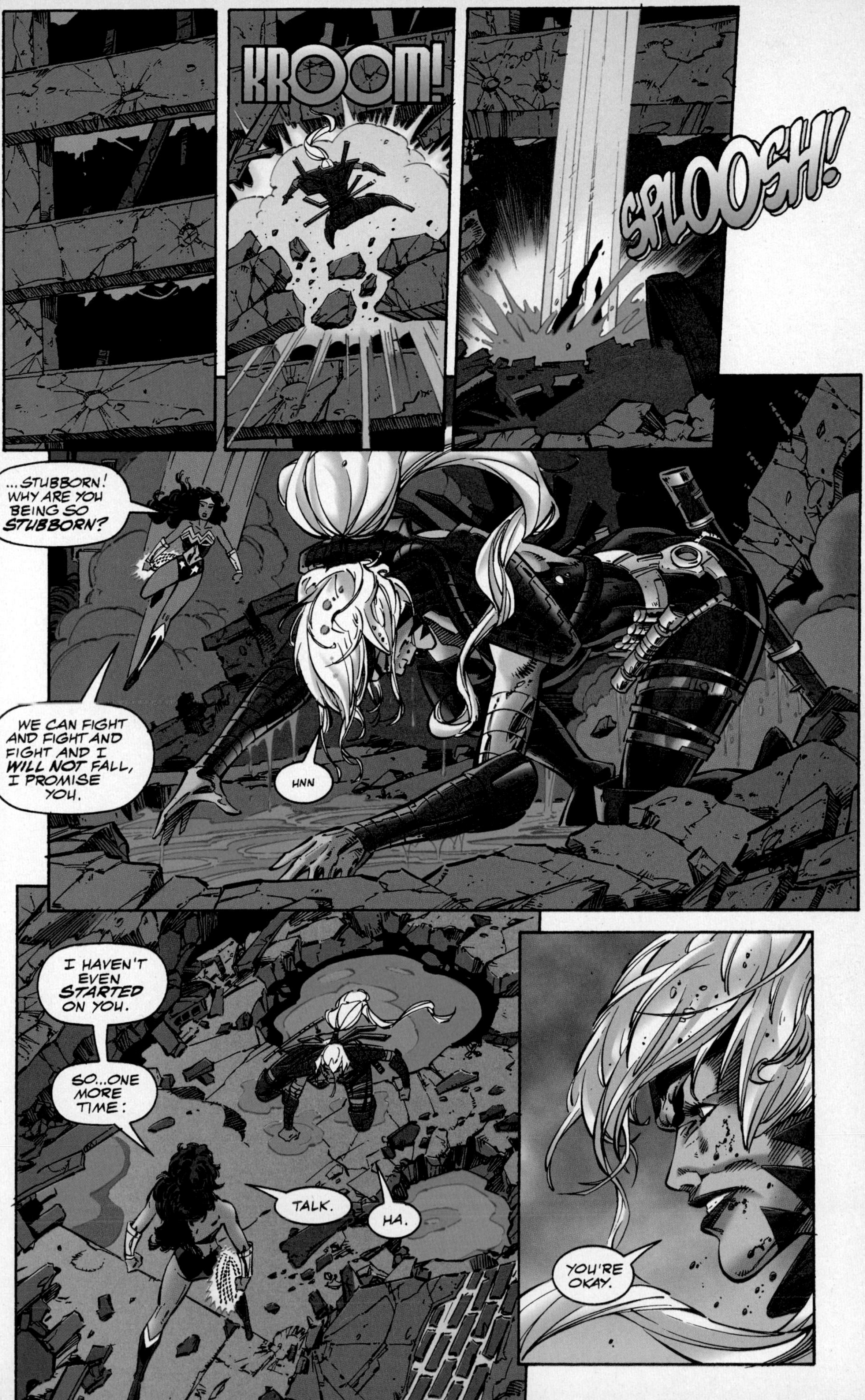
KROOM!
SPLOOSH!
...STUBBORN! WHY ARE YOU BEING SO STUBBORN?
WE CAN FIGHT AND FIGHT AND FIGHT AND I WILL NOT FALL, I PROMISE YOU.
HNN
I HAVEN'T EVEN STARTED ON YOU.
SO...ONE MORE TIME:
TALK.
HA.
YOU'RE OKAY.

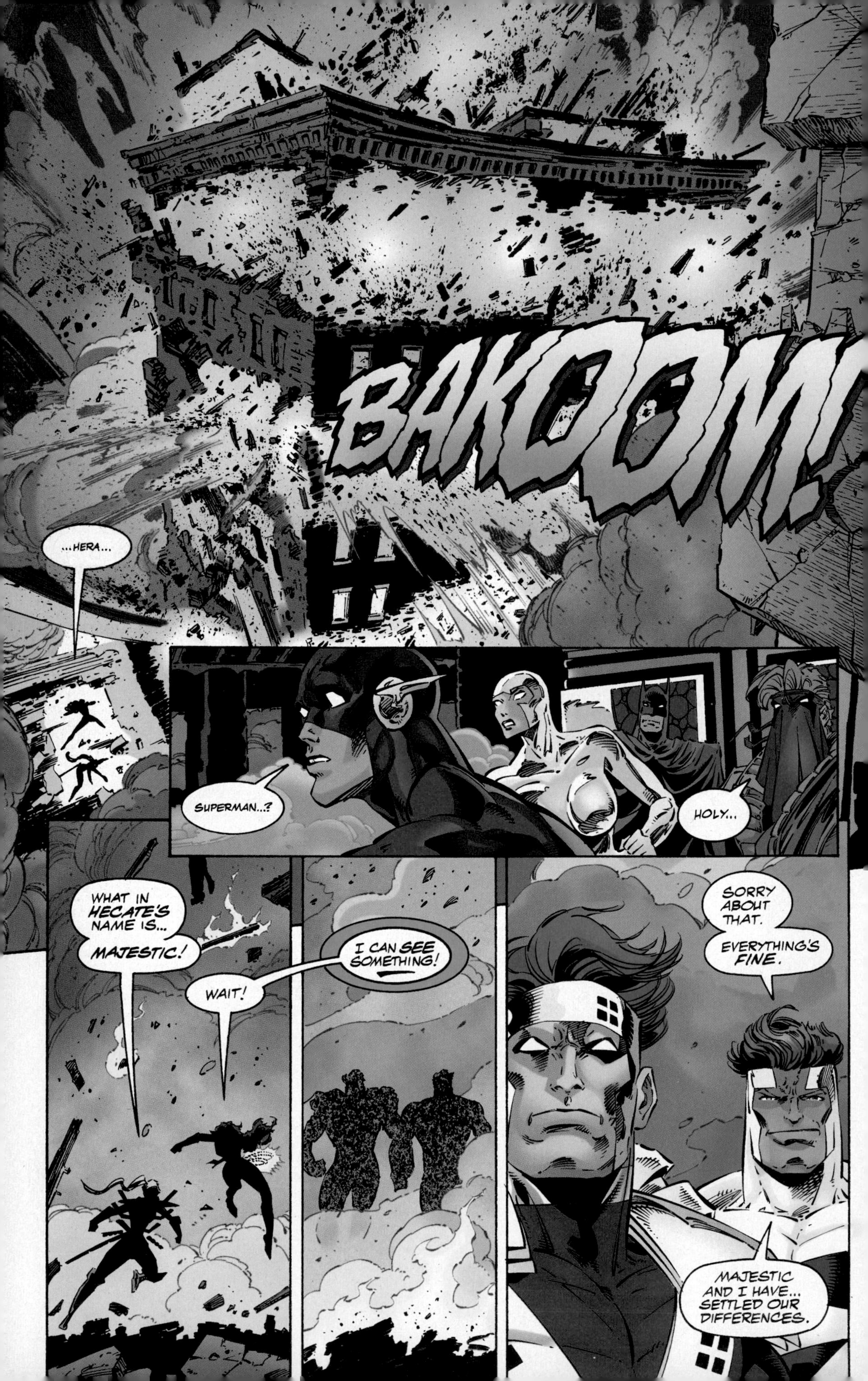
BAKOOM!
...HERA...
SUPERMAN...?
HOLY...
WHAT IN HECATE'S NAME IS... MAJESTIC!
WAIT!
I CAN SEE SOMETHING!
SORRY ABOUT THAT.
EVERYTHING'S FINE.
MAJESTIC AND I HAVE... SETTLED OUR DIFFERENCES.

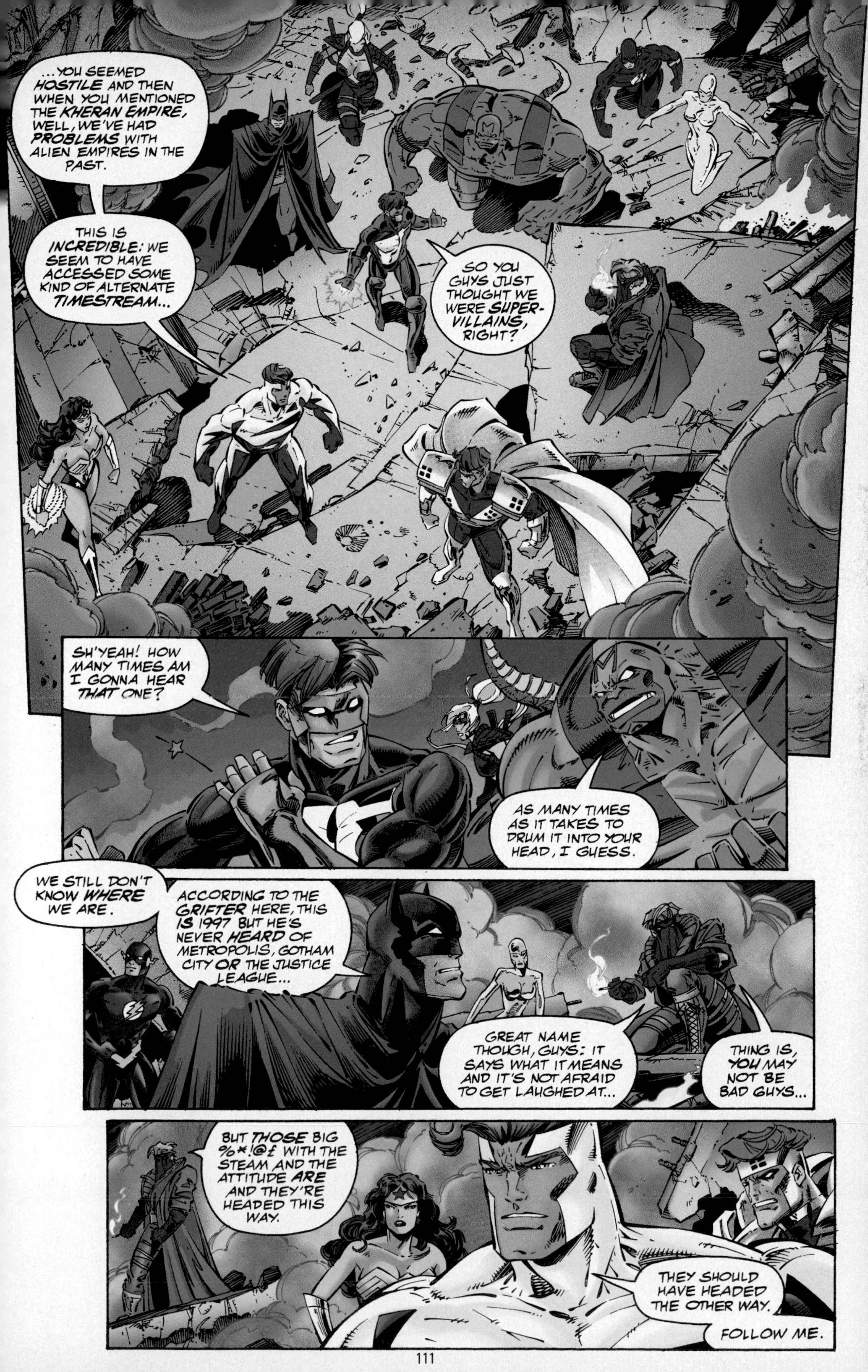
...YOU SEEMED HOSTILE AND THEN WHEN YOU MENTIONED THE KHERAN EMPIRE, WELL, WE'VE HAD PROBLEMS WITH ALIEN EMPIRES IN THE PAST.
THIS IS INCREDIBLE: WE SEEM TO HAVE ACCESSED SOME KIND OF ALTERNATE TIMESTREAM...
SO YOU GUYS JUST THOUGHT WE WERE SUPER-VILLAINS, RIGHT?
SH'YEAH! HOW MANY TIMES AM I GONNA HEAR THAT ONE?
AS MANY TIMES AS IT TAKES TO DRUM IT INTO YOUR HEAD, I GUESS.
WE STILL DON'T KNOW WHERE WE ARE.
ACCORDING TO THE GRIFTER HERE, THIS IS 1997 BUT HE'S NEVER HEARD OF METROPOLIS, GOTHAM CITY OR THE JUSTICE LEAGUE...
GREAT NAME THOUGH, GUYS: IT SAYS WHAT IT MEANS AND IT'S NOT AFRAID TO GET LAUGHED AT...
THING IS, YOU MAY NOT BE BAD GUYS...
BUT THOSE BIG %*!@£ WITH THE STEAM AND THE ATTITUDE ARE AND THEY'RE HEADED THIS WAY.
THEY SHOULD HAVE HEADED THE OTHER WAY.
FOLLOW ME.

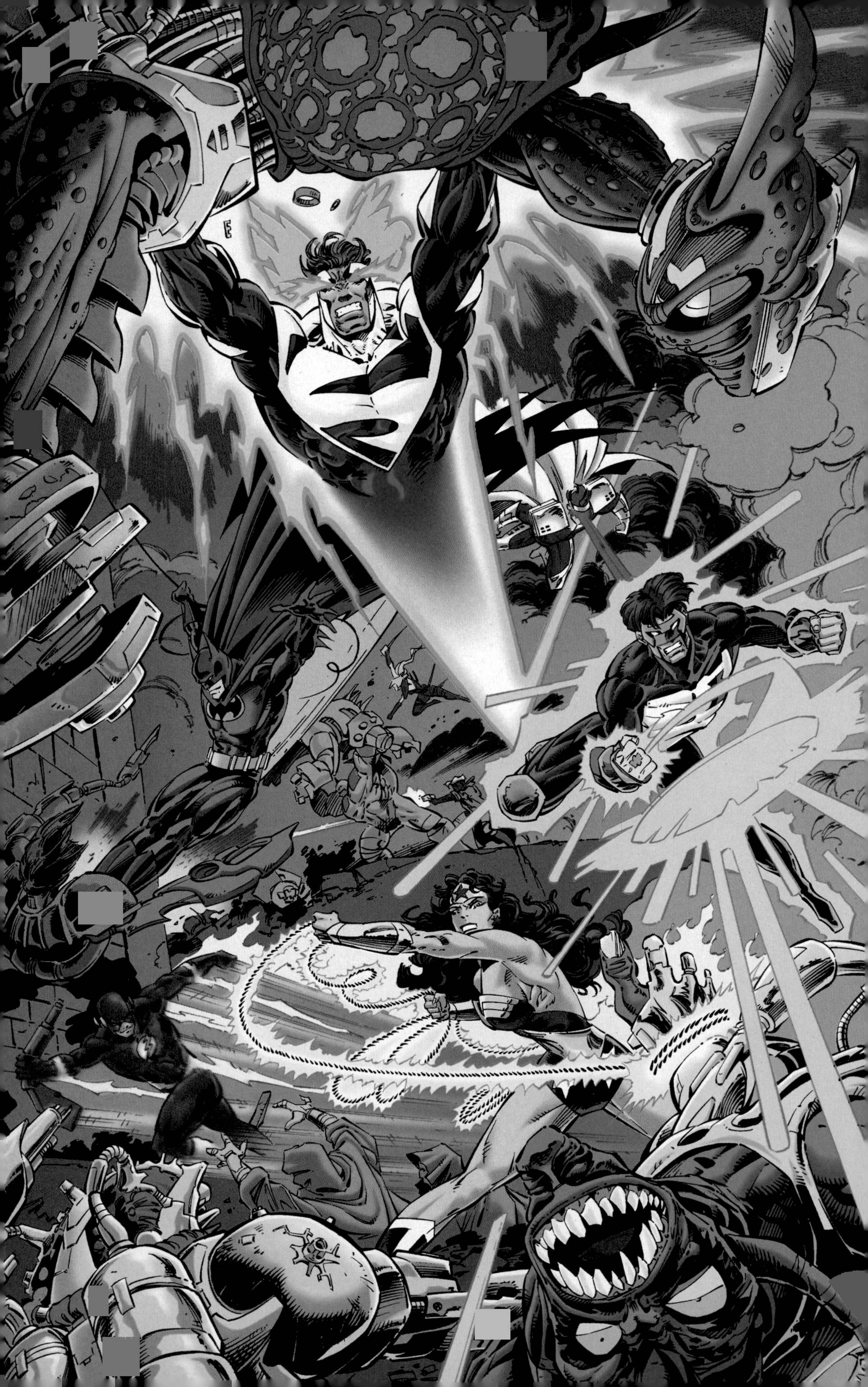

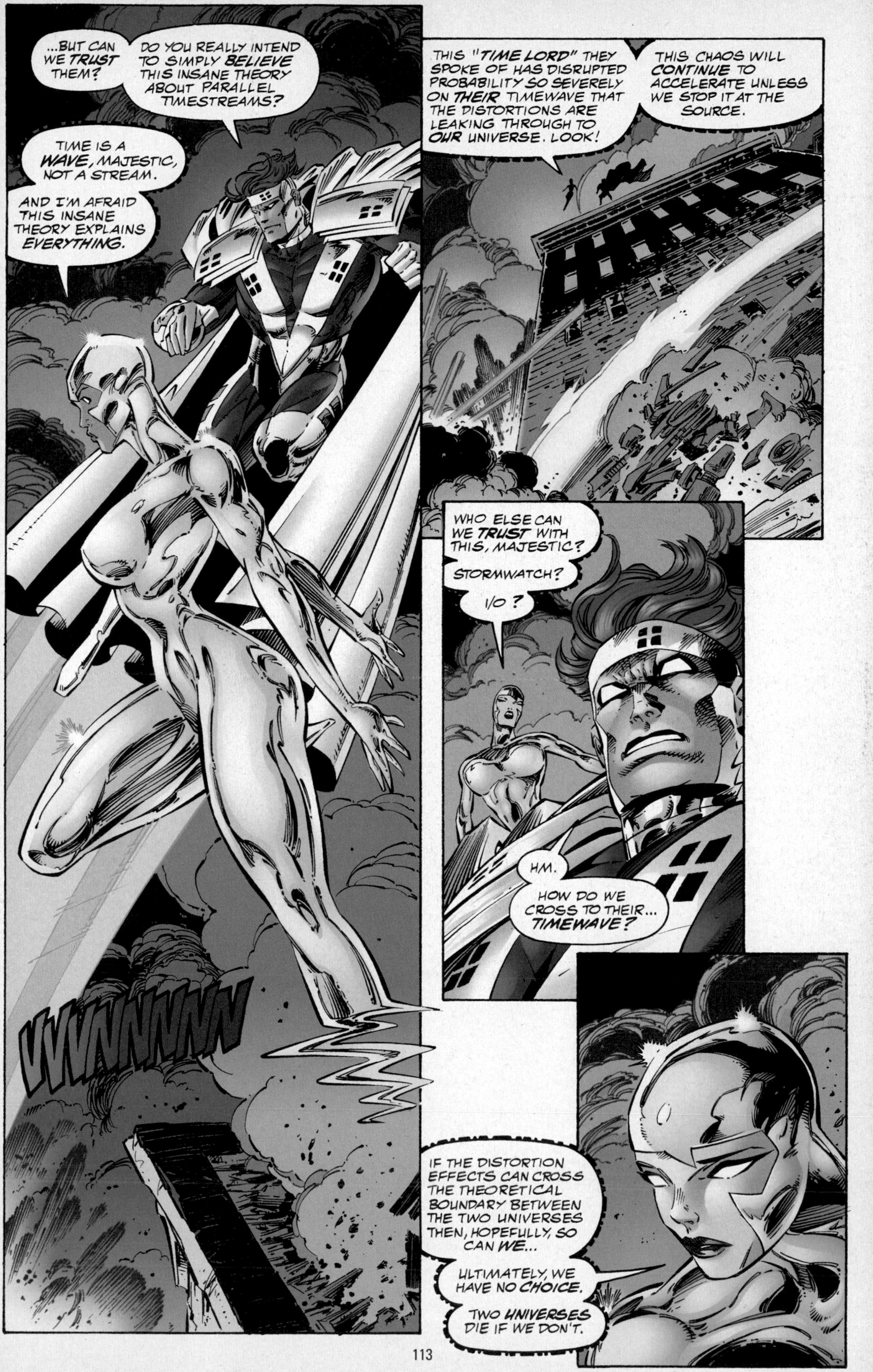
...BUT CAN WE TRUST THEM?
DO YOU REALLY INTEND TO SIMPLY BELIEVE THIS INSANE THEORY ABOUT PARALLEL TIMESTREAMS?
TIME IS A WAVE, MAJESTIC, NOT A STREAM.
AND I'M AFRAID THIS INSANE THEORY EXPLAINS EVERYTHING.
VVVNNNNNN
THIS "TIME LORD" THEY SPOKE OF HAS DISRUPTED PROBABILITY SO SEVERELY ON THEIR TIMEWAVE THAT THE DISTORTIONS ARE LEAKING THROUGH TO OUR UNIVERSE. LOOK!
THIS CHAOS WILL CONTINUE TO ACCELERATE UNLESS WE STOP IT AT THE SOURCE.
WHO ELSE CAN WE TRUST WITH THIS, MAJESTIC?
STORMWATCH?
I/O?
HM.
HOW DO WE CROSS TO THEIR... TIMEWAVE?
IF THE DISTORTION EFFECTS CAN CROSS THE THEORETICAL BOUNDARY BETWEEN THE TWO UNIVERSES THEN, HOPEFULLY, SO CAN WE...
ULTIMATELY, WE HAVE NO CHOICE.
TWO UNIVERSES DIE IF WE DON'T.

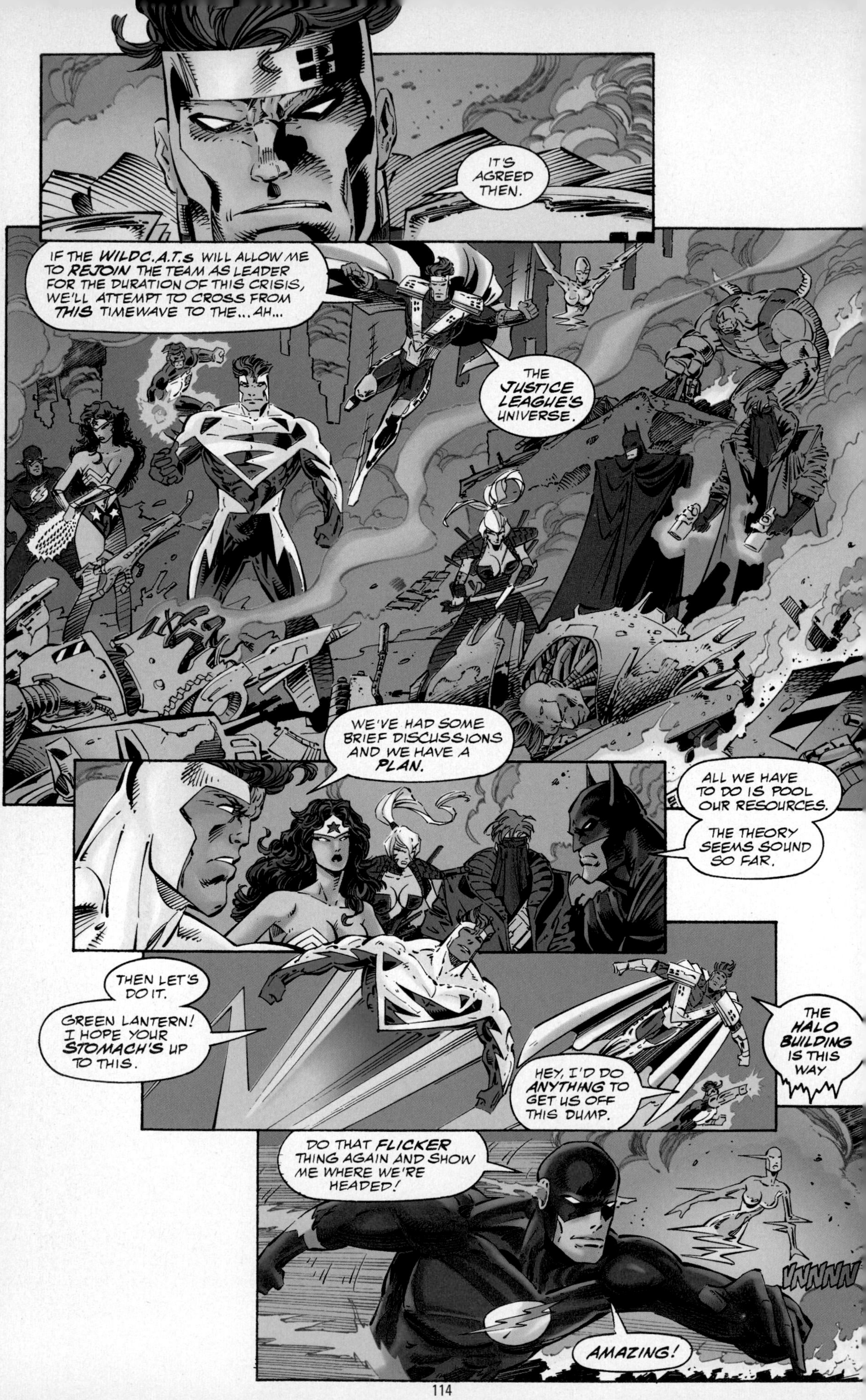
IT'S AGREED THEN.
IF THE WILDC.A.T.s WILL ALLOW ME TO REJOIN THE TEAM AS LEADER FOR THE DURATION OF THIS CRISIS, WE'LL ATTEMPT TO CROSS FROM THIS TIMEWAVE TO THE... AH...
THE JUSTICE LEAGUE'S UNIVERSE.
WE'VE HAD SOME BRIEF DISCUSSIONS AND WE HAVE A PLAN.
ALL WE HAVE TO DO IS POOL OUR RESOURCES.
THE THEORY SEEMS SOUND SO FAR.
THEN LET'S DO IT.
GREEN LANTERN! I HOPE YOUR STOMACH'S UP TO THIS.
HEY, I'D DO ANYTHING TO GET US OFF THIS DUMP.
THE HALO BUILDING IS THIS WAY
DO THAT FLICKER THING AGAIN AND SHOW ME WHERE WE'RE HEADED!
VNNNN
AMAZING!

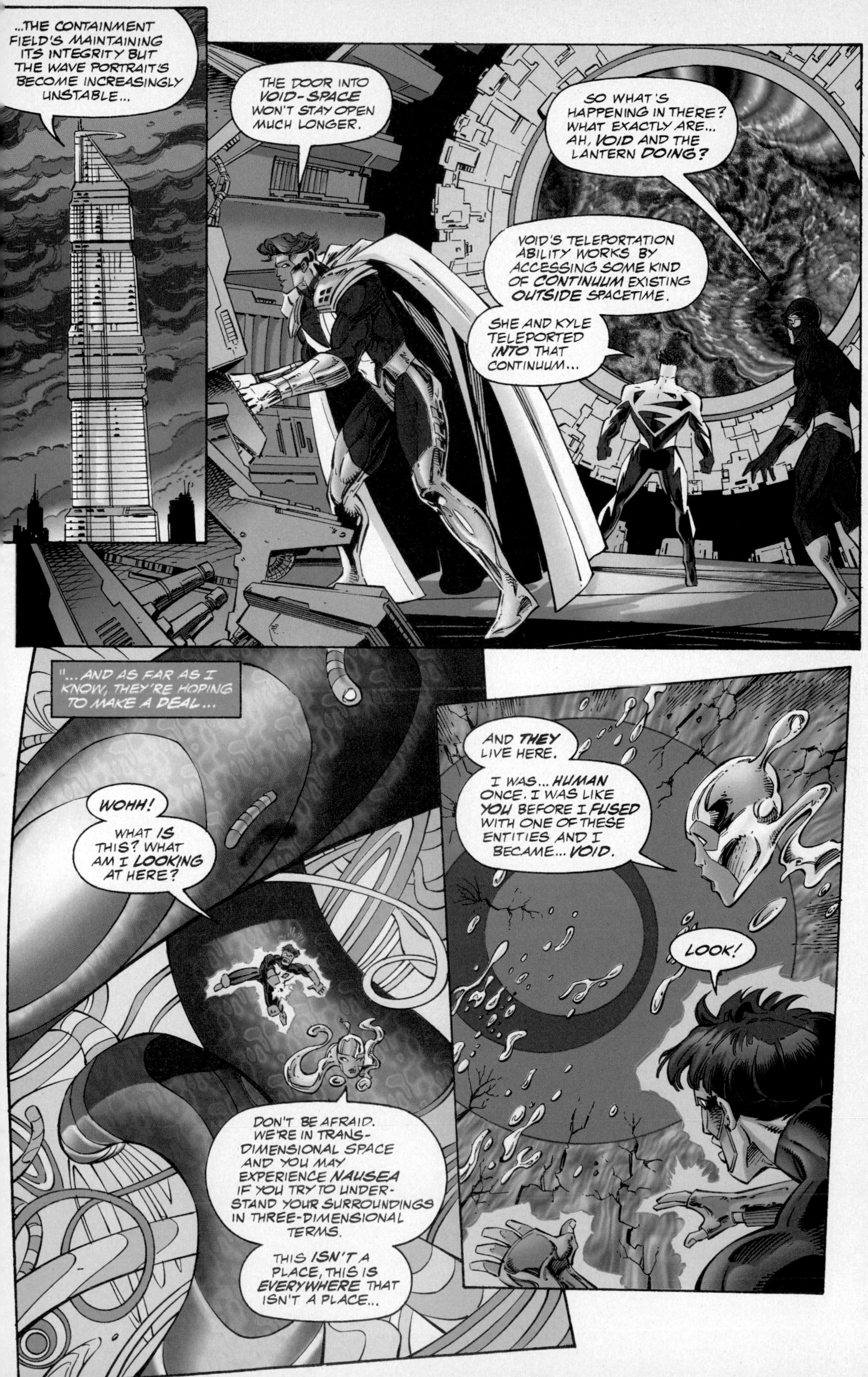

...THE CONTAINMENT FIELD'S MAINTAINING ITS INTEGRITY BUT THE WAVE PORTRAIT'S BECOME INCREASINGLY UNSTABLE...
THE DOOR INTO VOID-SPACE WON'T STAY OPEN MUCH LONGER.
SO WHAT'S HAPPENING IN THERE? WHAT EXACTLY ARE... AH, VOID AND THE LANTERN DOING?
VOID'S TELEPORTATION ABILITY WORKS BY ACCESSING SOME KIND OF CONTINUUM EXISTING OUTSIDE SPACETIME.
SHE AND KYLE TELEPORTED INTO THAT CONTINUUM...
"...AND AS FAR AS I KNOW, THEY'RE HOPING TO MAKE A DEAL...
WOHH!
WHAT IS THIS? WHAT AM I LOOKING AT HERE?
DON'T BE AFRAID. WE'RE IN TRANS-DIMENSIONAL SPACE AND YOU MAY EXPERIENCE NAUSEA IF YOU TRY TO UNDER-STAND YOUR SURROUNDINGS IN THREE-DIMENSIONAL TERMS.
THIS ISN'T A PLACE, THIS IS EVERYWHERE THAT ISN'T A PLACE...
AND THEY LIVE HERE.
I WAS... HUMAN ONCE. I WAS LIKE YOU BEFORE I FUSED WITH ONE OF THESE ENTITIES AND I BECAME... VOID.
LOOK!

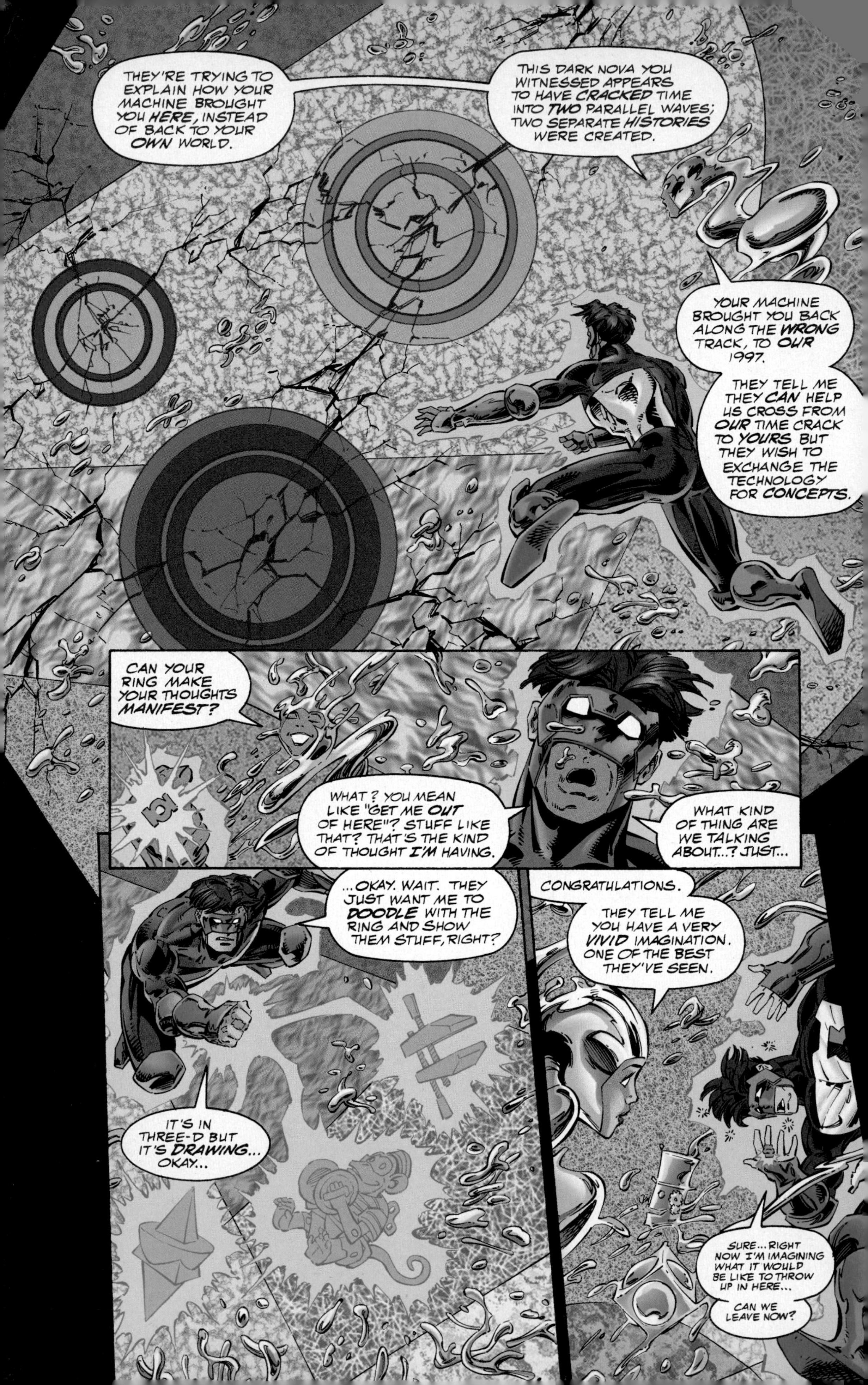
THEY'RE TRYING TO EXPLAIN HOW YOUR MACHINE BROUGHT YOU HERE, INSTEAD OF BACK TO YOUR OWN WORLD.
THIS DARK NOVA YOU WITNESSED APPEARS TO HAVE CRACKED TIME INTO TWO PARALLEL WAVES; TWO SEPARATE HISTORIES WERE CREATED.
YOUR MACHINE BROUGHT YOU BACK ALONG THE WRONG TRACK, TO OUR 1997.
THEY TELL ME THEY CAN HELP US CROSS FROM OUR TIME CRACK TO YOURS BUT THEY WISH TO EXCHANGE THE TECHNOLOGY FOR CONCEPTS.
CAN YOUR RING MAKE YOUR THOUGHTS MANIFEST?
WHAT? YOU MEAN LIKE "GET ME OUT OF HERE"? STUFF LIKE THAT? THAT'S THE KIND OF THOUGHT I'M HAVING.
WHAT KIND OF THING ARE WE TALKING ABOUT...? JUST...
...OKAY. WAIT. THEY JUST WANT ME TO DOODLE WITH THE RING AND SHOW THEM STUFF, RIGHT?
IT'S IN THREE-D BUT IT'S DRAWING... OKAY...
CONGRATULATIONS.
THEY TELL ME YOU HAVE A VERY VIVID IMAGINATION. ONE OF THE BEST THEY'VE SEEN.
SURE... RIGHT NOW I'M IMAGINING WHAT IT WOULD BE LIKE TO THROW UP IN HERE...
CAN WE LEAVE NOW?

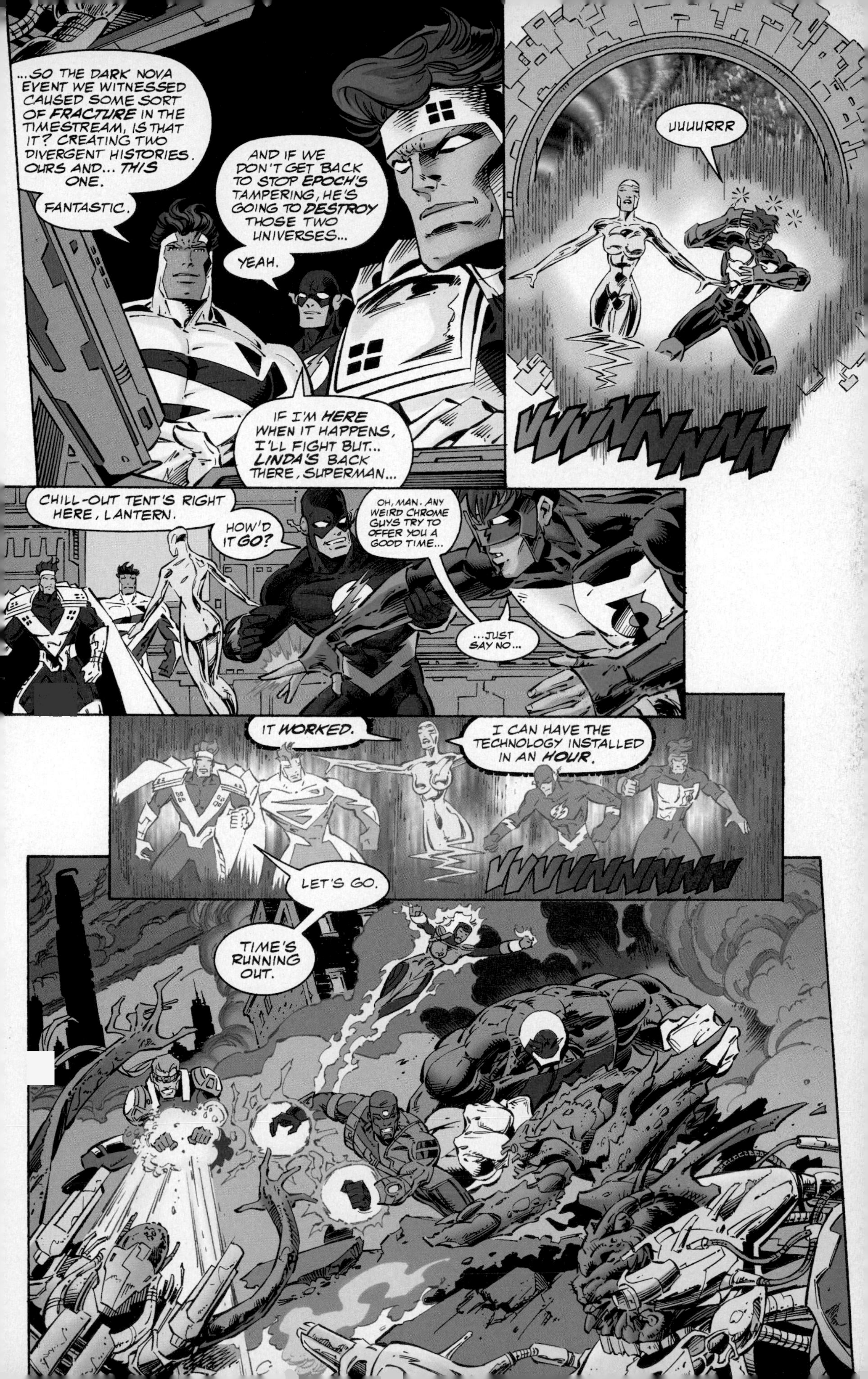
...SO THE DARK NOVA EVENT WE WITNESSED CAUSED SOME SORT OF FRACTURE IN THE TIMESTREAM, IS THAT IT? CREATING TWO DIVERGENT HISTORIES. OURS AND... THIS ONE.
FANTASTIC.
AND IF WE DON'T GET BACK TO STOP EPOCH'S TAMPERING, HE'S GOING TO DESTROY THOSE TWO UNIVERSES...
YEAH.
IF I'M HERE WHEN IT HAPPENS, I'LL FIGHT BUT... LINDA'S BACK THERE, SUPERMAN...
UUUURRR
VVVVNNNNN
CHILL-OUT TENT'S RIGHT HERE, LANTERN.
HOW'D IT GO?
OH, MAN. ANY WEIRD CHROME GUYS TRY TO OFFER YOU A GOOD TIME...
...JUST SAY NO...
IT WORKED.
I CAN HAVE THE TECHNOLOGY INSTALLED IN AN HOUR.
VVVVNNNNNN
LET'S GO.
TIME'S RUNNING OUT.

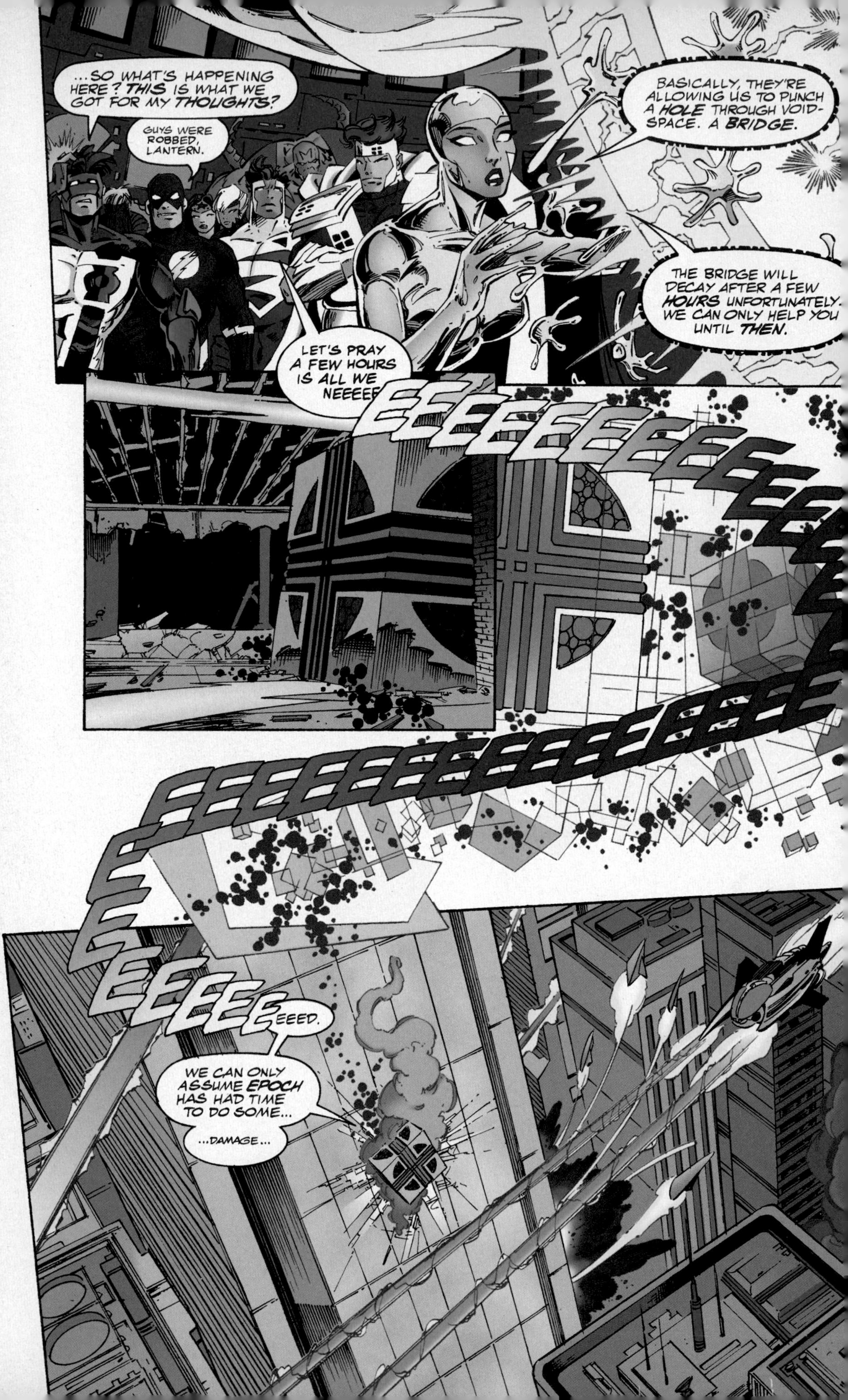
...SO WHAT'S HAPPENING HERE? THIS IS WHAT WE GOT FOR MY THOUGHTS?
GUYS WERE ROBBED, LANTERN.
BASICALLY, THEY'RE ALLOWING US TO PUNCH A HOLE THROUGH VOID-SPACE. A BRIDGE.
THE BRIDGE WILL DECAY AFTER A FEW HOURS UNFORTUNATELY. WE CAN ONLY HELP YOU UNTIL THEN.
LET'S PRAY A FEW HOURS IS ALL WE NEEEEEEEEEEEEEEEEEEEEEEEEEEEEEEEEEEEEEEEEEEEEEEEEEEEEEEEEEEEEEEEEEEEEEED.
WE CAN ONLY ASSUME EPOCH HAS HAD TIME TO DO SOME...
...DAMAGE...

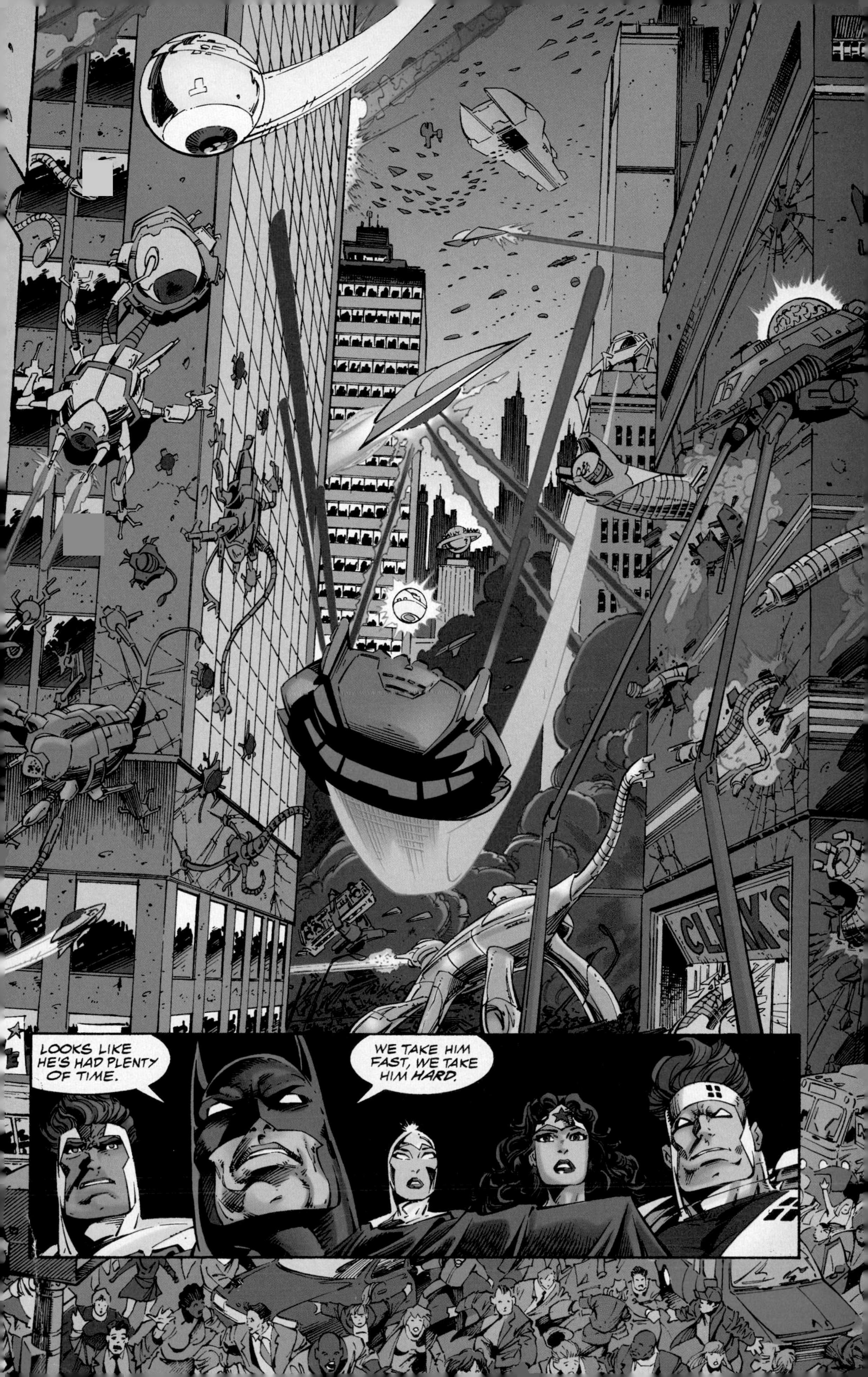
LOOKS LIKE HE'S HAD PLENTY OF TIME.
WE TAKE HIM FAST, WE TAKE HIM HARD.
CLARK'S

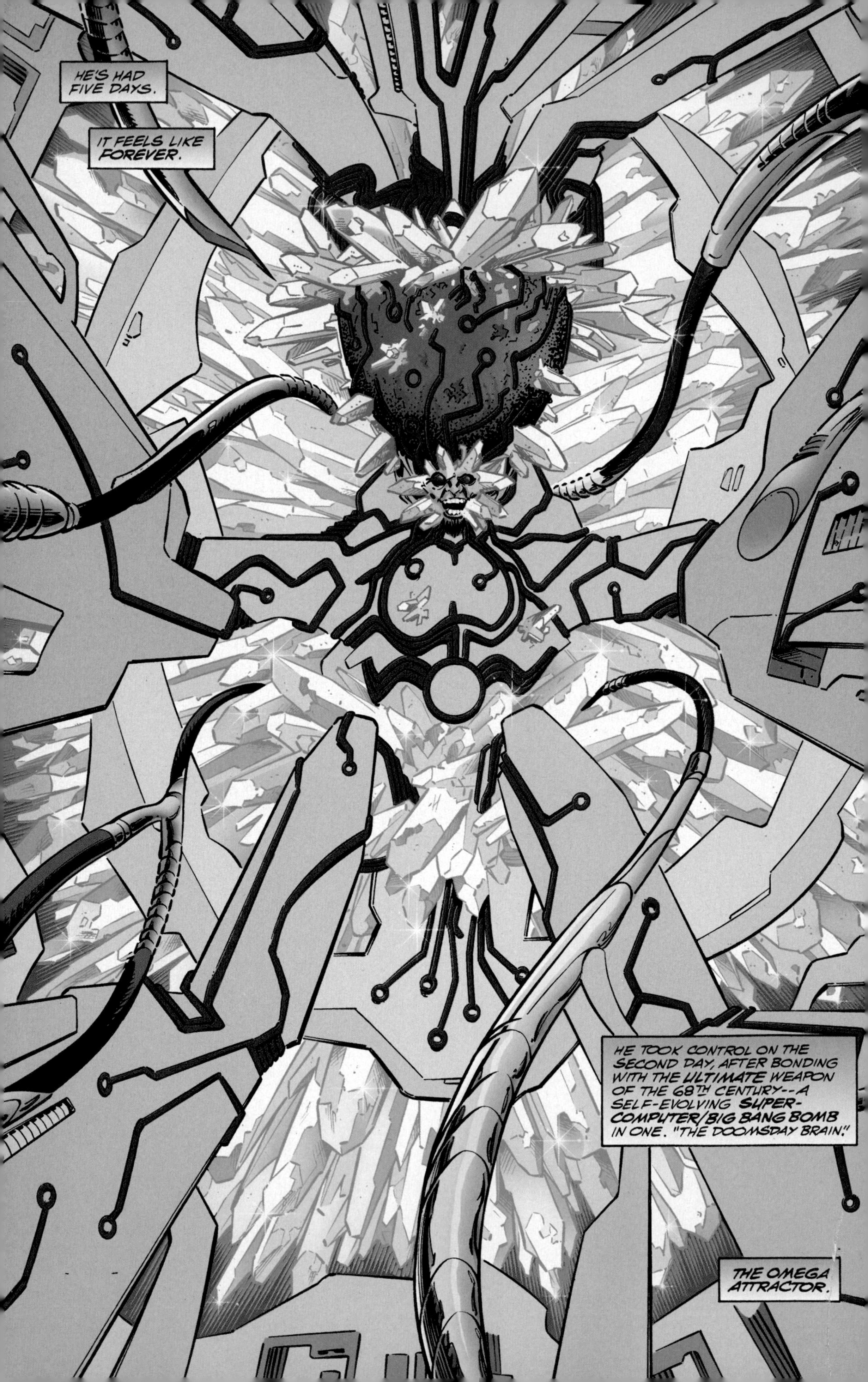
HE'S HAD FIVE DAYS.
IT FEELS LIKE FOREVER.
HE TOOK CONTROL ON THE SECOND DAY, AFTER BONDING WITH THE ULTIMATE WEAPON OF THE 68TH CENTURY--A SELF-EVOLVING SUPER-COMPUTER/BIG BANG BOMB IN ONE. "THE DOOMSDAY BRAIN."
THE OMEGA ATTRACTOR.

NOW HE CAN'T TELL WHERE HE ENDS AND IT BEGINS.

EVERYTHING IS THE OMEGA ATTRACTOR.

HIS THOUGHTS ARE ENORMOUS NOW.

BIG ENOUGH TO REACH EFFORTLESSLY ACROSS SPACE AND TIME. BIG ENOUGH TO COMMAND THE LEGIONS OF THE *FUTURE* AND SUBDUE THE EARTH.

INTELLIGENT CLOUD SURVEILLANCE SYSTEMS FROM THE 22ND CENTURY, RELEASE SHOWERS OF MIND-SOFTENING *RAIN* OVER THE EASTERN SEABOARD OF THE USA.

GARGOYLE-TROOPS FROM THE 98TH CENTURY GOTHIC IMPERIUM OF NEO-PANGEA HAUNT THE SPIRES OF *MOSCOW.*

THE SCALE OF HIS *PLANS* GROWS GRANDER EVERY HOUR AS HIS MIND OUTRACES *ALL* LIMITS.

28TH CENTURY *MACROSUITS* PROWL THE PACIFIC RIM.

ALL OF IT UNDER HIS CONTROL.

HE INTENDS NOW TO CONVERT THE ENTIRE EARTH INTO A VAST TIME-TRAVELING *ENGINE* POWERED BY ITS HUMAN SLAVE POPULATION.

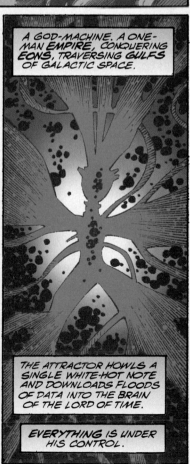

A GOD-MACHINE. A ONE-MAN *EMPIRE*, CONQUERING *EONS*, TRAVERSING *GULFS* OF GALACTIC SPACE.

THE ATTRACTOR HOWLS A SINGLE WHITE-HOT NOTE AND DOWNLOADS FLOODS OF DATA INTO THE BRAIN OF THE LORD OF TIME.

EVERYTHING IS UNDER HIS CONTROL.

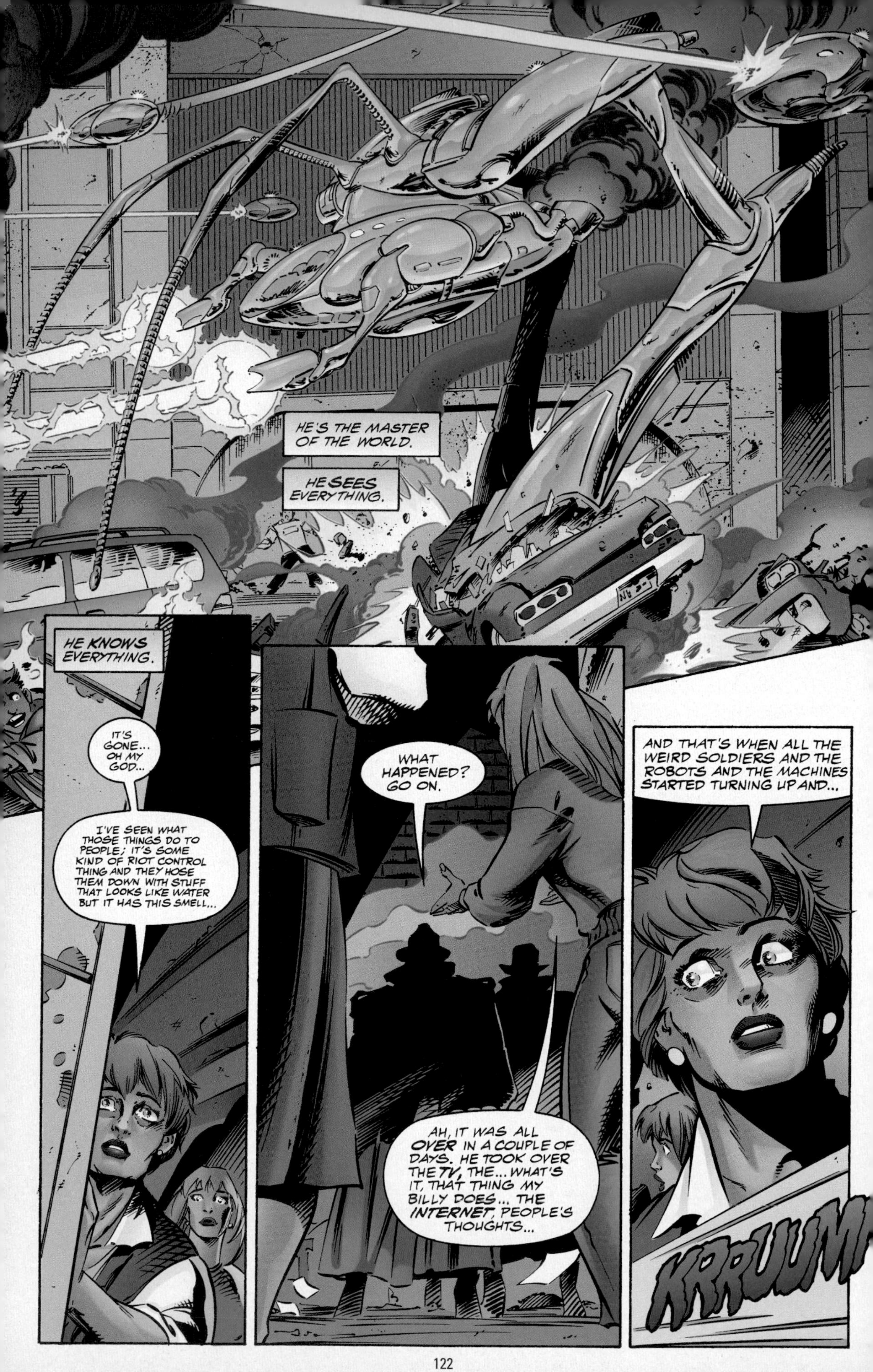
HE'S THE MASTER OF THE WORLD.
HE SEES EVERYTHING.
HE KNOWS EVERYTHING.
IT'S GONE... OH MY GOD...
I'VE SEEN WHAT THOSE THINGS DO TO PEOPLE; IT'S SOME KIND OF RIOT CONTROL THING AND THEY HOSE THEM DOWN WITH STUFF THAT LOOKS LIKE WATER BUT IT HAS THIS SMELL...
WHAT HAPPENED? GO ON.
AH, IT WAS ALL OVER IN A COUPLE OF DAYS. HE TOOK OVER THE TV, THE... WHAT'S IT, THAT THING MY BILLY DOES... THE INTERNET, PEOPLE'S THOUGHTS...
AND THAT'S WHEN ALL THE WEIRD SOLDIERS AND THE ROBOTS AND THE MACHINES STARTED TURNING UP AND...
KRRUUM

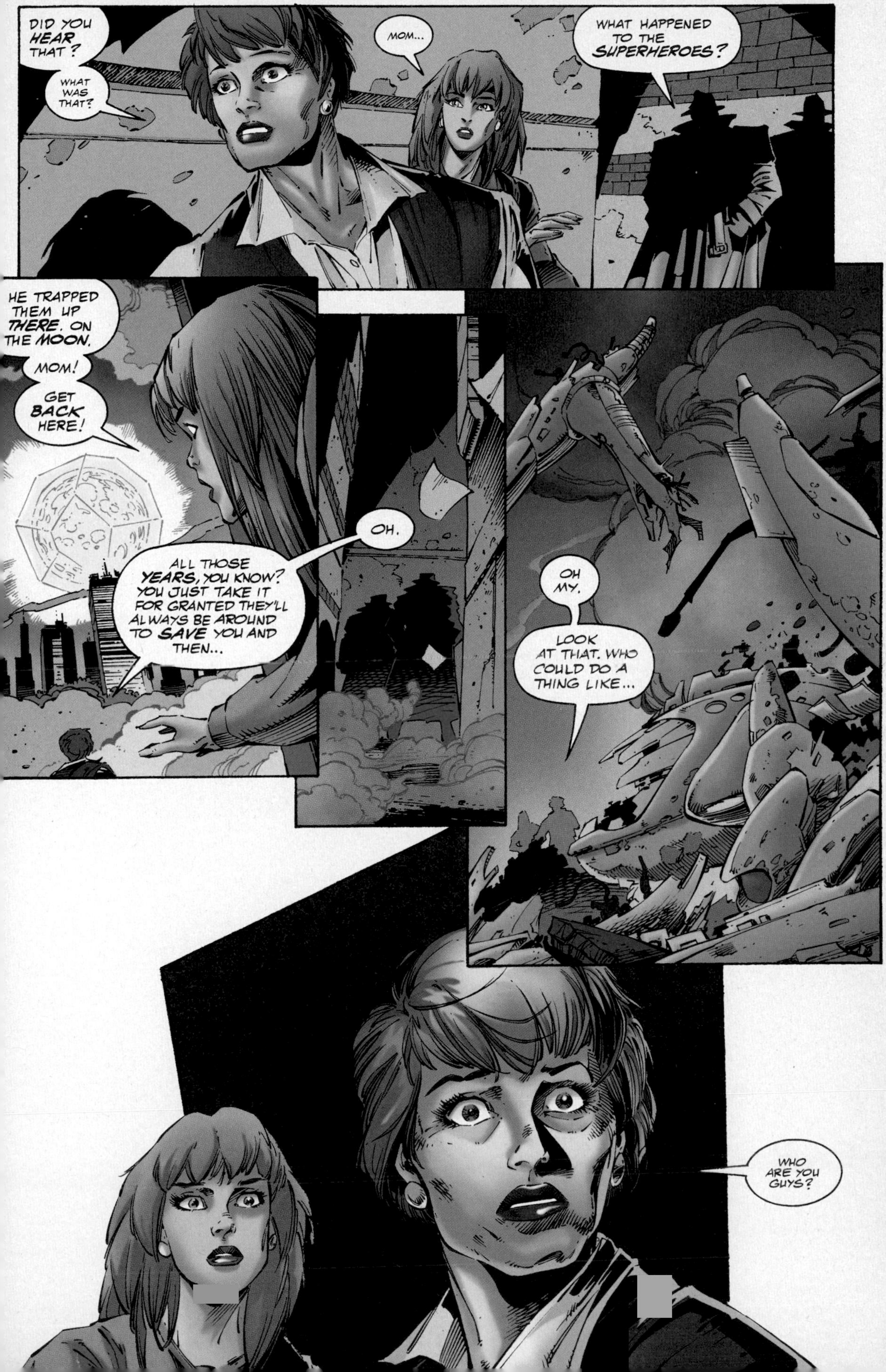
DID YOU HEAR THAT?
WHAT WAS THAT?
MOM...
WHAT HAPPENED TO THE SUPERHEROES?
HE TRAPPED THEM UP THERE. ON THE MOON.
MOM!
GET BACK HERE!
ALL THOSE YEARS, YOU KNOW? YOU JUST TAKE IT FOR GRANTED THEY'LL ALWAYS BE AROUND TO SAVE YOU AND THEN...
OH.
OH MY.
LOOK AT THAT. WHO COULD DO A THING LIKE...
WHO ARE YOU GUYS?

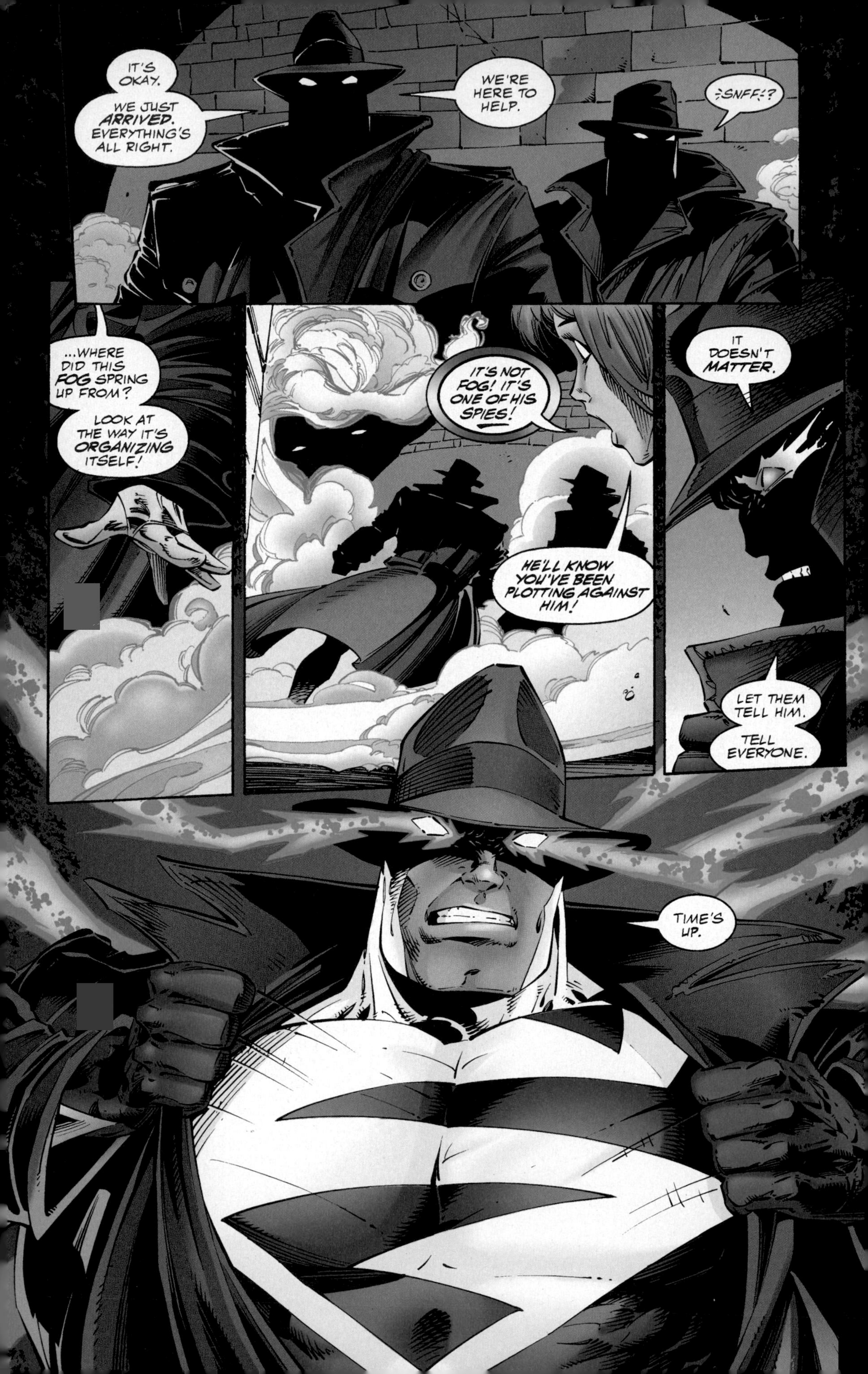
IT'S OKAY.
WE JUST ARRIVED. EVERYTHING'S ALL RIGHT.
WE'RE HERE TO HELP.
SNFF?
...WHERE DID THIS FOG SPRING UP FROM?
LOOK AT THE WAY IT'S ORGANIZING ITSELF!
IT'S NOT FOG! IT'S ONE OF HIS SPIES!
HE'LL KNOW YOU'VE BEEN PLOTTING AGAINST HIM!
IT DOESN'T MATTER.
LET THEM TELL HIM.
TELL EVERYONE.
TIME'S UP.

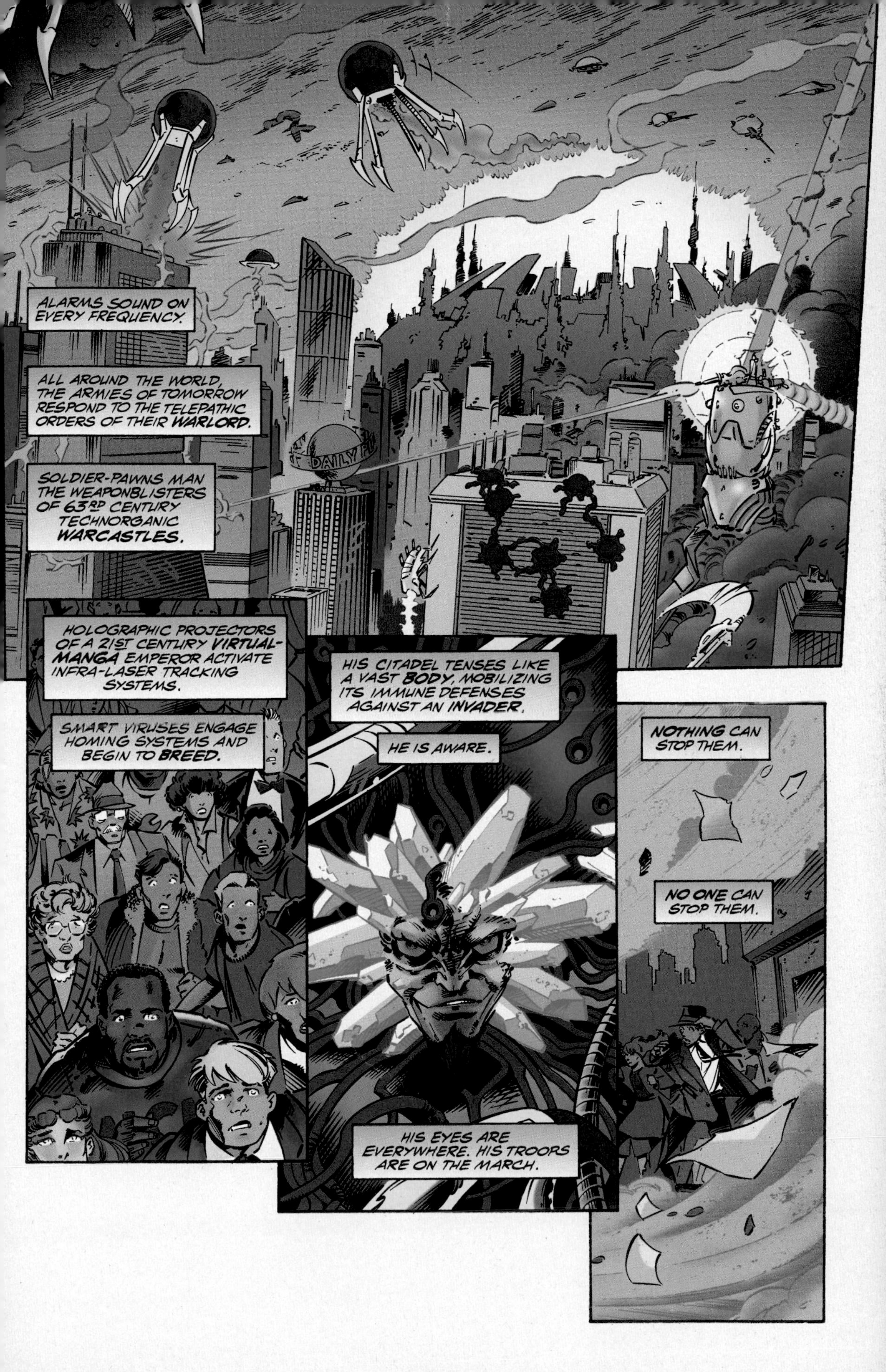
ALARMS SOUND ON EVERY FREQUENCY.
ALL AROUND THE WORLD, THE ARMIES OF TOMORROW RESPOND TO THE TELEPATHIC ORDERS OF THEIR WARLORD.
SOLDIER-PAWNS MAN THE WEAPONBLISTERS OF 63RD CENTURY TECHNORGANIC WARCASTLES.
DAILY PL
HOLOGRAPHIC PROJECTORS OF A 21ST CENTURY VIRTUAL-MANGA EMPEROR ACTIVATE INFRA-LASER TRACKING SYSTEMS.
SMART VIRUSES ENGAGE HOMING SYSTEMS AND BEGIN TO BREED.
HIS CITADEL TENSES LIKE A VAST BODY, MOBILIZING ITS IMMUNE DEFENSES AGAINST AN INVADER.
HE IS AWARE.
HIS EYES ARE EVERYWHERE. HIS TROORS ARE ON THE MARCH.
NOTHING CAN STOP THEM.
NO ONE CAN STOP THEM.

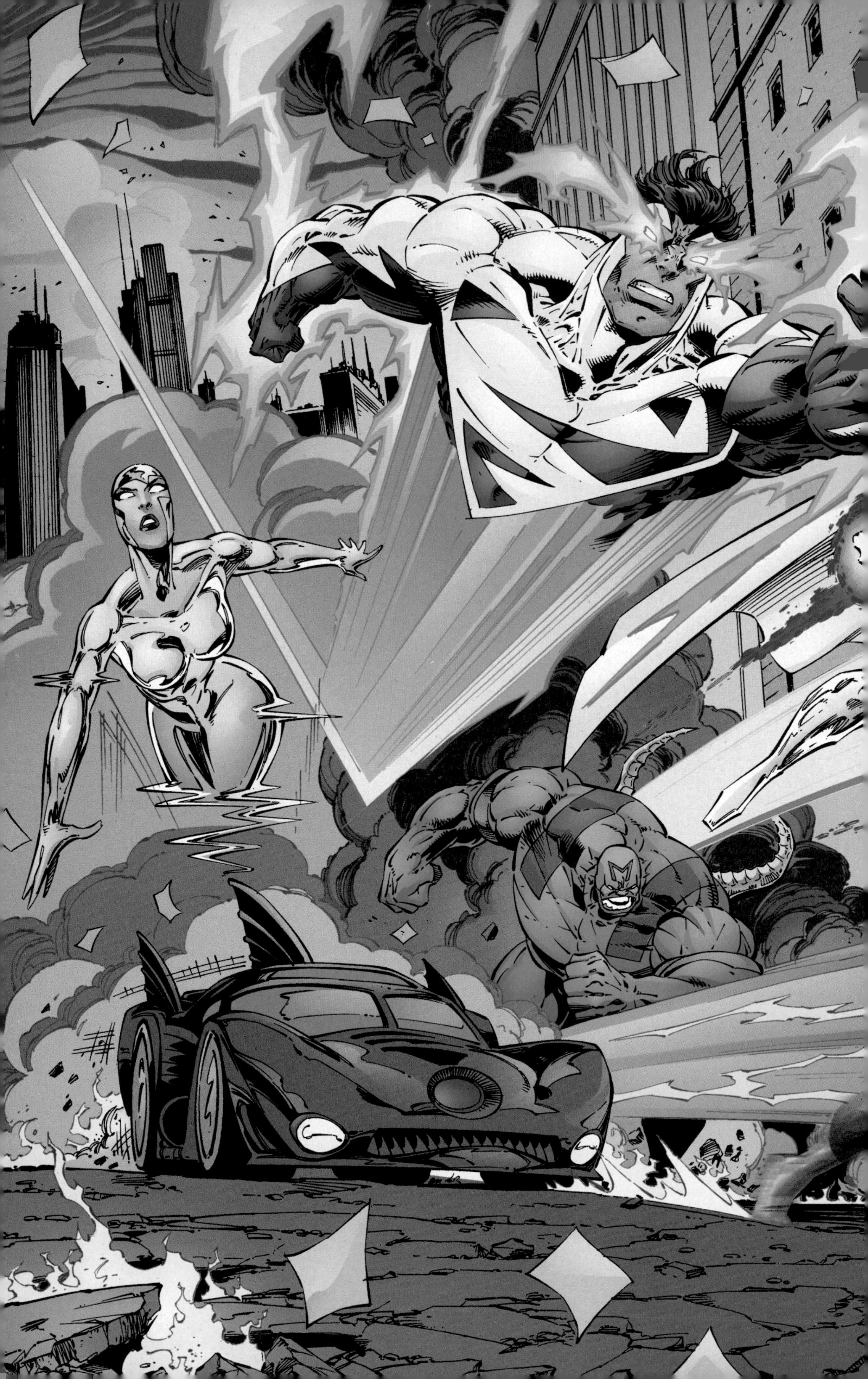

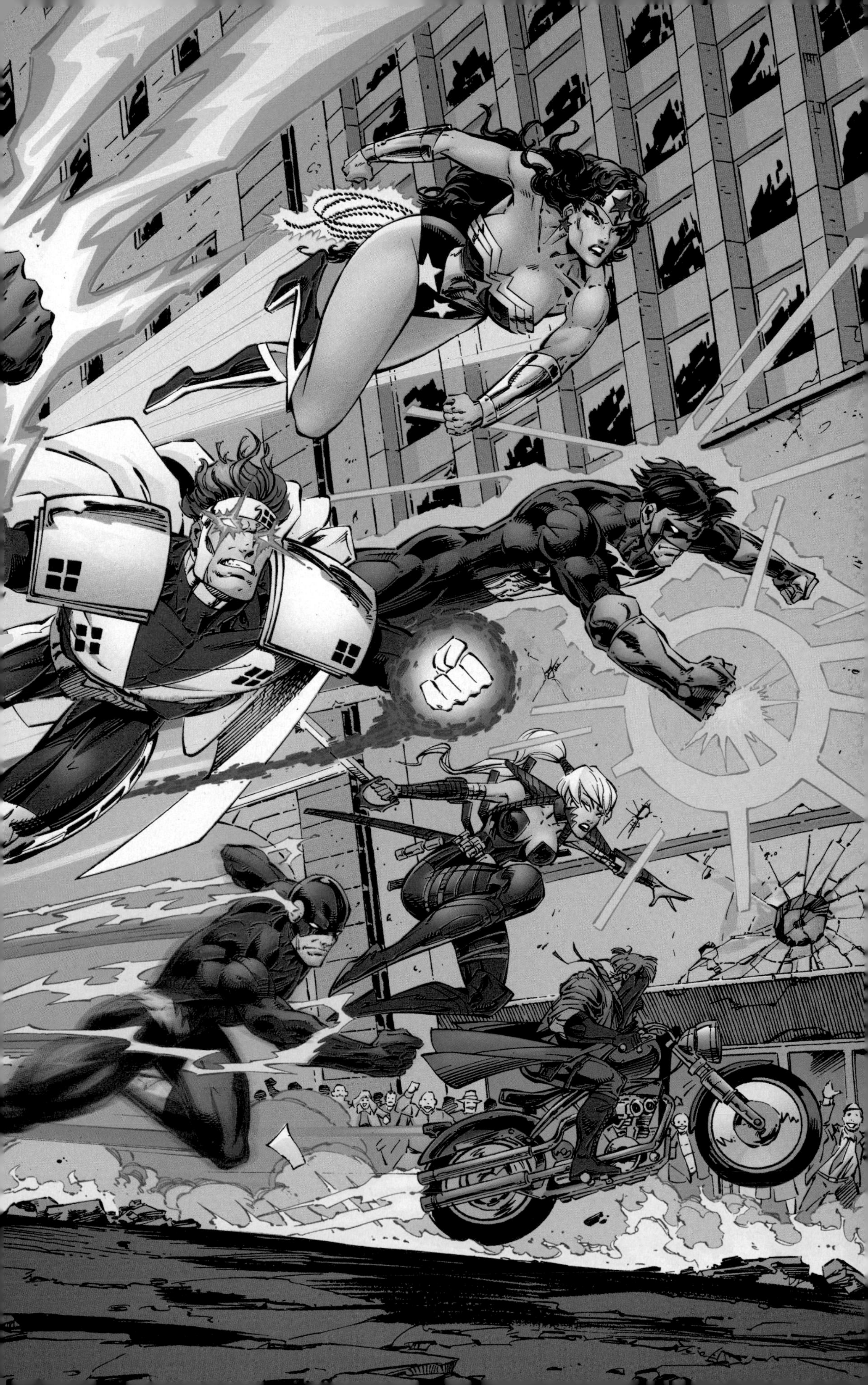

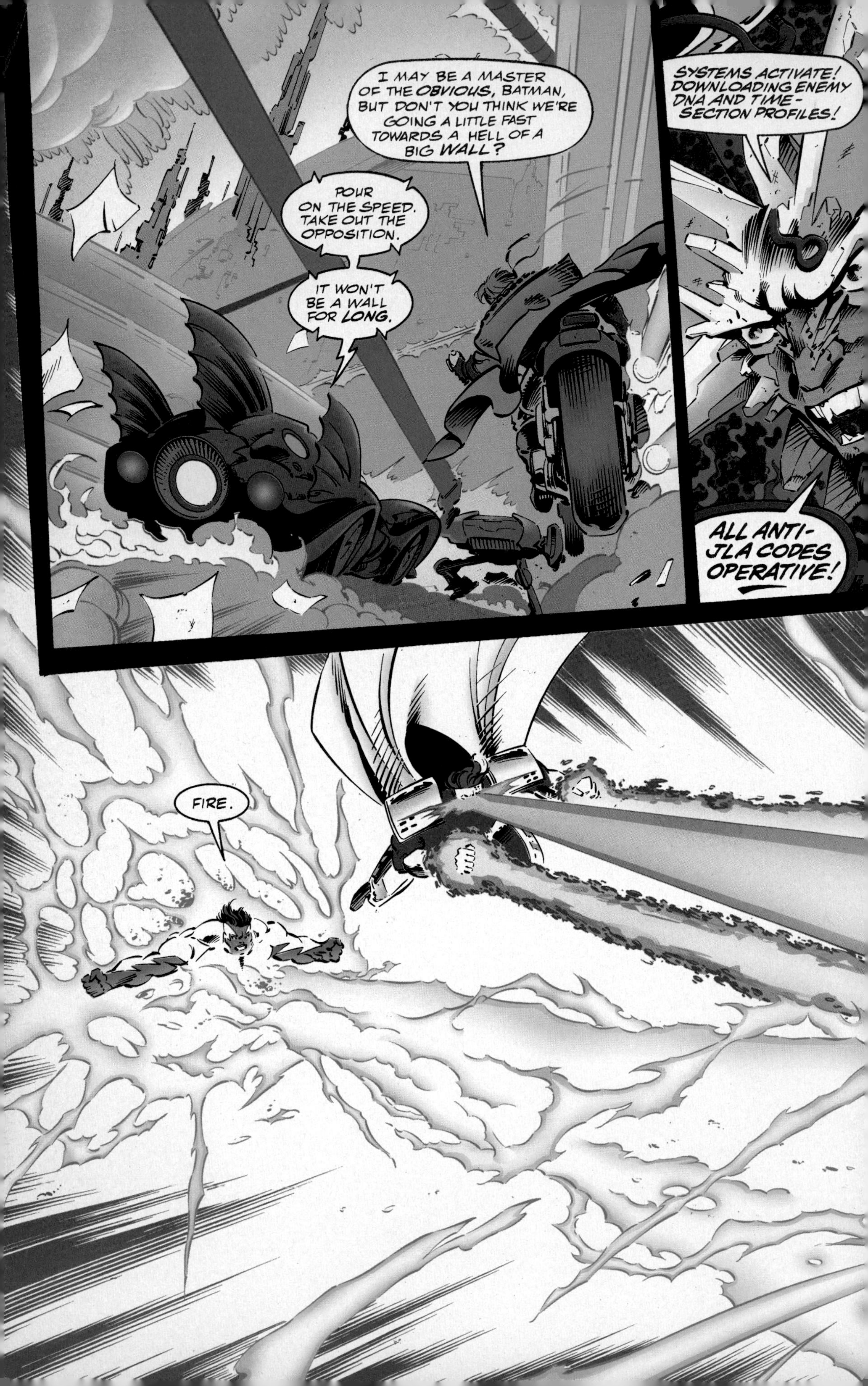
I MAY BE A MASTER OF THE OBVIOUS, BATMAN, BUT DON'T YOU THINK WE'RE GOING A LITTLE FAST TOWARDS A HELL OF A BIG WALL?
POUR ON THE SPEED. TAKE OUT THE OPPOSITION.
IT WON'T BE A WALL FOR LONG.
SYSTEMS ACTIVATE! DOWNLOADING ENEMY DNA AND TIME-SECTION PROFILES!
ALL ANTI-JLA CODES OPERATIVE!
FIRE.

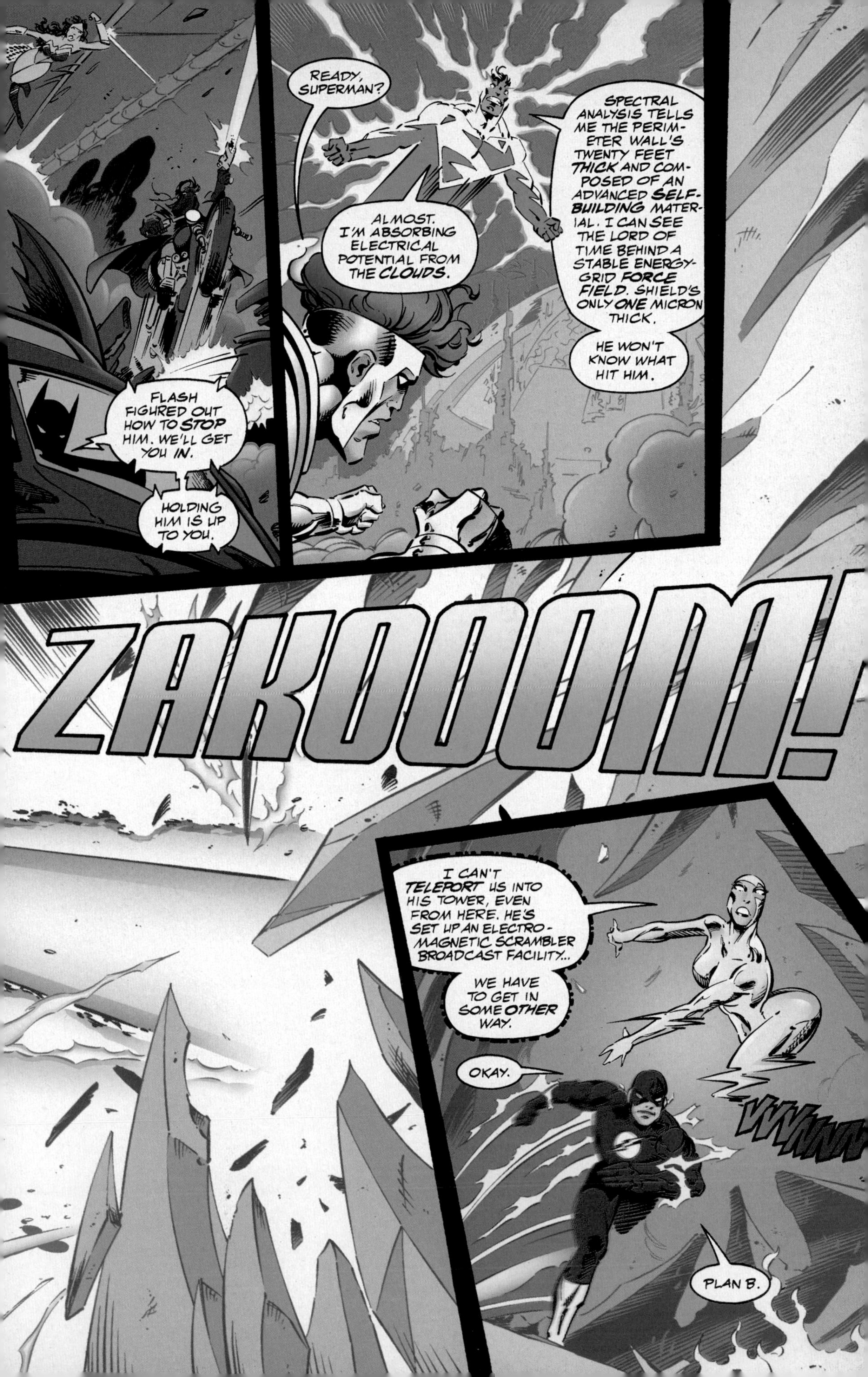
FLASH FIGURED OUT HOW TO STOP HIM. WE'LL GET YOU IN.
HOLDING HIM IS UP TO YOU.
READY, SUPERMAN?
ALMOST. I'M ABSORBING ELECTRICAL POTENTIAL FROM THE CLOUDS.
SPECTRAL ANALYSIS TELLS ME THE PERIMETER WALL'S TWENTY FEET THICK AND COMPOSED OF AN ADVANCED SELF-BUILDING MATERIAL. I CAN SEE THE LORD OF TIME BEHIND A STABLE ENERGY-GRID FORCE FIELD. SHIELD'S ONLY ONE MICRON THICK.
HE WON'T KNOW WHAT HIT HIM.
ZAKOOOM!
I CAN'T TELEPORT US INTO HIS TOWER, EVEN FROM HERE. HE'S SET UP AN ELECTRO-MAGNETIC SCRAMBLER BROADCAST FACILITY...
WE HAVE TO GET IN SOME OTHER WAY.
OKAY.
VVNNN
PLAN B.

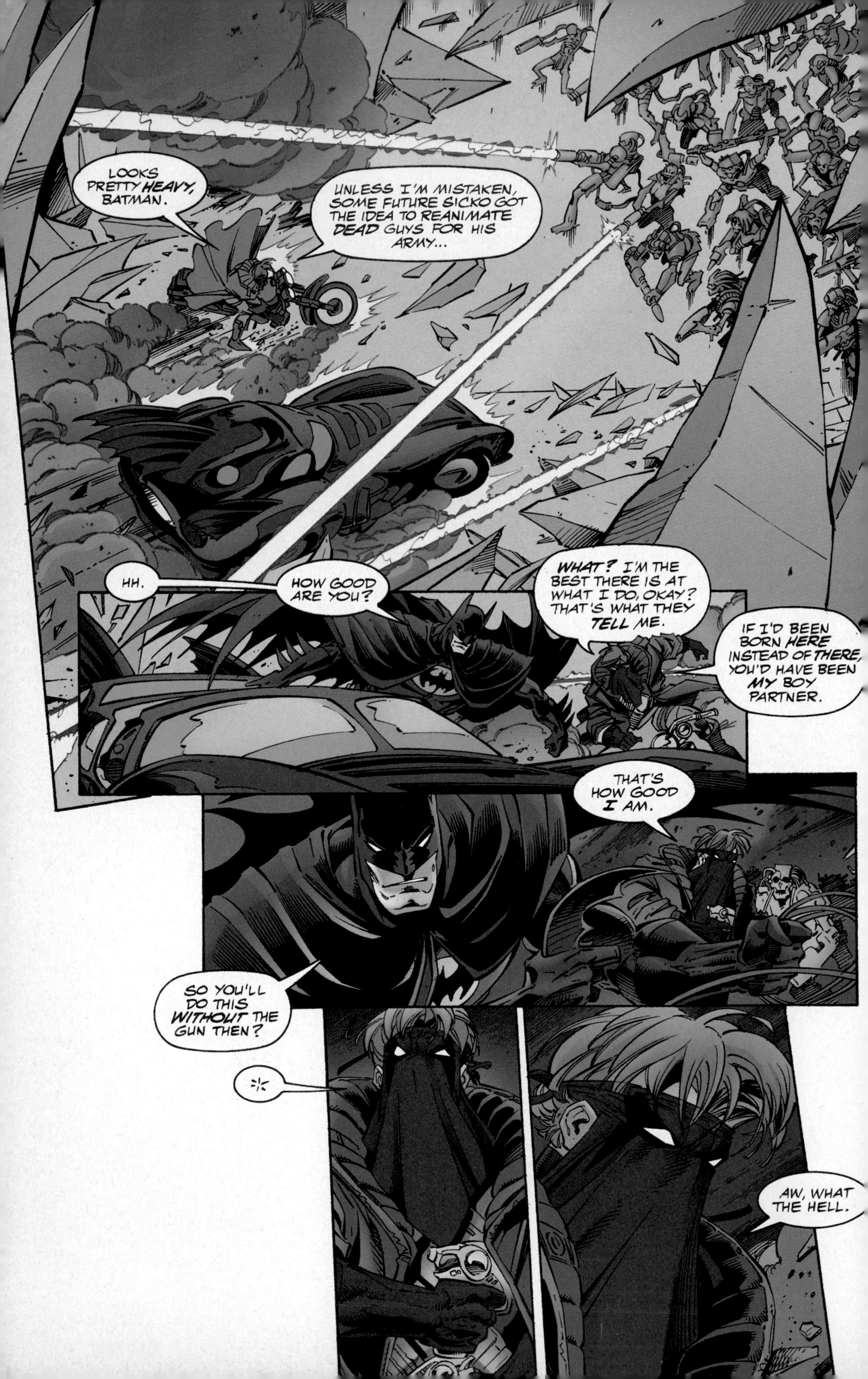
LOOKS PRETTY HEAVY, BATMAN.
UNLESS I'M MISTAKEN, SOME FUTURE SICKO GOT THE IDEA TO REANIMATE DEAD GUYS FOR HIS ARMY...
HH.
HOW GOOD ARE YOU?
WHAT? I'M THE BEST THERE IS AT WHAT I DO, OKAY? THAT'S WHAT THEY TELL ME.
IF I'D BEEN BORN HERE INSTEAD OF THERE, YOU'D HAVE BEEN MY BOY PARTNER.
THAT'S HOW GOOD I AM.
SO YOU'LL DO THIS WITHOUT THE GUN THEN?
AW, WHAT THE HELL.

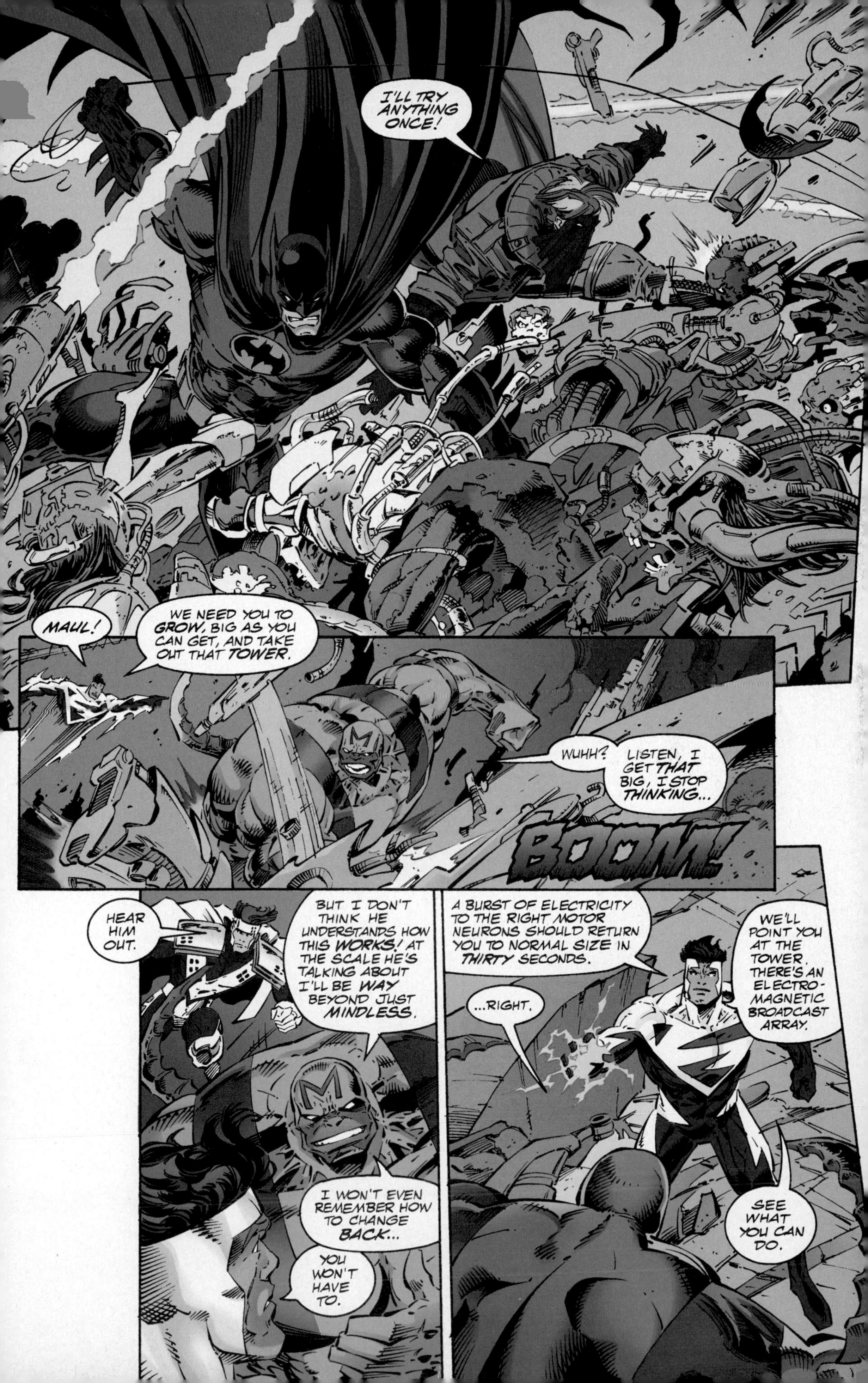
I'LL TRY ANYTHING ONCE!
MAUL!
WE NEED YOU TO GROW. BIG AS YOU CAN GET, AND TAKE OUT THAT TOWER.
WUHH?
LISTEN, I GET THAT BIG, I STOP THINKING...
BOOM!
HEAR HIM OUT.
BUT I DON'T THINK HE UNDERSTANDS HOW THIS WORKS! AT THE SCALE HE'S TALKING ABOUT I'LL BE WAY BEYOND JUST MINDLESS.
I WON'T EVEN REMEMBER HOW TO CHANGE BACK...
YOU WON'T HAVE TO.
A BURST OF ELECTRICITY TO THE RIGHT MOTOR NEURONS SHOULD RETURN YOU TO NORMAL SIZE IN THIRTY SECONDS.
...RIGHT.
WE'LL POINT YOU AT THE TOWER. THERE'S AN ELECTRO-MAGNETIC BROADCAST ARRAY.
SEE WHAT YOU CAN DO.

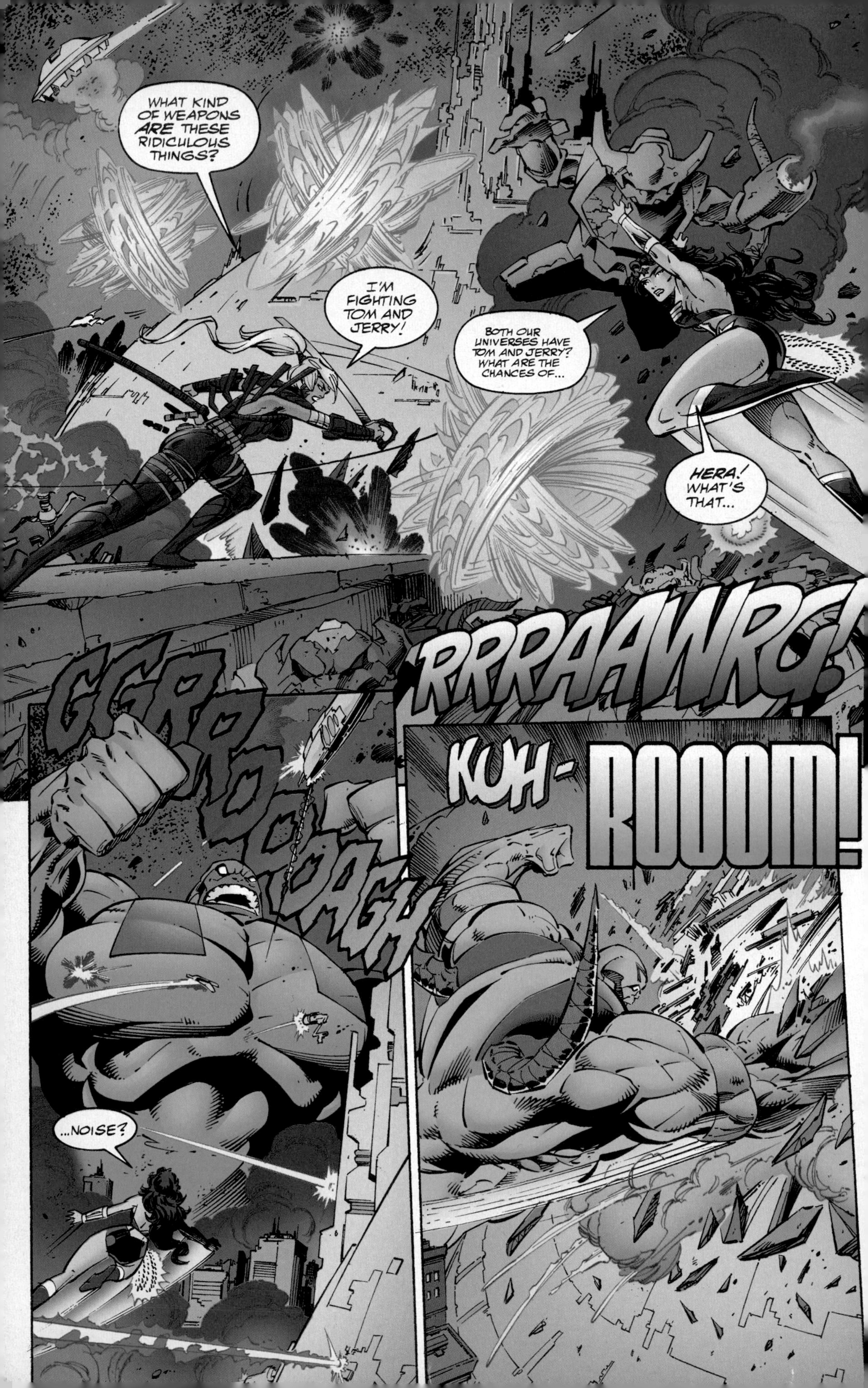
WHAT KIND OF WEAPONS ARE THESE RIDICULOUS THINGS?
I'M FIGHTING TOM AND JERRY!
BOTH OUR UNIVERSES HAVE TOM AND JERRY? WHAT ARE THE CHANCES OF...
HERA! WHAT'S THAT...
RRRAAWRG!
GGRROOOAGH
...NOISE?
KUH-ROOOM!

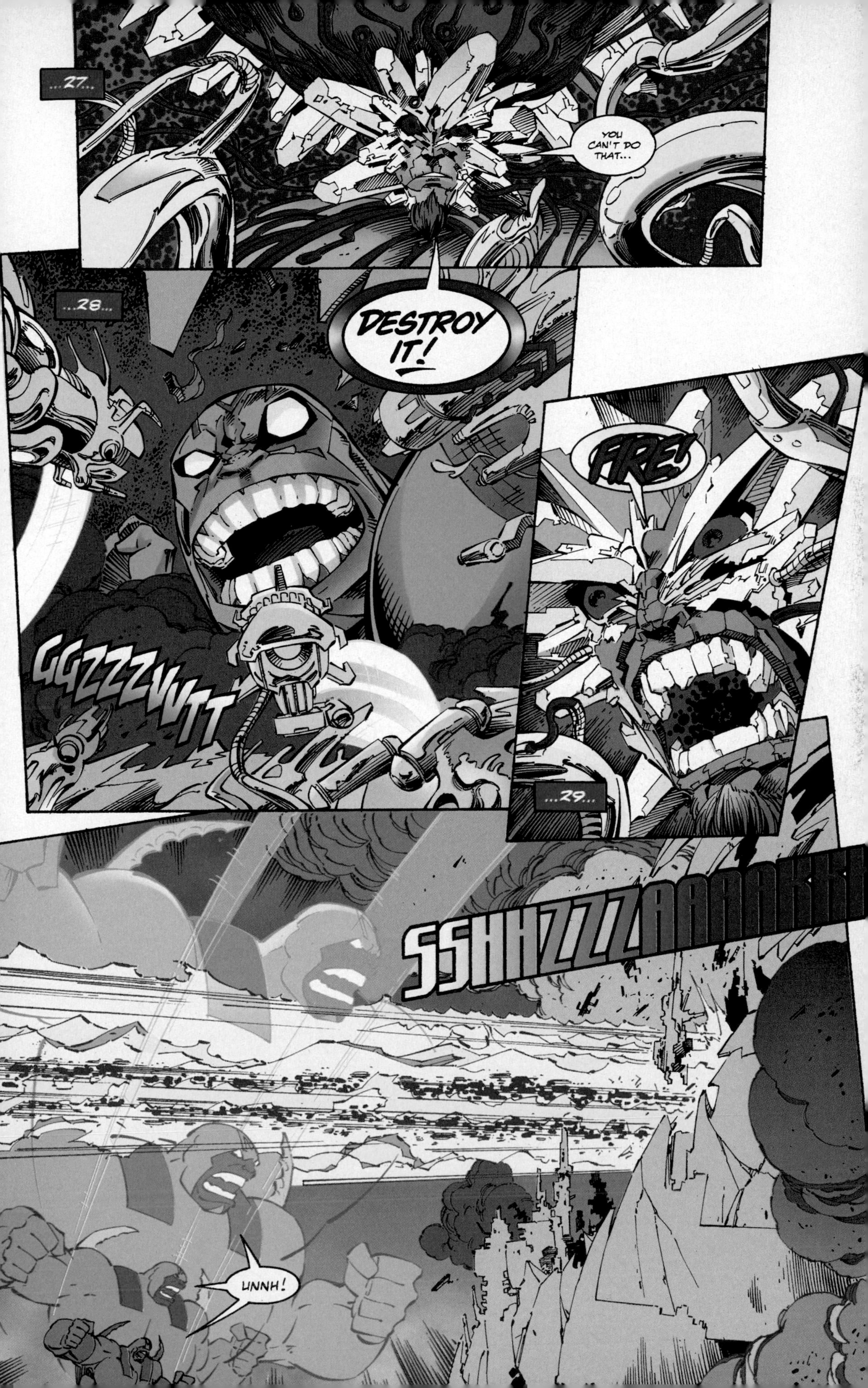
...27...
YOU CAN'T DO THAT...
...28...
DESTROY IT!
GGZZZVVTT
FIRE!
...29...
SSHHZZZZAAAAKKK
UNNH!

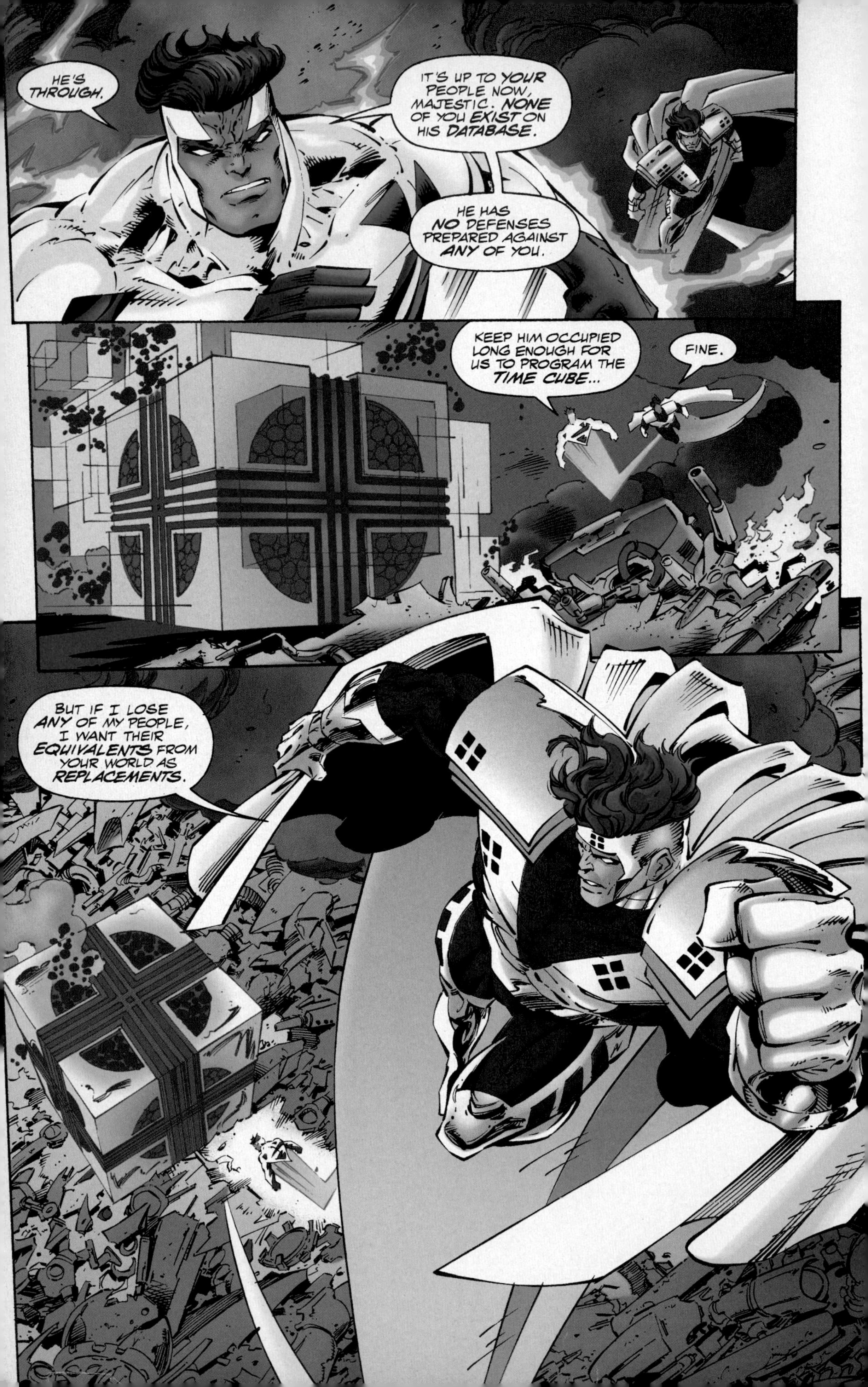
HE'S THROUGH.
IT'S UP TO YOUR PEOPLE NOW, MAJESTIC. NONE OF YOU EXIST ON HIS DATABASE.
HE HAS NO DEFENSES PREPARED AGAINST ANY OF YOU.
KEEP HIM OCCUPIED LONG ENOUGH FOR US TO PROGRAM THE TIME CUBE...
FINE.
BUT IF I LOSE ANY OF MY PEOPLE, I WANT THEIR EQUIVALENTS FROM YOUR WORLD AS REPLACEMENTS.

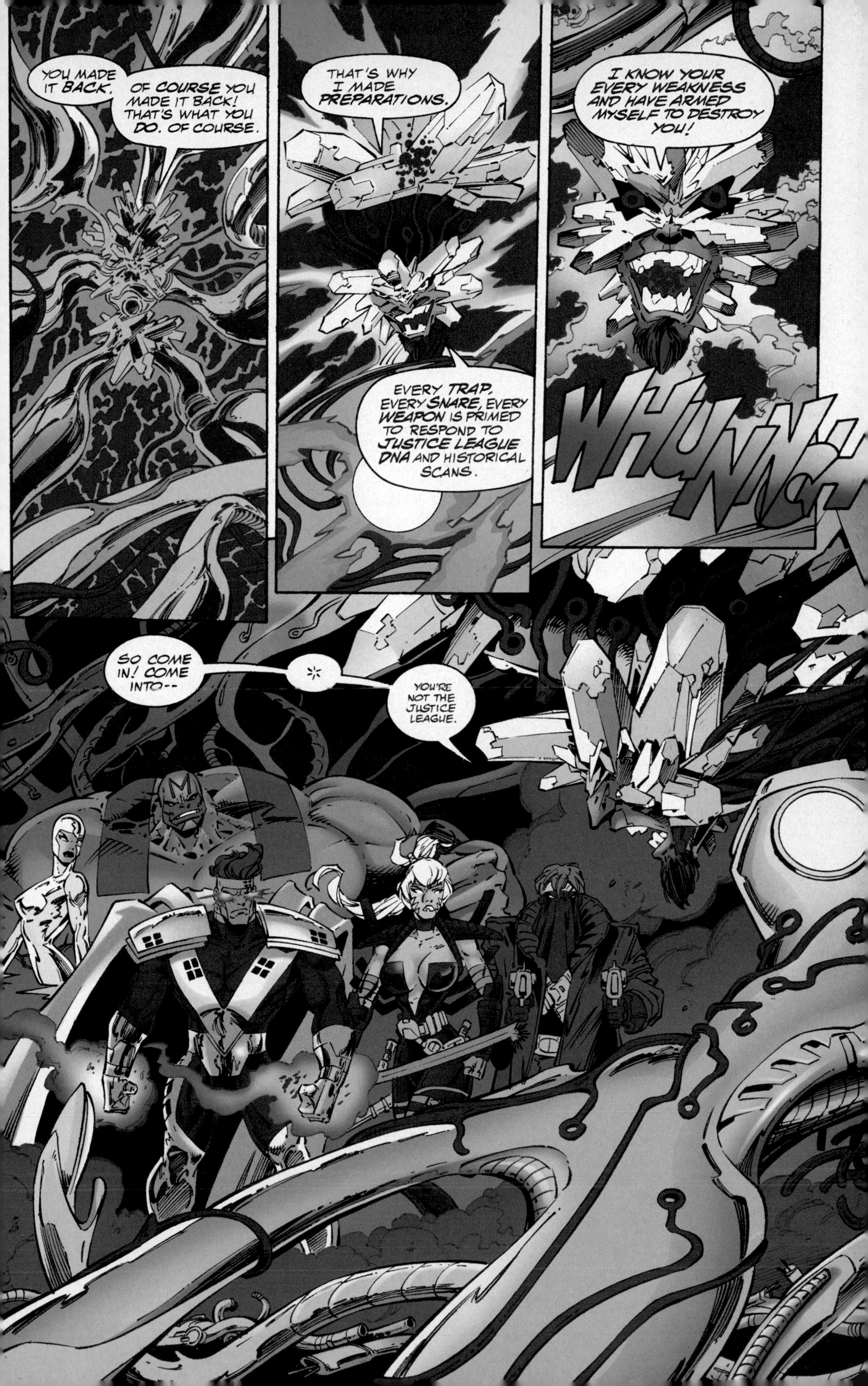
YOU MADE IT BACK.
OF COURSE YOU MADE IT BACK! THAT'S WHAT YOU DO. OF COURSE.
THAT'S WHY I MADE PREPARATIONS.
EVERY TRAP. EVERY SNARE, EVERY WEAPON IS PRIMED TO RESPOND TO JUSTICE LEAGUE DNA AND HISTORICAL SCANS.
I KNOW YOUR EVERY WEAKNESS AND HAVE ARMED MYSELF TO DESTROY YOU!
WHUNNNCH
SO COME IN! COME INTO--
YOU'RE NOT THE JUSTICE LEAGUE.

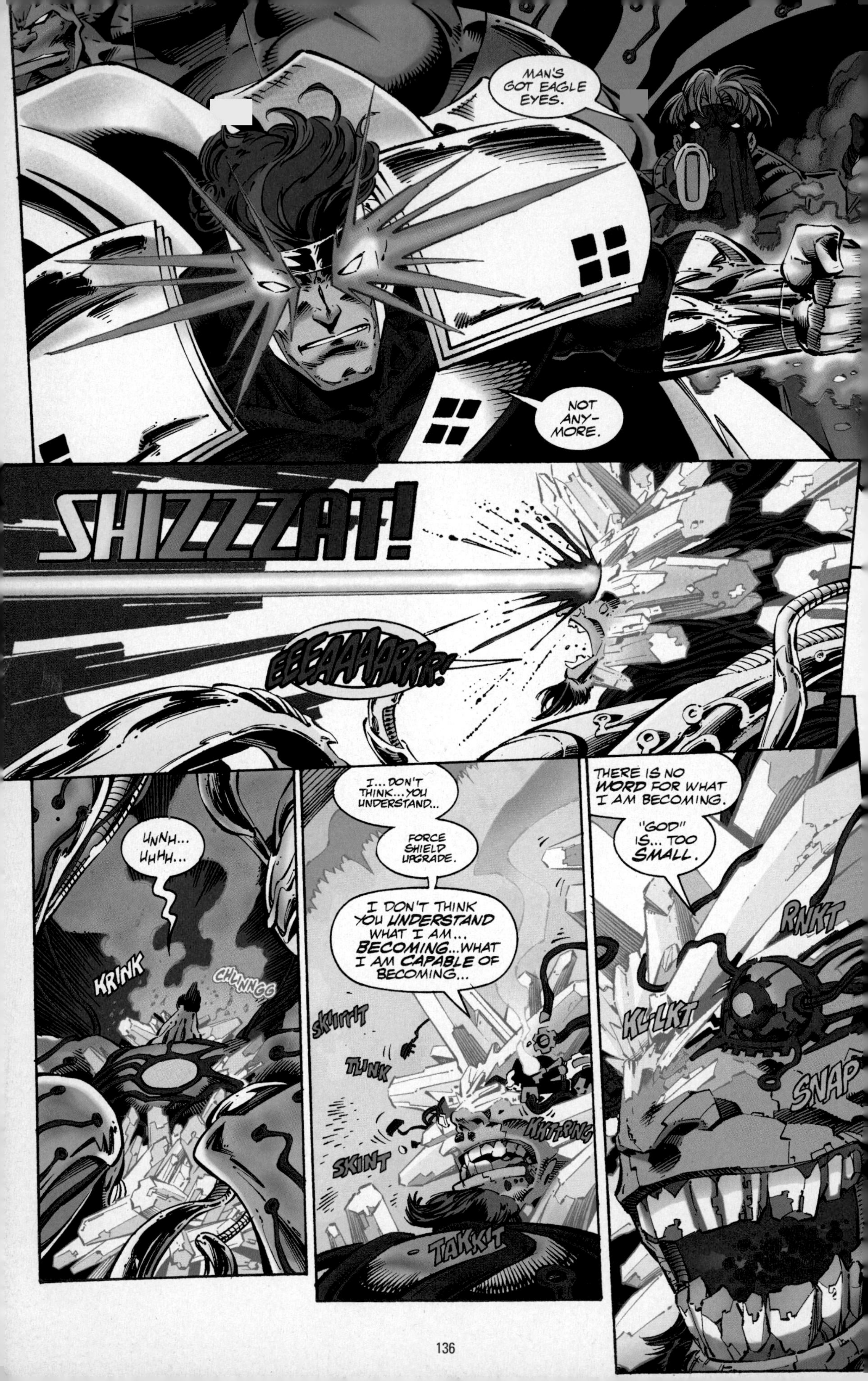
MAN'S GOT EAGLE EYES.
NOT ANY-MORE.
SHIZZZAT!
EEEAAAARRR!
UNNH... UHHH...
KRINK
CHUNNGG
I... DON'T THINK... YOU UNDERSTAND...
FORCE SHIELD UPGRADE.
I DON'T THINK YOU UNDERSTAND WHAT I AM... BECOMING... WHAT I AM CAPABLE OF BECOMING...
SKIIRRT
TLINK
KKTTRING
SKINT
TAKKT
THERE IS NO WORD FOR WHAT I AM BECOMING.
"GOD" IS... TOO SMALL.
RNKT
KL-LKT
SNAP

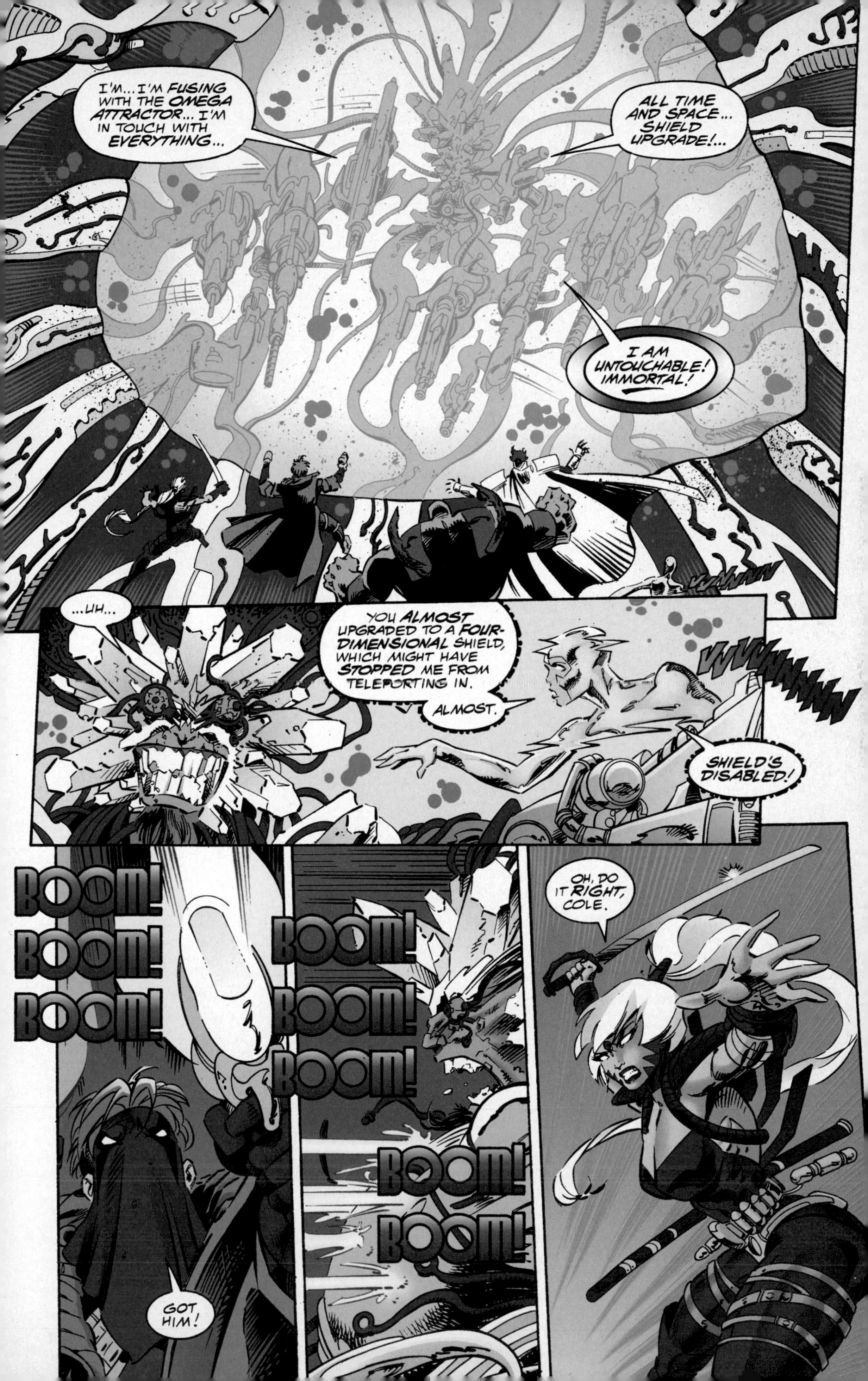
I'M... I'M FUSING WITH THE OMEGA ATTRACTOR... I'M IN TOUCH WITH EVERYTHING...
ALL TIME AND SPACE... SHIELD UPGRADE!...
I AM UNTOUCHABLE! IMMORTAL!
VVNNNN
...UH...
YOU ALMOST UPGRADED TO A FOUR-DIMENSIONAL SHIELD, WHICH MIGHT HAVE STOPPED ME FROM TELEPORTING IN.
ALMOST.
VVVNNNNNN
SHIELD'S DISABLED!
BOOM! BOOM! BOOM!
BOOM! BOOM! BOOM!
BOOM! BOOM!
GOT HIM!
OH, DO IT RIGHT, COLE.

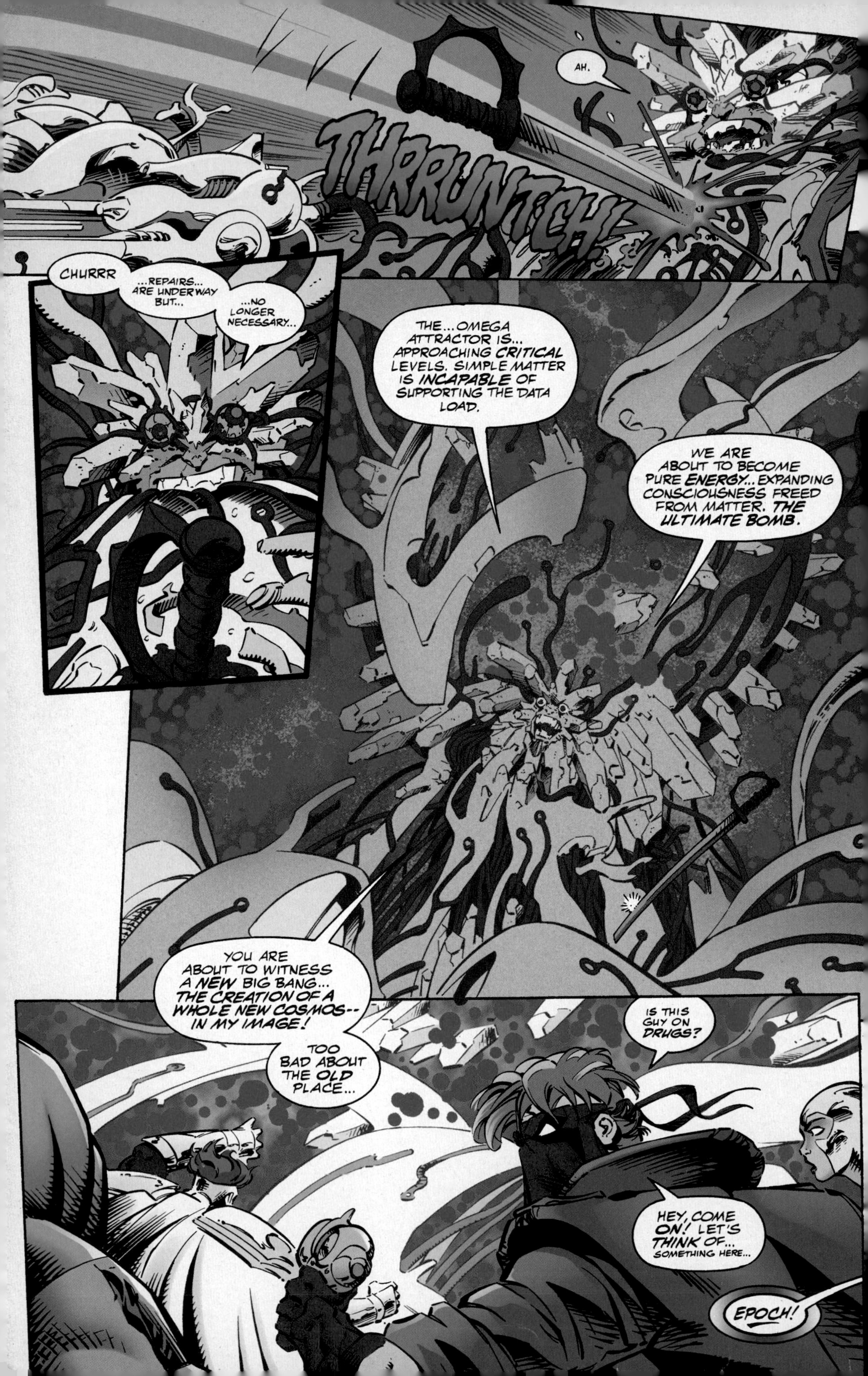
AH.
THRRUNTCH!
CHURRR
...REPAIRS... ARE UNDERWAY BUT...
...NO LONGER NECESSARY...
THE... OMEGA ATTRACTOR IS... APPROACHING CRITICAL LEVELS. SIMPLE MATTER IS INCAPABLE OF SUPPORTING THE DATA LOAD.
WE ARE ABOUT TO BECOME PURE ENERGY... EXPANDING CONSCIOUSNESS FREED FROM MATTER. THE ULTIMATE BOMB.
YOU ARE ABOUT TO WITNESS A NEW BIG BANG... THE CREATION OF A WHOLE NEW COSMOS-- IN MY IMAGE!
TOO BAD ABOUT THE OLD PLACE...
IS THIS GUY ON DRUGS?
HEY, COME ON! LET'S THINK OF... SOMETHING HERE...
EPOCH!

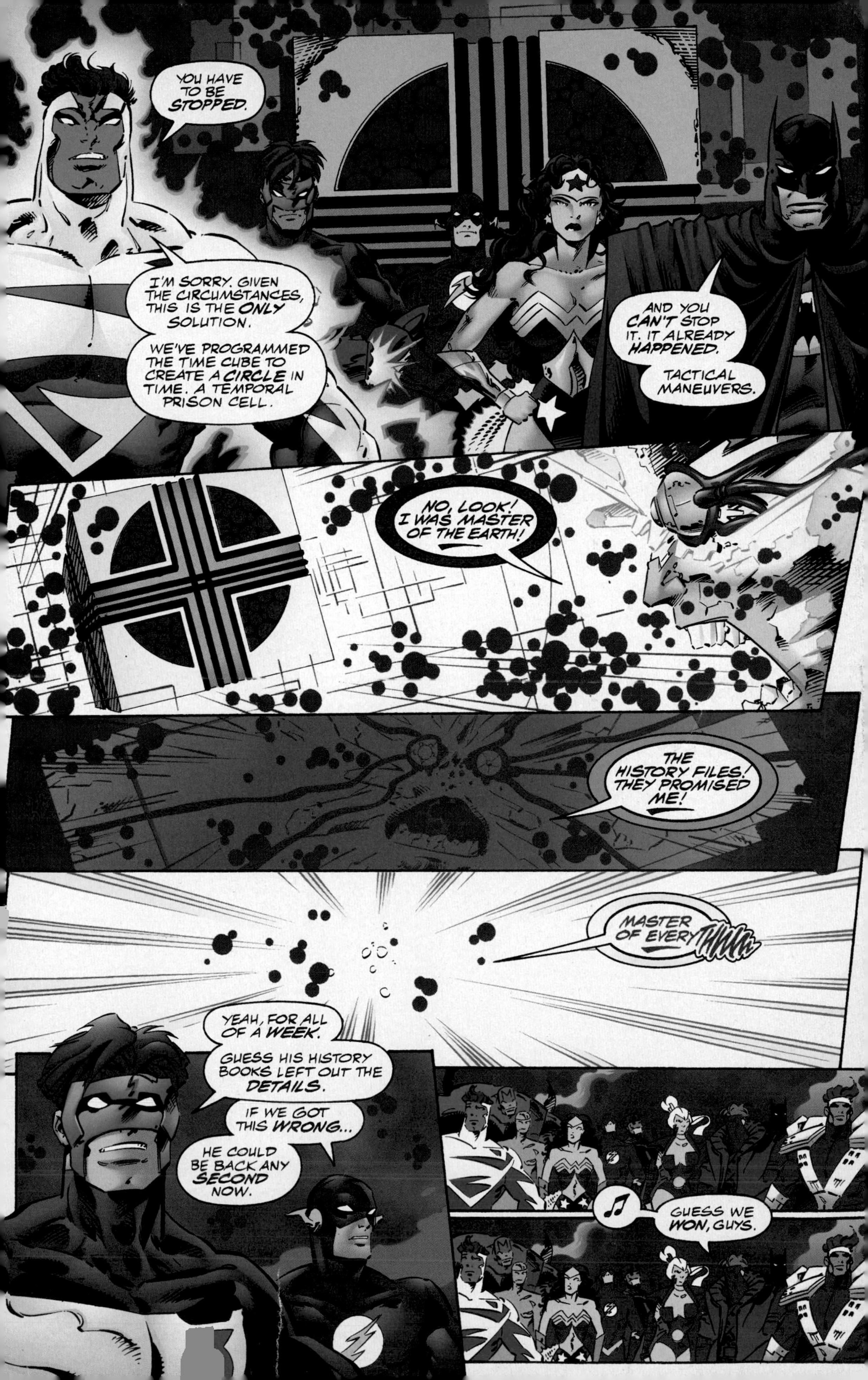

YOU HAVE TO BE STOPPED.
I'M SORRY. GIVEN THE CIRCUMSTANCES, THIS IS THE ONLY SOLUTION.
WE'VE PROGRAMMED THE TIME CUBE TO CREATE A CIRCLE IN TIME. A TEMPORAL PRISON CELL.
AND YOU CAN'T STOP IT. IT ALREADY HAPPENED.
TACTICAL MANEUVERS.
NO, LOOK! I WAS MASTER OF THE EARTH!
THE HISTORY FILES! THEY PROMISED ME!
MASTER OF EVERYTHNNN
YEAH, FOR ALL OF A WEEK.
GUESS HIS HISTORY BOOKS LEFT OUT THE DETAILS.
IF WE GOT THIS WRONG...
HE COULD BE BACK ANY SECOND NOW.
♫
GUESS WE WON, GUYS.

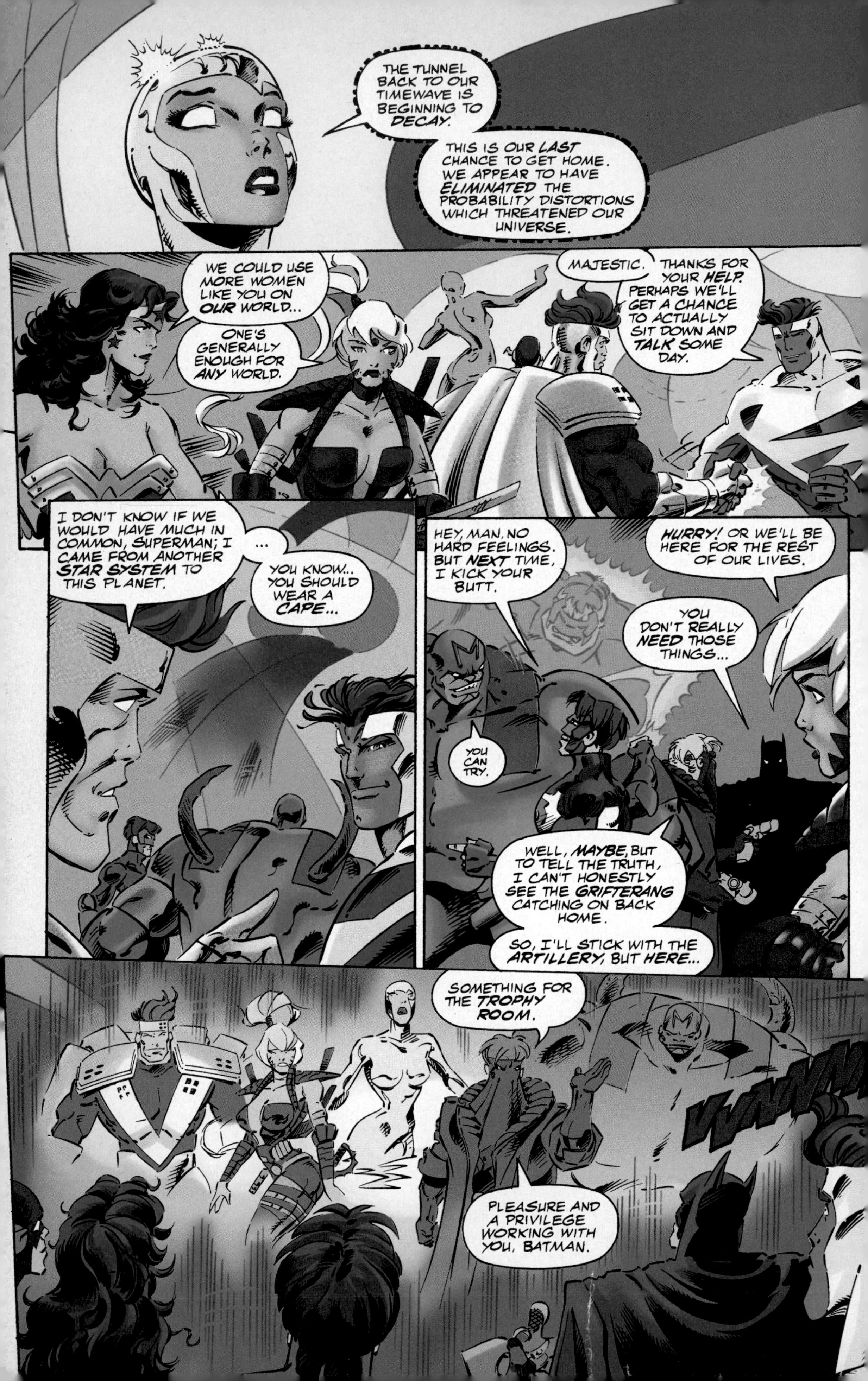
THE TUNNEL BACK TO OUR TIMEWAVE IS BEGINNING TO DECAY.
THIS IS OUR LAST CHANCE TO GET HOME. WE APPEAR TO HAVE ELIMINATED THE PROBABILITY DISTORTIONS WHICH THREATENED OUR UNIVERSE.
WE COULD USE MORE WOMEN LIKE YOU ON OUR WORLD...
ONE'S GENERALLY ENOUGH FOR ANY WORLD.
MAJESTIC.
THANKS FOR YOUR HELP. PERHAPS WE'LL GET A CHANCE TO ACTUALLY SIT DOWN AND TALK SOME DAY.
I DON'T KNOW IF WE WOULD HAVE MUCH IN COMMON, SUPERMAN; I CAME FROM ANOTHER STAR SYSTEM TO THIS PLANET.
...
YOU KNOW... YOU SHOULD WEAR A CAPE...
HEY, MAN, NO HARD FEELINGS. BUT NEXT TIME, I KICK YOUR BUTT.
YOU CAN TRY.
HURRY! OR WE'LL BE HERE FOR THE REST OF OUR LIVES.
YOU DON'T REALLY NEED THOSE THINGS...
WELL, MAYBE, BUT TO TELL THE TRUTH, I CAN'T HONESTLY SEE THE GRIFTERANG CATCHING ON BACK HOME.
SO, I'LL STICK WITH THE ARTILLERY, BUT HERE...
SOMETHING FOR THE TROPHY ROOM.
VVVVVNN
PLEASURE AND A PRIVILEGE WORKING WITH YOU, BATMAN.

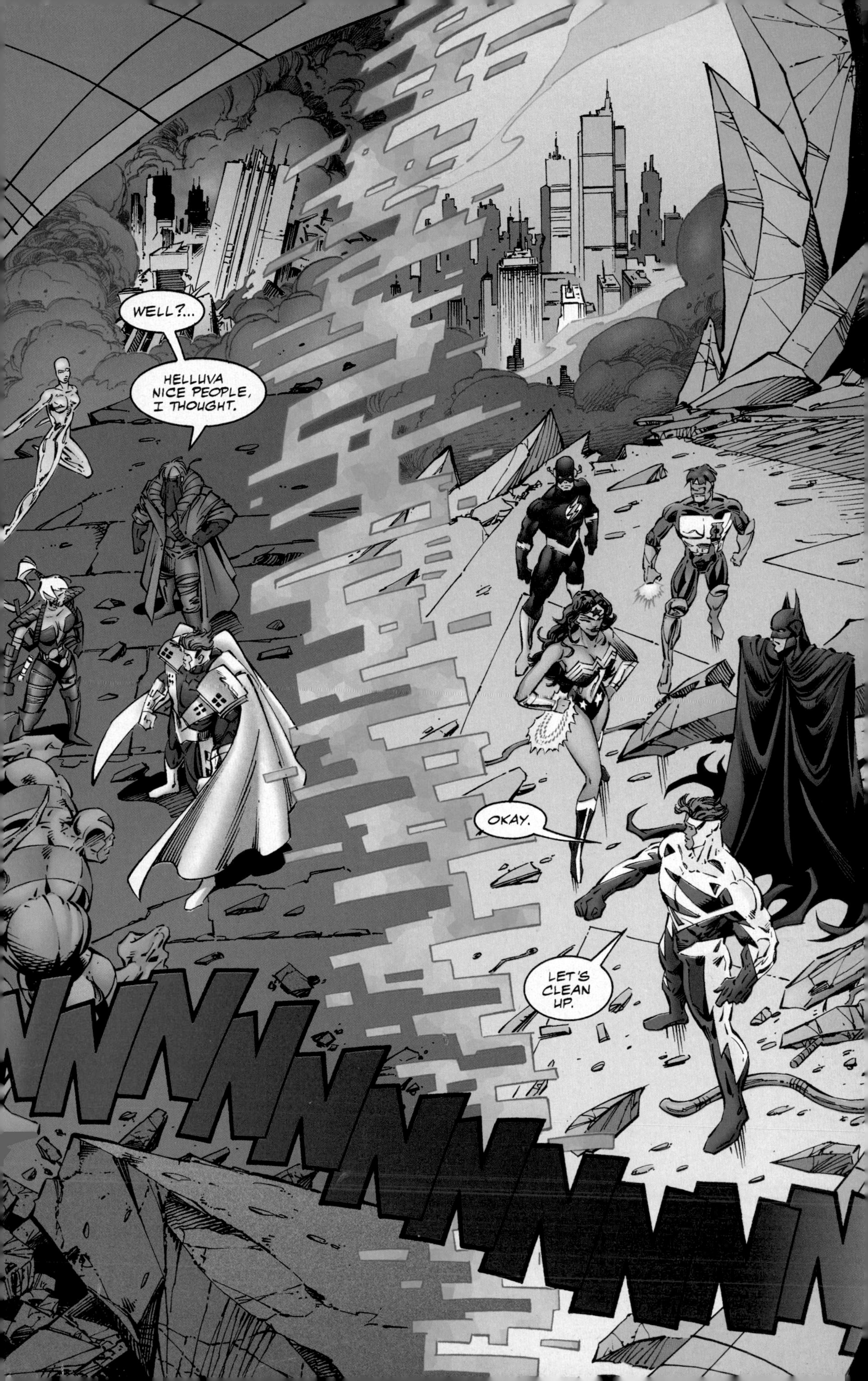
WELL?...
HELLUVA NICE PEOPLE, I THOUGHT.
OKAY.
LET'S CLEAN UP.
WNNNNNNNNNNNNNNNN

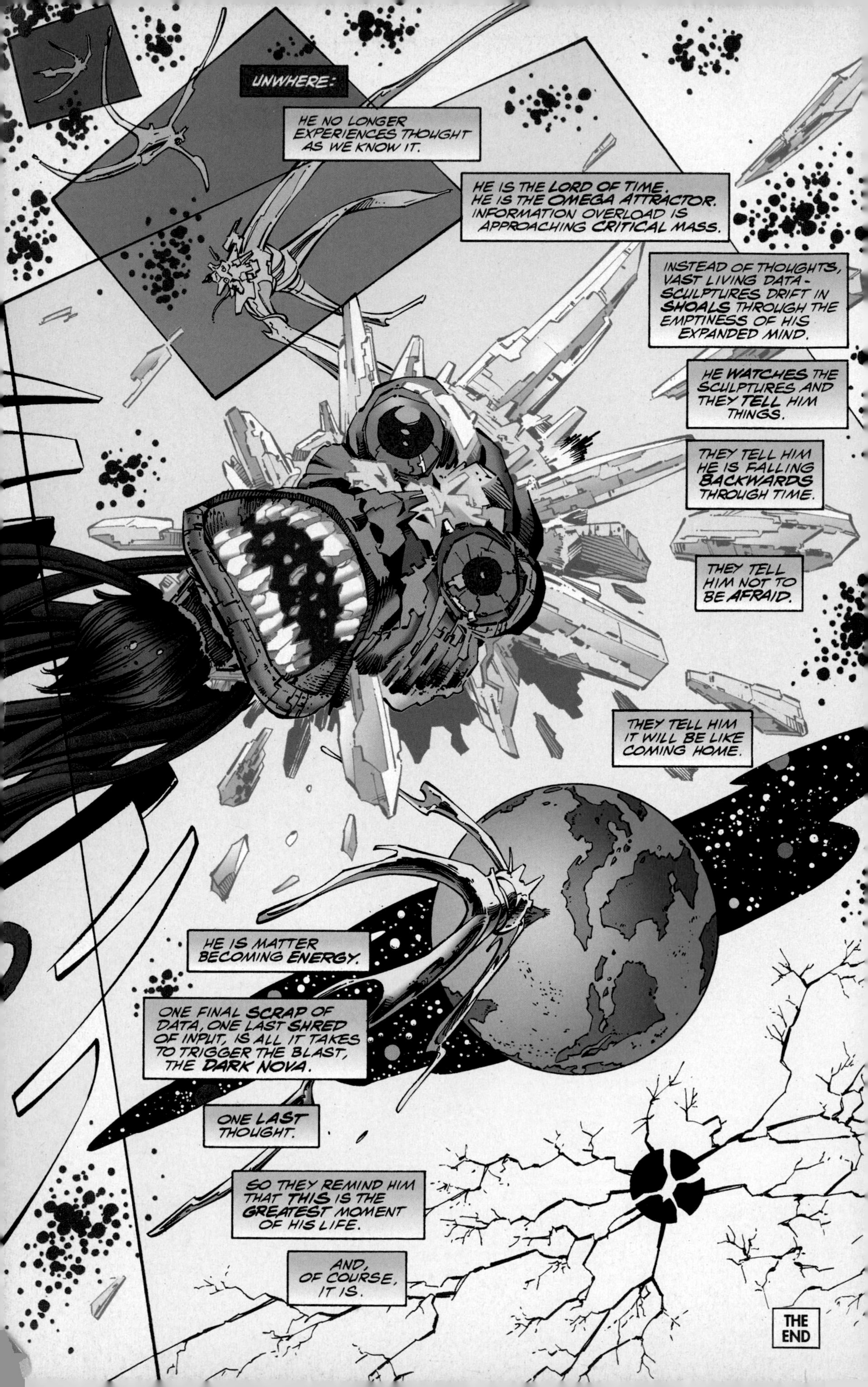
UNWHERE:
HE NO LONGER EXPERIENCES THOUGHT AS WE KNOW IT.
HE IS THE LORD OF TIME. HE IS THE OMEGA ATTRACTOR. INFORMATION OVERLOAD IS APPROACHING CRITICAL MASS.
INSTEAD OF THOUGHTS, VAST LIVING DATA-SCULPTURES DRIFT IN SHOALS THROUGH THE EMPTINESS OF HIS EXPANDED MIND.
HE WATCHES THE SCULPTURES AND THEY TELL HIM THINGS.
THEY TELL HIM HE IS FALLING BACKWARDS THROUGH TIME.
THEY TELL HIM NOT TO BE AFRAID.
THEY TELL HIM IT WILL BE LIKE COMING HOME.
HE IS MATTER BECOMING ENERGY.
ONE FINAL SCRAP OF DATA, ONE LAST SHRED OF INPUT, IS ALL IT TAKES TO TRIGGER THE BLAST, THE DARK NOVA.
ONE LAST THOUGHT.
SO THEY REMIND HIM THAT THIS IS THE GREATEST MOMENT OF HIS LIFE.
AND, OF COURSE, IT IS.
THE END

READ MORE ADVENTURES OF YOUR
FAVORITE HEROES IN THESE
COLLECTIONS FROM DC COMICS:

KINGDOM COME

Mark Waid and **Alex Ross** deliver a
grim tale of youth versus experience,
tradition versus change and what
defines a hero. KINGDOM COME is
a riveting story pitting the old guard —
Superman, Batman, Wonder Woman
and their peers — against a new
uncompromising generation.

**WINNER OF FIVE EISNER AND
HARVEY AWARDS, INCLUDING
BEST LIMITED SERIES
AND BEST ARTIST**

IDENTITY CRISIS

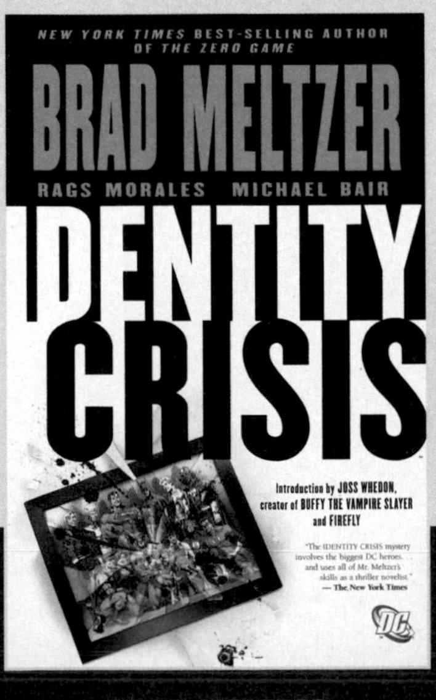

CRISIS ON
INFINITE EARTHS

DC: THE NEW FRONTIER
VOLUME 1

BRAD MELTZER
RAGS MORALES
MICHAEL BAIR

MARV WOLFMAN
GEORGE PÉREZ

DARWYN COOKE
DAVE STEWART

DON'T MISS THESE OTHER GREAT TITLES FROM AROUND THE **DCU!**

SUPERMAN:
BIRTHRIGHT

SUPERMAN
BIRTHRIGHT
THE ORIGIN OF THE MAN OF STEEL
MARK WAID LEINIL FRANCIS YU GERRY ALANGUILAN

MARK WAID
LEINIL FRANCIS YU
GERRY ALANGUILAN

BATMAN:
DARK VICTORY

Dark
Victory

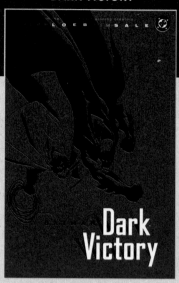

JEPH LOEB
TIM SALE

WONDER WOMAN:
GODS AND MORTALS

· GEORGE PÉREZ ·
WONDER WOMAN
LEN WEIN · GREG POTTER · BRUCE PATTERSON
GODS AND MORTALS

GEORGE PÉREZ
LEN WEIN/GREG POTTER
BRUCE PATTERSON

GREEN LANTERN:
NO FEAR

GREEN LANTERN
NO FEAR
Geoff Johns · Carlos Pacheco · Ethan Van Sciver
Darwyn Cooke · Simone Bianchi

GEOFF JOHNS
CARLOS PACHECO
ETHAN VAN SCIVER

GREEN ARROW:
QUIVER

KEVIN SMITH
GREEN ARROW
PHIL HESTER
ANDE PARKS
QUIVER

KEVIN SMITH
PHIL HESTER
ANDE PARKS

TEEN TITANS:
A KID'S GAME

Teen Titans
A KID'S GAME

GEOFF JOHNS
MIKE McKONE

SEARCH THE GRAPHIC NOVELS SECTION OF
www.DCCOMICS.com
FOR ART AND INFORMATION ON ALL OF OUR BOOKS!